Liberty, State, & Union

MERCER
UNIVERSITY PRESS

Endowed by
TOM WATSON BROWN
and
THE WATSON-BROWN FOUNDATION, INC.

Liberty, State, & Union

The Political Theory of Thomas Jefferson

LUIGI MARCO BASSANI

MERCER UNIVERSITY PRESS

MACON, GEORGIA

MUP/H802
ISBN   978-0-88146-186-2

© 2010 Mercer University Press
1400 Coleman Avenue
Macon, Georgia 31207

First Edition.

Books published by Mercer University Press are printed on acid
free paper that meets the requirements of American National
Standard for Information Sciences—Permanence of Paper for
Printed Library Materials.

Mercer University Press is a member of Green Press initiative
(greenpressinitiative.org), a nonprofit organization working to help
publishers and printers increase their use of recycled paper and
decrease their use of fiber derived from endangered forests. This
book is printed on recycled paper.

Cataloging-in-Publication Data
Bassani, Luigi Marco, 1963-
  Liberty, state & union : the political theory of Thomas Jefferson /
Luigi Marco Bassani. -- 1st ed.
      p. cm.
  "MUP/H802"--T.p. verso.
  Includes bibliographical references and index.
  ISBN 978-0-88146-186-2 (acid-free paper)
  1. Jefferson, Thomas, 1743-1826--Political and social views. 2.
Jefferson, Thomas, 1743-1826--Philosophy. I. Title.
  E332.2B27 2010
  973.4'6092--dc22
                                              2010003172

Contents

1

Thomas Jefferson
Icon of a Vanished Republic

Freedom in all just pursuits.[1]

It is uncommon for the man of action to be a philosopher. A political thinker is not usually a statesman nor is the political leader an original thinker. Thomas Jefferson is an exception to this rule, one of those rare individuals who could legitimately go down in history as both a thinker and a politician. Also, judging from the wealth of literature dedicated to him over the years, there are surely hardly more than a dozen or so great historical figures about whom more has been written than Jefferson. He was a politician and political thinker as well as a noteworthy scientist, naturalist, botanist, architect, and cultural organizer. In short, Thomas Jefferson seems to challenge the common perception that if talents, virtue, and the blessings of Providence are embodied within one and the same person, such a man can be successful in one field only.

Jefferson is a truly unique case in the history of political thought. Author of just one booklength work, *Notes on the State of Virginia* (written in 1781, published in 1785 in French, and two years later in English),[2] and of hundreds of documents of a straightforward political character—that is to say, submitted for the consideration of some representative assembly—Jefferson poured out the vast body of his political opinions in thousands of letters, often veritable essays, written during more than sixty years of his life (his earliest extant letter was written in 1762 and the last dates from 1826). Jefferson's correspondence was overwhelmingly prompted, as is typical of the American tradition, by contingent problems. If the history of political thought is to be understood as the attempt to uncover both the tangible evidence of ideas and that which remains below the surface—the living testimony of an author or a tradition as well as the voice of bygone times—then Jefferson is a particularly stimulating subject from the methodological point of view. His books, published essays, official documents, dispatches, legal/political opinions, and private letters all stand as statements of his thought and constitute equally authoritative sources. While for many great thinkers there is a body of work meant for publication that represents the core of their contribution, and a lesser, though at times relevant, private production, in the case of Jefferson, an equal dignity must be conferred by the interpreter to the vast sum of his writings.

The use of Jeffersonian writings in the general reconstruction of his thinking, however, can be fruitful only after a clear examination of the historical and temporal contexts surrounding the statements. Moreover, as Michael P. Zuckert has repeatedly pointed out, it must be borne in mind that the author of the Declaration abhorred unnecessary disagreements and was a kind, sociable person, both as a result of his upbringing and his natural bent. So, vigilant attention must also be paid to the recipient of the letter. To quote just one example, it is true that he stated that the *Federalist* (1788) is "the best commentary on the principles of government which ever was written."[3] However, the person to whom he made this remark was his friend and protégé James Madison, one of the writers of the essays and, therefore, this may not be regarded as his definitive opinion on the work of *Publius.*

In any event, as will be shown in this work, many of these letters had a lasting impact, and the statements contained in them make up the heart of Jeffersonianism. Dozens of these had undoubtedly an effect and a circulation comparable to that of a political pamphlet. His correspondence thus forms an extremely unusual collection of letters, not just a hermeneutic supporting material. A careful reading of his letters clarifies what Jefferson actually thought about large and small matters, and also serves to provide some insight, well in advance of its general recognition, into the formation of a political consensus within a very influential circle in the American politics of the time.

Notwithstanding the wealth of studies dedicated to him, or rather because of it, Jefferson's exact place in the history of political thought is still the subject of fierce controversy today. The famous cry, "Those of you who are for and against Robespierre, please tell us who Robespierre was!" is quite suitable for almost all historical research on great, widely discussed figures. But in the case of the third president, it would have to be reformulated more or less as follows: "Jeffersonians, decide what Thomas

Jefferson really thought." For the passions and controversies that the figure of the great Virginian still stirs up today focus primarily on the intellectual influences and the correct understanding of his thinking rather than on his standing in history. That he was a major figure of towering importance can never be called into doubt.

Author of the Declaration of Independence, minister to France, a prominent figure in the first American administration, undisputed leader of the opposition to the Federalists in the 1790s, president of the United States from 1801 to 1809, the critical conscience of the country until his death on 4 July 1826, Thomas Jefferson is the most widely studied, fascinating, and genuinely representative Founding Father of an entire era. Almost uniquely among America's great statesmen, Jefferson epitomizes this role both with regard to his contemporaries and his descendants.

Jefferson's contemporaries charged him with the drafting of the Declaration, a task he would never have been entrusted with had they not held him, then aged thirty-three, to be an excellent representative of the entire revolutionary generation. The very words of his friend and political rival, John Adams, pronounced on his deathbed on the 4 July 1826— "Thomas Jefferson survives," to be understood as "The spirit of the Revolution is not yet dead"—confirm the complete identification of the Virginian politician with the American Revolution; indeed, of Jefferson with America itself. It is difficult to find a comparable interplay of such strong, intertwined references between an historical figure and a country. Jefferson is the First Virginian and the First American—he himself invented the term "Americanism." Like many American intellectuals after him, he spent years in Paris, had an extremely cosmopolitan outlook, and felt part of that "Republic of letters" that united all learned men in the eighteenth century. Yet whenever he said "my country," he was always referring only to Virginia. He spent the whole of his life thinking about America and its infinite opportunities and remained convinced that what had been created great and free could not degenerate to become a second Europe.

The specific problem surrounding Jefferson is that of a historical figure transformed into an icon, of a man who wrote just one book and of whom hundreds of books have been written. It was James Parton, one of his first biographers of note, who recapped it in a nutshell: "If Jefferson was wrong, America is wrong. If America is right, Jefferson was right."[4]

The Political Theory of Thomas Jefferson

Perhaps the responsibility of evoking the entire "meaning" of a country, and of the country which has the greatest influence on contemporary mankind, is too much of a burden for Jefferson's legacy. The image of Jefferson studied so brilliantly by Merrill Peterson almost fifty years ago continues to be "a sensitive reflector, through several generations, of America's troubled search for the image of itself."[5]

In addition, Jefferson is better remembered than any other historical figure by Americans, even for what he did not do. According to a survey in the early 1990s, 30 percent of respondents indicated Jefferson as one of the Fathers of the Constitution.[6] While this is undoubtedly forgivable and only goes to show the extent to which the third president is the Founding Father best known to Americans today, it should be noted that one of the greatest European historians of the past century, Fernand Braudel, made this very same error.[7] The mistake is perhaps additional evidence of the complete lack of European regard toward American history, the latter having for far too long been thought of as a mere appendix to European history.

Many scholars regard Jefferson as the quintessence of contradictions and enigmas. The title of a book dedicated to the great Virginian's ideas, *American Sphinx*,[8] aptly sums up Joseph Ellis's anguish. In Merrill Peterson's opinion, Jefferson, like every great protagonist, "was a baffling series of contradictions: philosopher and politician, aristocrat and democrat, cosmopolitan and American. He authored the nation's birthright, but he also wrote the Kentucky Resolutions of 'nullification.'"[9] These supposed contradictions only show, in the case of Ellis, that the latter failed to divest himself of the mindset of a twentieth-century American liberal intellectual. In the case of Peterson, the contradictions stand out by choosing subsequent American history and the Jeffersonian image as the preferred viewpoint. From the vantage point of Monticello, on the other hand, the view is more linear than later historians would have one believe. Perhaps, if anything, it is American history that blatantly contradicts its own beginnings. In his time, Jefferson was no sphinx; it is the unbridgeable gap between the early republic and our age that makes him seem so.

The figure and thought of Thomas Jefferson is called upon to vindicate the most diverse and improbable constitutional arrangements. Students are constantly at work discovering the "striking similarity" between Jefferson and almost any other figure of national import, no matter how distant in time and space. As one of the most sophisticated and unique human products of the Enlightenment on either side of the Atlantic, Jefferson seems to find soul mates in unlikely eras and places. For instance, we learn that there is a "striking similarity of ideas" between Thomas Jefferson and Muhammad Ali Jinnah, Founding Father of Pakistan.[10] If this were not enough, according to Garrett W. Sheldon, the Founding Father of modern Turkey, Kemal Atatürk, is a *Geist* buddy of the author of the Declaration. Though the two leaders might seem quite distant in every respect, a closer look reveals "striking similarities in background, interests, and ideals."[11] Sheldon points to a specific similarity that most students of Jefferson would find quite unconvincing: "Jefferson and Atatürk...saw the integral place of economics to democratic society and the need for a mix of private enterprise and government regulation of business."[12]

The remarkable influence of the great Virginian was felt in an even more exotic setting. Yasushi Akashi, a Japanese United Nations official, reminisces on his early days and how he first became interested in Jefferson. "As a student brought up in postwar Japan, which was under the American occupation after its defeat in WWII, I was keenly interested in exploring Jefferson's ideas, which often seemed to lie behind reform policies carried out by the Occupation authorities."[13] Apparently, Jefferson is not only the numinous presence behind any great American leader from Lincoln to FDR, LBJ, and beyond, he is also the inspiration of none other than Douglas MacArthur, war general and peacetime dictator.

With regard to the use and misuse of the Jeffersonian heritage in a specifically American setting, we may observe that Thomas Jefferson belongs to everyone: historians, scholars, laymen, and politicians. Politicians who seek to put an elegant final flourish on their speeches can avail themselves of an endless number of useful phrases from the Sage of Monticello, as he is continually present in American political discourse. Joyce Appleby's remark is profoundly true: "The words *Washingtonian, Jacksonian, Wilsonian* direct us to a past political regime. Only *Jeffersonian* circulates in contemporary conversations."[14] In fact, "Jeffersonianism" has always been political legal tender in the United States—until one realizes that it is "as fake as a two-dollar bill,"[15] since everyone, especially politicians and academics, construct a Jefferson in his or her own image and likeness.

While the continuous revisiting of this figure can be interpreted benignly as a tribute to his stature, Jefferson's being considered in tune with the temper of this country more than 260 years after his birth makes the task of the historian of political ideas difficult beyond measure. Truly, Jefferson's spirit has never really died; it has migrated to the universities, to academic circles, among intellectuals, politicians, and mere political buffs. "What would Jefferson say?" is a question so recurrent in America that a scholar came up with the idea of a short book by the same title that analyzes the opinions Jefferson presumably would have held on contemporary political issues.[16] Needless to say, many scholars who have devoted years of study to the third president would not at all agree about "what Jefferson would have said," neither with the author of this particular essay, nor with one another.

The fact remains that Thomas Jefferson has been quoted in support of a whole host of different opinions and on the most disparate of matters. During Roosevelt's New Deal—the period in which federal government policy underwent the most radical transformation in American history, ditching for good a laissez-faire economic policy in favor of massive interventionism, affecting social groups in all walks of life—two books on Jefferson were published that upheld diametrically opposed arguments. In the first, *The Jeffersonian Tradition in American Democracy* (1935), Charles M. Wiltse maintained that the New Deal was in perfect tune with the social and political ideas of the most eminent Founding Father and that Roosevelt's political approach was basically Jeffersonian. By contrast, in the second work, *The Living Jefferson*, published the same year, James Truslow Adams portrayed Roosevelt's political experience as an abrupt departure from Jefferson's fundamental political policies and as a step toward a federal tyranny similar to that called for by Alexander Hamilton.[17] According to Adams, "The struggle going on almost everywhere today…is the struggle between the conception of a strong, centralized state, controlling the lives of the citizens for the sake of economics and national power, and the conception of personal liberty affording the greatest possible scope for the individual to live his life as he wills."[18]

Despite this, Samuel Pettengill, a somewhat nonconformist Democrat and the author of *Jefferson, the Forgotten Man*,[19] argued that the first New Deal stood for the true Jeffersonian heritage, as opposed to the authoritarian shift of the second. This work starts with the admission: "I was a New Dealer in 1932 when the New Deal was Jeffersonian. But as it has moved away from the principles of Jefferson to the principles of a centralized government, which would concentrate power at Washington far beyond the dreams of Alexander Hamilton, honest doubts have arisen as to the wisdom of the present trend."[20] In the preface, the congressman was carried away by his passionate analysis: "The most serious of all questions facing America and the masses of mankind everywhere is whether *Jefferson still lives.*"[21]

During the New Deal, Jefferson was thus understood in three distinct ways and was presented as the forerunner of the entire political landscape that was created following Roosevelt's "realignment." Wiltse contends that Jefferson would have been unconditionally in favor of the program of government intervention in the free economy, while according to James Adams, the Virginian would have unreservedly opposed the centralization of power in the hands of the federal government, and, finally, the figure presented by Pettengill is conceived as surely favoring the first steps but not the later developments of the system created by Franklin D. Roosevelt. Unfortunately, I wasn't able to find any mention of Jefferson to validate the embrace of the "second" New Deal by any former Republican opponent, a reading that, admittedly quite bizarre, would indeed close the political interpretation circle of the 1930s.

Yet in the biased simplifications by the politicians of the time, the New Deal represented the squaring of the circle, a modern way of rendering Jefferson and Hamilton, or liberty and coercion, compatible. Employing Hamiltonian means to obtain Jeffersonian goals "became the formula that was at once capable of dramatizing traditional democratic principles while at the same time strengthening the hand of the national government."[22]

The paradox is that of a clear political thinker who produced a contentious heritage (wrongly held to be ambiguous for the very fact of being contentious). This is, however, a constant of American politics and must not be judged merely as a deviation of the 1930s. As Senator George Hoar stated at the beginning of the last century, "Every party in this country to-day reckons Jefferson as its patron saint.... Every political sect finds its political doctrine in Jefferson, almost as every religious sect finds its doctrine in the Savior of mankind."[23]

The readings of Jefferson in the light of contemporary concerns crop up in all critical periods of recent American history. In the 1960s and 1970s, a fierce argument broke out on the subject of Jefferson and slavery, his vision of civil rights and political freedom. The same character described by some as the noble father of the movement for racial desegregation was, in the opinion of others, an advocate of slavery imbued with male chauvinism who, loath to forgo marital pleasures, caused his beloved wife to die in childbirth.

Leonard Levy's work of 1963 opens the period of criticism linked to the figure and the myth that cloaked him. According to Levy, there was really very little that was "libertarian" about Jefferson, who, on the contrary, was a fanatic, zealous, unscrupulous doctrinaire ready to accept dictatorship in order to save his idea of America. In particular, Levy argues, Jefferson had only scant respect for "civil liberties," above all, those of his military and political opponents.[24] As far as slavery is concerned, it was the "definitive" work by John Chester Miller, *The Wolf by the Ears*, that provided the basis for a condemnation of the inconsistencies between the flag-bearer of American freedom and the great slave owner.[25] Miller's essay was so enormously successful that it became the main source—as can readily be noted by any person who visits the splendid abode—of all Monticello's tour guides.

In 1974, the ingenious psychobiographical work by Fawn Brodie, *Thomas Jefferson: An Intimate History*, provided a breakthrough in studies on Jefferson that can only be fully appreciated today.[26] While presenting no definite proof—in fact, it would be more appropriate to speak of a heap of contrived conclusions based on weak evidence—the author touched a sensitive nerve by shifting the discussion to the Hemings affair, namely, the often-rumored but never conclusively proved affair between Jefferson and his young black slave Sally Hemings.[27] The sound part of Brodie's work, which for the rest conjures up a veritable love story between the president and the slave (possible but not verifiable), is based on a memoir published in 1873 by James Madison Hemings, who maintained he was one of the children of Thomas Jefferson and Sally Hemings.

In the 1990s, the issue became emblematic of the still uneasy relations between blacks and whites in America. Annette Gordon-Reed's work, *Thomas Jefferson and Sally Hemings: An American Controversy*,[28] strongly criticizes white, conservative historiography—with a particularly harsh assessment of Dumas Malone and Merrill Peterson, two of the greatest Jefferson scholars (white, males, and Southerners from Mississippi and Virginia, respectively)—for having denied the affair to the last and for having summarily dismissed the entire matter with words that were, to say the least, ill considered. Peterson, in particular, had gone so far as to declare that the "exaggeration" was the result of "the Negroes' pathetic wish for a little pride and their subtle ways of confounding the white folks."[29] A rather careless statement, as well as an inconsiderate one.

The current American obsession with relationships between genders and races helps explain precisely why Jefferson's relationship with Sally, a half-caste slave and half sister to his deceased wife, has come to represent the focus of the new Jeffersonian free-for-all. The spotlight trained on the Virginian's figure today seem to focus on the dispute among historians who believe it is of prime importance, for a better understanding of Jefferson, to endorse the ever-growing rumors about his relationship with the young slave girl (Sally was no more than fifteen when her relationship started with the then Ambassador to Paris) and about the various children he fathered.[30] If the spokesman of American freedom had, in fact, fathered children with a slave woman and kept them in slavery, then the ultimate hypocrisy of the way America was founded, and of a history told only through Dead White Males, as has always been claimed in radical circles, would be exposed once and for all. In 1998, the prestigious periodical *Nature*, on the basis of a DNA test, published a sensational finding: The slave woman's children were of pure presidential descent. The tests conducted on the offspring of Sally's son leave little room for doubt: Jefferson (or someone with a compatible genetic makeup) was the man's father.[31] But the clue to the mystery was already available by 1968 in a book by Winthrop Jordan, *White over Black*.[32] Jefferson was invariably at home nine months before the birth of each of Sally's children. The chance that this was just a coincidence appears to be quite slim. Thus, according to the official version of the Thomas Jefferson Memorial Foundation, the evidence offered by DNA results and Jefferson's place of residence at the times when Sally's children were conceived speak clearly: "Although paternity cannot be established with absolute certainty, our evaluation of the best evidence available suggests the strong likelihood that Thomas Jefferson and Sally Hemings had a relationship over time that led to the birth of one, and perhaps all, of the known children of Sally Hemings."[33]

Conceivably, the father could have been Jefferson's brother, whose life is in the main obscure. Of course, whenever Jefferson returned to Monticello, his house was full of visitors, some of whom were his brother's children, who also had the same genetic heritage.[34]

Although the soap opera that has enthralled the entire nation seems to have reached its final installment, many important scholars are not at all convinced about the authenticity of the accusations and have made their misgivings public. In fact, John Works, a Jefferson descendant in radical disagreement with the Foundation's report, has established a "Thomas Jefferson Heritage Society," charging a board of well-known scholars (including Lance Banning, Robert Ferrel, Harvey C. Mansfield, William R. Kenan, Jr., and Paul Rahe—the latter dissenting) with the task of looking anew at the whole matter. In spring 2001, the results were published without much fuss, since the conclusion was that the charges weren't proved and that they were in all likelihood a hoax.

Although not at all interested on the subject per se, I have dwelt on this matter at some length because it seems to plainly illustrate a critical point: Jefferson, who has already been enlisted by the progressive establishment as the unlikely champion of government intervention in the free economy, appears even more unlikely as the paragon of American virtues in the politically correct climate of our times. The few who try to remember the third president's basic personal details and insist on him being placed in history as a man of the Enlightenment, appear swamped by the chorus of those who want him to be a timeless figure, a contemporary of everyone and everybody. There are no issues concerning American public life, from government intervention in the free economy to race relations, civil rights, even sexual relationships, which—for the sole fact that he is at the center of the debate—do not lead to a painstaking reinterpretation of Jefferson.

Much more critical to my discussion of Jefferson is his alleged protosocialist outlook on the rights to property. The current interpretation of the third president as an opponent of property rights can be dated back to Vernon Parrington, who wrote the classic account of American thought for the generation who came of age between the two world wars, and it is as unfounded as it is entrenched.[35] Parrington reiterated the typical historiographical formula of the "Progressive Era," namely, the opposition between human rights (stated in the Declaration) and "property rights" (upheld by the Constitution). Jefferson, so the argument goes, was the champion of the former, while the framers, and above all, Madison, are depicted as being obsessed by the protection of property. In fact, the author of *Main Currents in American Thought* (1927–1930) was merely echoing ideas already expressed by Abraham Lincoln—blending them with the theories of the Progressive school—when he declared his party to be the true heir of Jeffersonianism and, in the case of a conflict between "the man and the dollar," to put "the man before the dollar."[36] This epic as well as phantasmagoric struggle between man and dollar was subsequently taken up repeatedly by Parrington, who sought to transform Jefferson into one of the great champions of a titanic, and, needless to say, totally far-fetched battle between man and the dollar.

The view of a nonindividualistic, antiproperty Jefferson, with possible communitarian if not even protosocialist undertones, was to prove fairly impervious to change and has also influenced foreign works on Jefferson in various ways.[37] There are even some who have presented the third president as a forerunner of Karl Marx and Friedrich Engels,[38] while others have preferred to read his ideas in the light of Gramscian concepts, in the wake of a fashion that was popular some years ago in American universities.[39] A Soviet scholar even bestowed on the author of the Declaration the distinction of being the herald of the American proletariat and a figurehead of the "enlightened bourgeois," accusing his followers of having utterly misinterpreted his message.[40] An actual ideological "marriage of Jefferson and Marx"[41] was allegedly the one celebrated by a group of Oklahoma Socialists in the beginning of the past century. According to Jim Blissett, they "conceptualized their response to capitalism in the United States in a way that rendered Marx's ideas more congruent with the particular experience of American workers.... In the resulting symbiosis, both traditions were legitimized to create an ideological system that was peculiarly American symbolically joining...Karl Marx and Thomas Jefferson."[42]

The works that form part of this "revisionist" interpretation, spanning the whole range from pale pink to bright red, have very few textual footholds to rest on for support, as I hope to show in this work. Still, they have been taken seriously by a large part of the academic world and contribute significantly to shaping the "scholars' Jefferson," who is by now far removed from the popular opinion that still rates him as a champion of limited government, of natural rights, and antagonism of the states toward interference by federal powers.

Parrington's fault, however, lies not only in the (almost) indestructible antiproperty paradigm built up around Jefferson, but also in the fact that, by associating the latter with Tom Paine in a section of the book entitled "The French group,"[43] the Harvard professor started a long and not-yet-concluded series of poorly founded arguments concerning the supposed French influence on his ideas. Over the years, many fanciful things have been written about Jefferson and his relations with France, both with the French Revolution and with French culture. Lawrence Kaplan, for example, believes that the French Revolution and French political and social thought held great sway over him.[44] A work by Conor Cruise O'Brien analyzes the entire relation between the Virginian and the French Revolution, vastly overestimating the influence that French political thought and the events of those years allegedly had on him.[45] The slip ups flowing from the pen of this scholar are such as to undermine the entire edifice of his arguments. This is particularly true when he states that a number of passages that are clearly referring to foreign policy, in which Jefferson is simply claiming that the United States ought to forge an alliance with France, are instead evidence of a concurrence between Jefferson's political thought and French revolutionary thinking.[46] But his dubious masterstroke is the attempt to demonstrate that Jean-Jacques Rousseau and Jefferson shared a common body of ideas, including the notion of general will, a subject about which Rousseau's ideas were at the furthest removed from Jeffersonian political thought. Thus, O'Brien states that Jefferson shared "the most audacious of Rousseau's paradoxes: the notion that people may be 'forced to be free.'"[47]

Certainly, the third president loved France and the French. Like all eighteenth-century educated men, he was aware that scientific research was generally more advanced there than anywhere else. But his entire political education had been built up in an English-speaking background, and there is little or no evidence of his being genuinely influenced by anyone other than authors belonging to the British and American tradition. In particular, as has been correctly noted, "the *Commonplace Book*, this repertory of Jefferson's ideas on government, contained not a single extract from Jean-Jacques Rousseau."[48] Paul M. Spurlin, author of a study on the fundamental irrelevance of Rousseau for the American revolutionaries, affirms: "I have nowhere uncovered in the writings of Jefferson a reference to the *Social Contract*."[49] In fact, there is no reference at all to the political thought of Jean-Jacques Rousseau, not even during Thomas Jefferson's French years.

In spite of his favorable attitude toward the French Revolution and some of the subsequent developments, Jefferson was later to reach a conclusion that is not only correct but also still worthy of being examined in greater depth today. Further, it clearly establishes that he took no part in revolutionary Jacobin fervor on one point that is so crucial that to call it central would truly be a gross understatement: "The republican government of France was lost without a struggle, because the party of 'une et indivisible' had prevailed; no provincial organizations existed to which the people might rally under authority of the laws, the seats of the directory were virtually vacant, and a small force sufficed to turn the legislature out of their chamber, and to salute its leader chief of the nation."[50]

Overall, the fact that in the 1790s Jefferson's political opponents at home called him a "Jacobin" while some historians continue to maintain that he was a follower of Rousseau by no means makes him one. In effect, the inchoate Jacobin and the protosocialist Jefferson are but two faces of the very same coin, or two phases of possible cultural operations that have no historical or philological basis whatsoever. Either the intent is to "disengage" Jefferson from the political context of the origins, or else the aim is more simply to portray a different foundation of America than the real historical picture by resorting to a fanciful interpretation of its most representative figure.

Until the early twentieth century, Jefferson was invariably and properly described as the champion of small government. For instance, an important writer of the next generation after his, William Leggett, sums up the Jeffersonian creed in the following terms: "The noble and just sentiment of Jefferson [is] that the sum of a good government is to restrain men from injuring one another; to leave them otherwise free to regulate their own pursuits of industry and improvement; and not to take from the mouth labour the bread it has earned."[51]

Even the classic liberal adage for which Jefferson is known to the layman—"That government is best that governs least" (actually not his own saying but adapted for the masthead of *The United States Magazine and Democratic Review*) —has always been at the center of reflection on his political heritage, at least since the time of Henry D. Thoreau. Note, for example, that in 1904 the American senator Charles A. Culberson stated correctly that Jeffersonian thought was "grounded in distrust of rulers, in the idea that free government is founded in jealousy and not in confidence, in the theory that the government is best which governs least, in individualism and not paternalism, in hatred of caste, in dispersion not concentration of power, and in the education and uplifting of the people, with a supreme faith in their capacity for self-government."[52]

Jefferson was undoubtedly a typical liberal, although quite obviously this characterization has nothing to do with the twentieth-century American liberal tradition, since, to quote a definition attributed to political scientist Giovanni Sartori, "Liberals are the socialists of a country without socialism." In this respect, an interpretation such as E. M. Halliday's—who, after a scanty analysis of the "Jefferson-Hamilton feud," concluded that Thomas Jefferson was the "guiding light...[of the] political left...usually meaning the Democrats,"[53] while his antagonist was the hero of the Republicans—is to be considered as completely missing the point.

Jefferson was a liberal firmly rooted in the Whig tradition and also, from time to time, a forerunner of later views, such as Herbert Spencer's "law of equal freedom." What he sought was the triumph of "a sound spirit of legislation, which, banishing all arbitrary and unnecessary restraint on individual action, shall leave us free to do whatever does not violate the equal rights of another."[54] His battle for the "holy cause of freedom,"[55] his lifelong commitment, was aimed entirely at the achievement of a freedom understood as the absence of coercion of individuals. So true is this that a liberal scholar, in the effort to find some similarity with his own ideas within Jeffersonian thinking, had to unhappily but honestly concede that "Jefferson's idea of liberty was, in fact, very much in the tradition of what the English philosopher, Sir Isaiah Berlin, has called 'negative' freedom. In this formulation the individual is free when he is completely exempt from the coercion of other men or institutions."[56] Further, the author also takes Jefferson to task for some alleged gaps in his understanding of liberty, particularly the fact that "men can become truly free only as a result of a deliberate, self-induced effort to change the nature of their desires and aspirations."[57] Of course, such opinions may have a certain validity only if it is clearly understood that the terms "positive" and "negative" freedom are perhaps useful as a mental reference, but they by no means corresponded to the theoretical framework of an eighteenth-century American Whig.

The present work is, therefore, a sort of "revision of revisers" and seeks to restore Jefferson to that foremost place among the classical liberal "philosopher-kings" that America bequeathed to the world in the birth throes of the Republic. And yet my criticism of the various interpretations does not imply an immediate charge of political bias on those scholars who have advanced them. At times, one can sense an authentically blinkered spirit, or, rather, the desire to marshal the great Virginian in support of latter-day battles, but in other cases there is an honest interpretive divergence.

The aim of this work is a reconstruction of Jefferson's political views in the twofold articulation—the rights of man and states' rights—that represents the core of all his ideas. As the author of the Declaration was part of a tradition, his thought must not be investigated in a vacuum. While my claim is that Jefferson's real mentor was John Locke, the quarrels with his contemporaries, John Adams, Alexander Hamilton, and James Madison, among others, serve to place the Jeffersonian thought in the right perspective, emphasizing its innovative nature as well as the surest philosophical legacies.

The work will start with a critical survey of the most recent paradigms of the historiography of the American founding era, in particular those spawned by the "republican school," which inevitably reverberate through Jeffersonian studies. The argument then will move to natural law, property, the idea of civil society, and consensus building in order to demonstrate that Jefferson's thought was perfectly in tune with the ideas of Locke on every important doctrinal issue. The last two chapters will place Jefferson within the political circumstances of his day, delving into his constitutional and doctrinal considerations on federalism and political representation.

My thesis is that far from being a radical democratic theorist who made some concessions in the sphere of the rights of the individual, Jefferson was a classical liberal who believed that individuals were the best guardians of their own liberties and natural rights. As Michael P. Zuckert appropriately states, "Jefferson's theory bears all the marks of the liberal theory of government as necessary evil."[58] This is the core of my entire analysis. Obviously, we also need to ask ourselves whether, and to what extent, Jefferson was an original political thinker. It is worth pointing out that absolute originality is always synonymous with madness and belongs more to eccentrics than to the great figures of the history of political thought. The notion of "general will" existed before Rousseau,[59] and the strength of Locke's reasoning derives from the fact that it is was grafted onto on an issue—that of natural law—which spanned the entire Middle Ages. These examples could be extended indefinitely.

Jefferson's ideas long represented the benchmark of political power (and resistance to it) in America. The author of the Declaration visualized America as a new beginning for mankind, in which the Whig political tradition would have its full, radical fulfillment. This tradition, reconstructed by present-day historians according to a number of different viewpoints, was understood by Jefferson as a body of doctrinal precepts that were to be found in the writings of thinkers ranging from Edward Coke to John Locke, but it was also felt to be enshrined in the *Cato's Letters* by John Trenchard and Thomas Gordon. The Whig tradition was the subtext of liberty and reached its crowning height with the godfather of classical liberalism.

The Jeffersonian interpretation of Lockean liberalism is, in a certain sense, the mirror image of the fortune of Locke in continental Europe. While in the latter case there was a gradual weakening of his postulates and a progressive segregation of Locke in the "conservative" or "liberal-democratic" field (culminating in the apogee of Marxist criticism), in Jefferson's case it was quite the opposite. The grafting occurred, in fact, as a radicalization, in the classical liberal and libertarian sense—antistatist and individualist—of the most important political thinker in the English language. While in Europe, John Locke was progressively domesticated and the most revolutionary underpinnings of his political philosophy almost forgotten, Jefferson advanced a sort of radicalization of Lockean thought.

In this work, the innovations that Jefferson brought to the Whig tradition will be highlighted, but overall it is worth noting that his thought would carry less weight were it not so strongly rooted in the American experience and not basking in the glow of the success—for all its shadows—of the American experiment in self-government and limited government prior to the Civil War. The proviso notwithstanding against the hackneyed image of "Jefferson standing for America and carrying the moral character of the country on his back,"[60] the link between Jeffersonian thought and the dawn of the Republic clearly cannot be severed lightly. The image of America as the shining orb of liberty is such an important part of the Jeffersonian vision that it cannot be neglected in any way whatsoever. As he wrote to John Adams in 1821:

I shall not die without a hope that light and liberty are on steady advance. We have seen, indeed, once within the records of history, a complete eclipse of the human mind continuing for centuries.... Even should the cloud of barbarism and despotism again obscure the science and liberties of Europe, this country remains to preserve and restore light and liberty to them. In short, the flames kindled on the 4th of July, 1776, have spread over too much of the globe to be extinguished by the feeble engines of despotism; on the contrary, they will consume these engines and all who work them.[61]

In short, those who understand the great originality of the early American republic, with a distinct and relatively autonomous tradition with respect to the European one, can only see in Jefferson the greatest exponent of American distinction. Those who fail to appreciate the specificity of the "natural rights republic," as Zuckert aptly called it, are bound to see only doctrinal assonances and dissonances vis-à-vis European thinkers, but nothing new under the sun of Monticello. To the latter, Jefferson himself must be made to reply: "We can no longer say there is nothing new under the sun. For this whole chapter in the history of man is new. The great extent of our republic is new. Its sparse habitation is new. The mighty wave of public opinion which has rolled over it is new."[62]

The American "novelty," as well as the Jeffersonian political vision that legitimized it, lasted for no more than two generations after his death. The Civil War shattered the Jeffersonian world. Jefferson, or rather his political vision, could be bearing America on his shoulders only as late as Fort Sumter. Afterward, it was left to other shoulders and to a completely different political outlook to carry the weight of the country. To render Jefferson comprehensible, coherent, consistent, and not the web of paradoxes most scholars claim he was, there is only one sure path: to dissolve the bond between the "author of America" and the country-empire we know nowadays. While it might be difficult to say whether Jefferson would like contemporary America, it is a safe bet that he would not recognize this country as the "natural" offspring of the one he helped to shape.

2

Jefferson and the Republican School

> This is Mr. Locke's doctrine, it is the doctrine of reason
> and truth, and it is…the unvarnished doctrine of the
> Americans.[1]

Natural Law in the Revolutionary Age

The single most important work for which Thomas Jefferson is known is undoubtedly the authorship of the Declaration of Independence. The Unanimous Declaration of the Thirteen United States is probably the document most closely related to the natural rights doctrine ever written in the history of mankind. Its preamble contains a sweeping array of notions about power, man and his rights, and the legitimate ends of government; in brief, about the substance of a just political order. Jefferson was the best representative of a revolutionary generation that grew up in a natural rights mindset, as political arguments based on natural rights permeated the thinking of the Founding Fathers, as well as the debates of the early republic.

Such was the preeminence accorded to natural law that one of the first congressional debates, occasioned by the contested eligibility of the congressman William Loughton Smith to his seat, was centered on the question of whether America, by virtue of the Declaration of Independence, had reverted to a state of nature, thereby invalidating the election of Smith, born in South Carolina but residing in England in that fateful year 1776. The supporters of this opinion stated that by virtue of the return to a state of nature between Americans, Smith lacked the requisite seven years of uninterrupted residence in America. Their opponents, led by James Madison, countered that the Declaration had indeed dissolved the links with the motherland, but not those between the citizens of the former colonies. The latter having retained the character of organized polities, a return to a state of nature was out of question, and Smith, never having relinquished his privileges, had acquired his American citizenship while residing in the Old World.

In the end, Congress opted for the view espoused by Madison, and the whole debate can be regarded as a vote on the Lockean doctrine of the "state of nature," as all the participants to the dispute seem to be perfectly familiar with "Of the Dissolution of Government," the last chapter of John Locke's *Second Treatise on Government*.[2]

It is important to stress the preeminence accorded to the philosophy of natural law in the thinking of the Founding Fathers, since this notion—commonplace among scholars of the founding period until not long ago—has been challenged by a historiographical school bent on diminishing, if not on denying outright, the spread of such philosophy during the formation of the United States.

Natural Rights versus Common Law: A Hopeless Dichotomy

The first reflections on the nature of the Revolution and on the sources of revolutionary ideas began fairly early, both in America and in Europe, especially as the other great Revolution, or what Europeans simply call "the Revolution," was taking place at around the same time. The comparison between the French and the American revolutions became a favorite pastime for Euro-American intellectuals in the beginning of the 1800s, and it remains quite popular to this day. One of the first of these endeavors was a book written by Friedrich von Gentz and translated in 1800 by the young John Quincy Adams, who was at the time ambassador in Berlin.[3] Gentz's thesis is important because it became quite popular among scholars for two centuries. The French Revolution was seen as the product of a fanatic zeal for natural rights, the "abstract natural rights of mankind," while the American one was rather viewed as a "conservative revolution." "The American revolution was from beginning to end...merely a defensive revolution."[4] It was a revolution forced upon Americans by the inflexibility of the British, and thus it was "a revolution of necessity...America had contended ten years long, not against England, but against the Revolution."[5]

From works such as Gentz's, a commonplace narrative began to take shape: The colonists had to break their ties with the mother country because they claimed the customary rights of the Englishmen and the British Empire denied to them the status of British subjects. It was thus a revolutionary separation that had very conservative implications; in order to safeguard their juridical and cultural heritage, the Americans were forced to break their ties with the British Empire.

Gentz was clearly following in the footsteps of Edmund Burke, who commented widely on what was to become the American Revolution as the news reached London, and was adamantly sympathetic to it from the very beginning. His support of the colonial stance was based on a "conservative" reading of the struggle. Britain was failing to come to terms with the colonies because this was the lowest point of its long love affair with liberty. In contrast, Burke said that in the English colonies, "The fierce spirit of liberty is stronger...than in any other people on earth" because they were Englishmen, and "not only devoted to liberty, but to liberty according to English ideas and on English principles. Abstract liberty, like other mere abstractions is not to be found [in the colonies]."[6]

John Philip Reid is one of the many contemporary scholars who, following this long train of interpretations, contends that "the familiar platitudes about natural law" are nothing but "pet beliefs cherished by American historians."[7] Instead of a commitment to the natural rights doctrine, it was, in fact, the absolute devotion of the colonists to the constitutional principles of the British tradition that prompted them to overthrow British rule. In Reid's analysis, the Declaration of Independence—far from having any significance for the political philosophy it expounded—was nothing more than an indictment of King George, according to common-law rules. The rights petitioned for in the Declaration are not the rights of mankind, but "English constitutional principles sanctioned by English constitutional history, and guaranteed by English common law."[8] Thus, the dissolution of the Empire, as far as the Americans were concerned, was firmly based in the common law.

It might seem quite staggering that scholars of such learning and clear mind entertained the idea that the British constitution included a right to withdraw from the British Empire, or the right to resist the authority of the English Parliament. However, the argument made by these scholars is stated inflexibly, if not persuasively, and it revolves around one single proposition: "The revolutionary controversy was concerned with positive constitutional rights, not abstract natural rights."[9] The colonial rebels wanted to be accepted as British citizens abroad and were actually fighting within the framework of the constitutional "positive" rights granted by British law in the course of history. Thus, the end of the American Revolution was to preserve an "already existing social order."[10] This position also seems to be very appealing to conservatives, such as Russell Kirk, who stated, "The American Revolution was not innovating upheaval, but a conservative restoration of colonial prerogatives."[11]

But to construe an opposition between the common law heritage and a defense of natural rights is seriously misleading. No such conflict existed. The customary laws of Englishmen were, in fact, venerated in America mainly because they were seen as a yardstick of what nature prescribed to men. In theory, a natural basis or an historic foundation for laws are two quite different things, but these views actually have much in common; they deny that law can be a power totally estranged from human beings and society, a simple volition of the sovereign authority, be it a number of citizens, an assembly, or a king.

Anglo-Saxon customary rights were understood differently in America and in Britain. As correctly remarked already in 1930 by Otto Vossler (in a book otherwise full of outdated and misleading interpretations), natural rights and common-law rights were so intertwined in the American mind of the Revolutionary era that it was impossible to distinguish one from the other.[12] In fact, to distinguish clearly between colonial claims based upon natural law and those proceeding from common-law considerations seems—and seemed at the time—rather problematic, if not impossible, causing the whole dichotomy between common law and natural law (underpinning the explorations described above) to be a rather fruitless exercise.

The Americans were actually following a venerable European tradition, which could be traced back to the Middle Ages, that tended to equate common law and natural law, customs and nature. Even in England, such views were not infrequent among jurists. Sir John Davis stated in 1615:

> As the lawe of nature, which the Schoolmen call *Ius Commune*, and which is also *Ius non scriptum*, being written onely in the heart of man, is better then all the written lawes in the world to make men honest and happy in this life.... So the customary law of England, which we doe likewise call *Ius Commune*, as coming nearest to the lawe of Nature, which is the root and the touchstone of all good lawes, and which is also *Ius non scriptum*, and written

onely in the memory of man...doth far excel our written lawes, namely our Statutes or Acts of Parliament.[13]

Customary rights and those derived from nature were impossible to set apart. James Otis stated, in one of the first revolutionary pamphlets, that "every British subject born on the continent of America or in any other of the British dominions is by the law of God and nature, by the common law, and by the act of Parliament...entitled to all the natural, essential, inherent and inseparable rights of our fellow subjects in Great Britain."[14] He was asking that the British grant to their colonial citizens both their rights as British subjects and their natural rights as human beings. He was appealing at one and the same time to the authority of rights founded on reason and nature and to the rights that had crystallized during the centuries in the body of the common law. And the rights sanctioned by nature came first. According to young John Adams, "The liberty, the unalienable, indefeasible rights of men, the honor and dignity of human nature, the grandeur and glory of the public, and the universal happiness of individuals, were never so skillfully and successfully consulted as in that most excellent monument of human art, the common law of England."[15] Thus, the common law as it developed was validated by nature, and its authority rested ultimately on the fact that it pointed toward the appreciation of the rights of all mankind. For many revolutionaries who admired and even loved the traditional liberties of Englishmen, the common law was nothing other than the history of natural law, a sort of natural history of liberty. After the Revolution, liberty had clearly found a new home. As Jefferson wrote in 1787 about England: "The sun of her glory is fast descending to the horizon. Her philosophy has crossed the Channel, her freedom the Atlantic."[16]

It was indeed in revolutionary America that the notion of a full identity between common and natural law, as well as their supremacy vis-à-vis statute law, became the standard assumption in political discourse. In the very first important writing of Thomas Jefferson, *A Summary View of the Rights of British America* (1774), both arguments blend inseparably together in an outright assault against the rule of Westminster over the colonies.[17] As an aside, and not unrelated to our subject, it is interesting to note that this brief work is centered upon the idea—central in the old Whig view of history—of the "Norman yoke," namely that Anglo-Saxon liberties preexisted the Norman conquest and were actively suppressed by the new rulers. This historical myth found a particular favor during the Puritan era in seventeenth-century England and was transplanted into America, where it flourished, as Jefferson's booklet clearly shows.[18]

The fact is that Americans did not start the Revolution because of their ideas on constitutional positive rights of Englishmen. Rather, it was their notion of rights—a notion that clearly was influenced, though not exclusively, by the fact that they were British subjects—that shaped and gave meaning to the Revolution as well as to the many constitutional endeavors that were part of the revolutionary process.

The moral doctrine of the Founding Fathers was definitely rooted in "a cluster of ideas that has little or no forebear in history, and that has left an indelible mark on our civilization."[19] In America, to use the words of Walter Berns, "In the beginning it was not the word...in the beginning was the state of nature and the word was with the philosophers of natural rights."[20] More than forty years ago, Yehoshua Arieli described the triumph of natural law doctrines in terms that still command attention:

> The revolutionary separation from the mother country involved a radical break with its own past, the transformation of English sub-jects into American citizens and of the rights of the Englishmen into the rights of nature. The...consciousness of English national traditions and rights, of the continuity of history and belonging, had to be reinterpreted in new terms which replaced the traditional element by concepts taken from the natural-rights philosophy."[21]

Edward Erler restated the same concept: "It was the change from historical prescription to natural rights that represents the radical core of the American Revolution and the American Founding. It was not the rights of the Englishmen...that was the subject of the Declaration, but the rights of man derived, not indeed from any particular constitution or positive law, but from nature."[22] If these are platitudes or commonplaces, they nonetheless represent the basic beliefs of the colonists.

The Republican Synthesis

In spite of all the doubts and reservations that historians shared on the strict adherence of the Founding Fathers to the natural law dogma, in the first part of the last century a consensus was forming at least on one thing, namely the paramount importance of John Locke for Americans. In his seminal work of 1922, Carl Lotus Becker, analyzing the theoretical framework of the Declaration of Independence, concluded, rather unsurprisingly, that Jefferson had added Lockean natural rights philosophy to the birth certificate of the country.[23] According to Becker, who claimed that the natural law tradition was crucial to the American mind, "[t]he lineage is direct, Jefferson copied Locke and Locke quoted Hooker."[24] During the 1950s, the "Lockean consensus"—an agreement among historians on the ideological consensus of the revolutionary generation— reached its pinnacle in Louis Hartz's *The Liberal Tradition in America*. He stated in simple and effective terms: "Locke dominates American political thought, as no thinker anywhere dominates the political thought of a nation."[25]

In the past half a century, this conventional wisdom has changed to a surprising extent.[26] There has been such a general attack on the influence of Locke that not only has the whole generation of Founding Fathers been purged of any Lockean influence, but no historical figure of importance has been allowed to remain a Lockean, despite anything the individual might have written or said.

The case of Thomas Jefferson is paradigmatic. Jefferson thought quite highly of Locke. To him, Locke, Bacon, and Newton "were the greatest men that ever lived without any exception."[27] And he reiterated this thought some twenty years later in a recollection of a conversation with Alexander Hamilton: "The room being hung around with a collection of the portraits of remarkable men, among them were those of Bacon, Newton and Locke, Hamilton asked me who they were. I told him they were my trinity of the three greatest men the world had ever produced, naming them. He paused for some time: 'the greatest man, said he, that ever lived, was Julius Caesar.'"[28] In a letter of 1790, Jefferson stated, "Locke's little book on Government, is perfect as far as it goes."[29] If this were not enough, at the age of thirty-three, the Virginian drafted the Declaration of Independence, which, in spite of some recent interpretations,[30] is nothing other than a Lockean manifesto. Garry Wills, Richard Matthews, and a cluster of other scholars, though, have devoted much time and effort trying to prove that Jefferson was *not* a Lockean, that he believed property was *not* a natural right, and that the Declaration is a product of some communitarian version of Scottish Enlightenment, and so on.[31] In truth, the proper title of Wills's work should be *Inventing Jefferson (and Hutcheson)*, as the author tries to argue that the Virginian was "enlightened" in his political thought by the authors of the Scottish Enlightenment and totally ignorant of Locke's work (one really wonders if there is anything we can be sure about, as the author claims that Jefferson had not read Locke's *Second Treatise*). After construing a fictitious Jefferson, Wills goes on to build up a totally deceptive Hutcheson, who supposedly influenced the Declaration's ideas on property, natural rights, and moral philosophy in general. As for another oft-quoted interpretation, Matthews contends that Jefferson was a fierce adversary of property rights and free markets and envisioned a radical redistribution of wealth in the early republic. There is no evidence, though, in either Jefferson the thinker or Jefferson the politician to support such an extravagant interpretation. Matthews's book is called *The Radical Politics of Thomas Jefferson. A Revisionist View*, but by the time Matthews was writing the forces of historiographical revisionism were at work through the "republican synthesis," and his view was not revisionist at all; rather, for quite a while, it became the orthodox interpretation.

In any case, with few notable exceptions, academics in the past forty years have tried to present a revolutionary mind that is more or less "debugged" of any sort of Lockean influence. As far as the whole revolutionary period is concerned, it has been the task of the republican school to challenge the long-accepted notion of a Lockean influence on the colonists.

This new historical category, republicanism, with its wealth of suggestive facets, began to be sketched in the 1950s with the ponderous essay by Caroline Robbins, *The Eighteenth-Century Commonwealthman*.[32] In it, the universe of Anglo-Saxon political ideas is presented as strongly influenced by classical and republican notions, rather than by a modern and Lockean political thought. Since that time, the number of works influenced by this school has proliferated.[33]

The works of John Pocock, Bernard Bailyn, Gordon Wood, and Lance Banning, just to name the front-runners of this deep revisionist movement, have been a powerful challenge to what was considered to be "The Myth of John Locke and the Obsession with Liberalism."[34] In the past forty years, these authors developed an influential school that revolves around the devaluation of any influence of classical liberalism, particularly of the Lockean inclination, on the men of eighteenth-century America.

These scholars have modified the notion of "republicanism," transforming what was once considered merely a form of government into a powerful political ideology. Such an ideology was so dynamic that it was hard for the crafters of this "new tradition" to agree on its main features. There are, in fact, almost as many variants of republicanism as there are historians. Pocock's republicanism is centered on the notion of self-fulfillment as political participation, while Wood's is built on the sacrifice of self to the common good. In Gordon Wood's reconstruction of America's dawn, there is no place for the individualistic tradition that we have heard about since grade school, since "ideally republicanism obliterated the individual."[35] Another variety of republicanism, one that might be termed soft republicanism, is Bernard Bailyn's view based on the conflict between liberty and power. For years, the varieties of republicanism, especially Pocock's and Wood's, were not even on speaking terms with each other.[36]

Republican scholars maintain that this ideology shaped both the ancient world and the modern one, and, in particular, that it dominated the Florentine political universe of the 1500s, reaching England in the 1600s and America in the revolutionary and early republic era. The history of the intellectual influences on the colonists had to be totally rethought as "an intellectual route from the Renaissance to the Revolution that bypassed Locke altogether."[37] The key modern figures of this novel interpretation are Machiavelli, Harrington, and...Thomas Jefferson.

It is to be stressed that the figure of Niccolò Machiavelli sketched by the republican school followers shares very little with the forerunner of the notion of "political modernity" and of the triumph of the state that is commonly offered in history books. Rather, the author of *The Prince* is understood as the go-between who allowed the survival of classical republican thought during the Renaissance. This tradition was to be continued by James Harrington and his English followers, so that republicanism could be handed over to the revolutionary generation in America, becoming the ideological cement holding together the rebellion against the British Empire. In the view of the adherents to the republican school, Harrington utilized the Florentine notion of civic humanism in his *Oceana* (1656) to reformulate the whole English political discourse. The

Harringtonian political concepts—centered on the ideal of the smallholder, who actively participated in the making of public policy and was dedicated to overcoming the corruption of power by means of republican virtue—became the leading themes in the opposition (Country) to Whig oligarchy (Court).

The terms Country and Court were already in use to refer to the opposition between the Whig and Tory parties, respectively. After the turnover occasioned by the Glorious Revolution of 1688, the Whig faction had embraced the conservative and aristocratic policies of the former ruling class, favoring the increase of the public debt, an oppressive taxation and the establishment of a standing army. This had brought about the emergence of an unlikely coalition, ranging from the conservative Bolingbroke to the radicals Trenchard and Gordon, which went up against the power of the Whigs and fashioned the ideology of the opposition, a new "Country ideology," full of agrarian and anticommercial suggestions and upholding a variety of republican virtues, understood as *vivere civile*.[38]

As related by the followers of the republican school, this opposition was grafted in its entirety in the soil of America, to the point that two crucial moments in the history of the new nation—namely the Revolution and the struggle of the Jeffersonian-Republican Party against the Federalist Party—were little more than a reenactment of the struggle between Country and Court begun on English soil a century earlier.[39]

The most brilliant historian of the republican school, J. G. A. Pocock, asserted in the 1970s: "An effect of the recent research has been to display the American Revolution less as the first political act of revolutionary enlightenment than as the last great act of the Renaissance."[40]

To be sure, the republican "discoverers" had, in point of fact, exposed a language of "corruption" and "virtue" in the Revolutionary period that was at odds with much of the natural rights discourse.[41] Moreover, it is true that much of this political jargon went unnoticed in the works of previous generations of historians. But Republican scholars have not confined themselves to the task of uncovering an almost forgotten tradition of "civic virtue" and classical republicanism in the American ideology, presenting it to the profession as a problem to be addressed. They actually went on to build a full-scale explanation of such a political discourse, and to display the irrelevance of John Locke, for England, the colonies, and the rest of the world.[42] As Steven Dworetz noted, "The fall of liberalism and the rise of

The Political Theory of Thomas Jefferson   27

republicanism in the historiography of the American Revolution—arguably the most stunning reversal in the history of political thought—...began with a hostile interpretation of Locke."[43] Or, as Joyce Appleby stated more bluntly, "Locke must be banished because he is offensive to the sensibilities cultivated by classical republicanism."[44]

Another part of the story, not irrelevant according to many, that is totally missing from the republican perspective is Christianity. Allegedly, centuries of Christian thought had no effect on the revolutionary generation in America. The political meaning of the peculiar Protestant thought that was supposed to be of vital importance in forming the climate that led to the Revolution is handily dismissed in republican historiography. If Lockean liberalism is the primary target of the republican artillery, the main collateral casualty is the relevance of Christianity for the Founding Fathers. One could really sense a classical paradigm at work, as the Republicans really believe in pagan theory. The doctrine that man is a brute beast bereft of individual rights who can only be saved by the state is indeed a reformulation of ancient political theories that were obliterated by Christianity.

Republicanism and Lockean Liberalism

Republicanism's most important assumption is that the supreme political end is the pursuit of the "public good," which, in turn, is defined almost always *ex negativo* as the opposite of the search for private interests. It follows that liberty is essentially the Florentine ideal of *vivere civile*, or civic virtue, and it has nothing to do with the classical liberal definition of liberty in terms of noninterference of public authorities in the lives of the individuals.[45] The republican thesis centers on a premodern view of man as a social animal, driven by social needs, "whose realization of self occurs only through participation in public life."[46] The "common good" is something totally different from the sum of all private goods, as Wood states nicely, if somewhat unpersuasively: "This common interest was not, as we might today think of it simply the sum of consensus of the particular interests that made up the community. It was rather an entity in itself, prior to and distinct from the various private interests of groups and individual."[47]

For Republicans, freedom is essentially "civic participation." The conception of liberty mostly in tune with republicanism is, of course, positive liberty. The Republican historians grew very fond of Berlin's categories and used them freely in their research. Pocock, for instance, argues that "the republican vocabulary...articulated the positive conception of liberty: it contended that *homo*, the *animale politicum*, was so constituted that his nature was completed in a *vita activa* practiced in a *vivere civile*, and that *libertas* consisted in freedom from restraints upon the practice of such a life."[48]

However, Republican historians and theorists tell us that it is not a simple restoration of the liberty of the ancients, according to the notorious classification of Benjamin Constant. Between the negative liberty of the moderns and the positive one of the ancients there is a third alternative: the republican idea of liberty. That is, "Freedom as non-domination which requires that no one is able to interfere on an arbitrary basis—at their pleasure—in the choices of the free person."[49] Freedom in the republican context is always defined as independence (from the will of other men), and thus it is clearly different from the classical liberal view (liberty as absence of coercion) or from the democratic one (liberty as voluntary, self-imposed restraint).

The cardinal category of the republican school is that of "virtue," defined as a sacrifice of the self (especially of self-interests) in order to perfect the individual as he participates in the construction of the republic, the sole fulfilling political end. This larger scheme, higher than the private individual and located in the public sphere, represents the object for which virtue is the means. Virtue consists of meekly following the path that is bound to lead all citizens to live in a "well-ordered republic." It would be difficult to find any meaningful difference with the unquestioned acceptance of the "general will" that was the paramount virtue of the Rousseau worshiped by the Jaco-bins. The ideal, both for the American revolutionaries and for the main cur-rent in the Anglo-Saxon political universe in the seventeenth and eighteenth century, would thus be "civic humanism," variously depicted by the authors mentioned above, but always implying an unqualified refusal of the individualism extolled in the thought of John Locke and his adherents. The central thesis of Gordon Wood's *The Creation of the American Republic, 1776–1787*, one of the most radical assessments of the republican view, is that "the sacrifice of individual interests to the greater good of the whole formed the essence of republicanism and comprehended for Americans the idealistic goal of their Revolution."[50]

In this framework, property cannot be much more than an instrumental tool, a pathway to public participation and a safeguard of autonomy and independence. As Wood put it, "Property in a republic was still conceived of traditionally...not as means of personal profit or aggrandizement but rather as a source of personal authority or independence."[51] But property was no natural right; rather, it was a conventional and society-given right. Pocock concurs: "The citizen required the autonomy of real property, and many rights...were necessary in order to assure it to him; but the function of property remained the assurance of virtue."[52] So one had to become rich in order to show one possessed virtue, and thus could be a productive participant to the political life of the community (whether getting rich was the spinach might be open to question, but obviously, according to the republican theorists, political participation was the dessert).

It is also very important to note that "there is no suggestion of limiting the power of government in the classical tradition as long as that power serves the common good."[53] The limitation of governmental power cannot be a political end of a republican community devoted to the search of the public good; clearly, this is at odds with Lockean liberalism.

Wood is sure that Americans shared a "willingness of the individual to sacrifice his private self-interests for the good of the community."[54] According to Pocock, Americans were actually trying to resist capitalism and modernity during their revolution. In particular, it was the division of labor that tantalized them. "Specialization...was a prime cause of corruption; only the citizen as amateur, propertied, independent, and willing to perform in his own person all functions essential to the polis, could be said to practice virtues."[55] One really wonders how this antimarket mentality could have flourished in societies that were on the verge of becoming the most successful capitalistic ventures on the planet.

Conversely, classical liberalism, most notably as embodied in Lockean political thought, guarantees full moral and political legitimacy to the pursuit of purely private interests. "In a liberal polity there is no duty to participate actively in politics, no requirement to place the public above the private and to subordinate personal interest to the common good."[56] This vision implies that the individual is seen in duplicity of relations, with other fellow human beings in the free market and with agents acting on behalf of the government. The free-market consensual relations regulate the legitimate order of dealings with other individuals and the natural rights doctrine (the idea that there are certain inalienable rights that cannot be encroached upon by the state) limits legitimate government actions. The boundaries of the political sphere are watertight, at least in principle: Government should provide a safe environment for the individual's enjoyment of his natural rights. As Thomas Jefferson, the most improbable hero of republicanism, stated, "Our legislators are not sufficiently apprized of the rightful limits of their power; that their true office is to declare and enforce only our natural rights...and to take none of them from us. No man has a natural right to commit aggression on the equal rights of another; and this is all from which the laws ought to restrain him...and the idea is quite unfounded, that on entering into society we give up any natural right."[57] The limitation of power being so clearly linked to liberty becomes, indirectly, the most important political end of the classical liberal tradition.

It is possible to outline, with all due caution, a number of dichotomies as useful tools to better identify the contrast lines between republicanism and Lockean liberalism. The ultimate political end for republicanism is virtue, while for classical liberalism, it is liberty. With regard to power, limited government is the aim of liberalism, and government for the sake of the common good is the object of republican theory. And, lastly, "individual autonomy" and "inviolable natural rights" best describe how the two schools of thought have historically viewed the individual.

As Michael Zuckert, author of some of the most convincing critical studies of republicanism,[58] has argued, both traditions were present in early American history. In the opinion of this author, the error made by the followers of republicanism is rooted in the confusion between the notion of "political science" and "political philosophy" in the eighteenth century. Whereas republicanism was the political science of the Founding Fathers, their moral philosophy was strongly grounded in natural law and enjoyed the precedence that first principles have on institutional expediency: "Most of what is currently discussed as classical republicanism is political thought at the level of political science; most of what is discussed as liberalism is reflection at the level of political philosophy. Lines of thought at these different levels, as both Locke and Jefferson implied so clearly, do not necessarily conflict."[59]

The Political Theory of Thomas Jefferson

Richard Fallon, Jr., summarizes very well what seems to be wrong with republicanism. Though one may find it difficult to share his optimism, which seems to be based on the soundness of contemporary political theory, his analysis is right on target:

> The paradigm of classical republicanism seems a poor candidate for contemporary adoption. Too many of its central assumptions—that human nature has a uniform purpose or telos that can be fulfilled only through participation in political activity, that there exists an objective public good apart from individual goods, and that this objective good can be discovered through virtuous political debate—are highly uncongenial to modern ontology and epistemology. Most of us no longer believe that the good of the public could be anything other than some function of the good for individuals, we are skeptical that there is a uniform human nature capable of fulfillment only through politics, and the idea that republican politics would yield unanimity over the nature of the good strikes us as either delusive or tyrannical.[60]

The Republican as a Timid Communitarian

While most of the early works of republican revisionists were indeed scholarly ("magisterial" is the adjective most commonly associated with Pocock's *Machiavellian Moment*) and not ideologically oriented, the coming together of Republicans and Communitarians was a done deal by the 1980s. The Republicans were unearthing a too-palatable as well as usable past for Communitarians to pass. Also, contemporary liberals must have been reassured in their opinion that America had always been a Rooseveltian haven. As the preoccupation with the common good was of paramount importance for classical Republicans, the American past comes out very much in tune with the present. Liberty and equality turn out to be perfectly compatible. The republican Founding Fathers speak to contemporary man and, considering their (supposed) fondness for the common good, they suggest that America's political past is not at odds with the present-day political landscape. The New Deal, the welfare state, and government intervention in the free economy were there from the beginning, if not as a political practice, at least in the minds of the revolutionary generation. The American political horizon seems to be almost prefigured from the start, as virtue, common good, and all the other republican concepts can never be construed against taxation, redistribution, and salvation by government.[61]

Communitarians have started to adopt republican themes from the early 1980s, that is, from the beginning of their assault on liberalism. Michael Sandel, America's public intellectual, if there is one, has probably been the most honest about blending communitarianism and republicanism.[62] As one of "the contemporary critics of liberalism who would revitalize American public discourse by reclaiming a republican past,"[63] Michael Sandel was probably the most consistent Communitarian to perceive a civic humanist solution to the problem of community and of the unencumbered self. As early as 1984, Sandel advocated the need "to revitalize those civic republican possibilities implicit in our tradition but fading in our time."[64]

But the sympathy runs actually deeper. The contempt for natural rights, for instance, is just as vociferous among Communitarians as it is with Republicans. As MacIntyre tells us, the belief in natural rights "is one with the belief in witches and unicorns."[65] He must have been glad to learn from republican historians that almost nobody, with the possible exception of the unimposing John Locke, actually believed in such a lunacy.

Michael Walzer was ready to admit, more than ten years ago, that "a revival of neoclassical republicanism provides much of the substance of contemporary communitarian politics."[66] And he easily predicted an ideological alliance: "Perhaps the doctrine [of classical republicanism] can be extended to account for a 'republic of republics,' a decentralized and participatory revision of liberal democracy."[67] It is impossible to overlook how significant it was for Communitarians to find a political doctrine, supposedly very ancient but of vital importance in the modern world, which focuses on virtue. As "virtues…will sustain us in the relevant quest for the good,"[68] it is clear that virtue plays a central role in the communitarian intellectual pursuit for what is best for us as human beings.

However, republicanism is to a degree intellectually independent of communitarianism. While the former has no problem with the historical upshot of political communities (that is, the nation-state), the latter sponsors a radical redefinition of communities all around the globe and the dismantling of existing states. While the communitarian dream is a highly decentralized form of coercion, Republicans are quite happy with the centralized one we enjoy today.

Communitarianism may be the most important contemporary effort to rethink the political community in a collectivist fashion. A complex society cannot be entrenched in the welfare utopia as a set of social rights, allegedly stemming out of human needs. However, Communitarians end up in the same quagmire as latter-day "liberals," since they portray society as an archipelago of historical tribes, sexual preferences, social categories, and ethnic, religious groups. Communitarians, liberals, and Republicans are actually much closer to each other than it appears. To the old tradition of social democratic theory, oriented to the satisfaction of individual needs, Communitarians have added a new concern for differences and group identities. Modern liberals are ready to accommodate such concerns, as they work to combine the welfare state with the multicultural jungle.

Republicans and Communitarians share a fierce opposition to classical liberalism (the Republicans, as we have seen, contend that this attitude was shared by the Founding Fathers). But "liberalism" so understood is unsophisticated to a fault, because the mantle of liberalism is used to denote belief systems that are different, both historically and ideologically. For the communitarian intellectual, "liberal" is a perfectly good label for classical liberals and social democrats alike: Locke and Rawls, Constant and Keynes, Hayek and John Stuart Mill, and Mises and Darhendorf are just some of the thinkers who, according to these pundits, would belong to the same school of thought. Liberalism becomes a term so vague that it encompasses the whole Western tradition—give or take Hegel and Marx. One may wonder what clarity could come out of concocting a tradition that never existed, one that puts together the critics of laissez-faire and the enemies of social planning.

The republican works have had an enormous influence on the realm of legal scholarship as well. Cass Sunstein has been the front-runner of a number of constitutional thinkers who argue in favor of accepting the "republican synthesis," not only as an historical explanation, but also, and more importantly, as a normative criterion.[69] According to this influential legal scholar, the courts should make sure that government decisions are not the product of private interests, but rather the fruit of an ample and open "public deliberation."[70] Which is to say that the courts should investigate the legislative process with substantial latitude and purge the legal system of those laws that were not formed according to an "open republican process." If we follow Sunstein to his logical conclusions, the courts should simply nullify the existing laws that were passed in contempt of a just republican process, and thus judge every law according to a test of "procedural republican legitimacy."

Rousseau, the Authentic Republican Hero

Republican thought in its purest form is to be found not in sixteenth-century Florence or in seventeenth-century England, but, rather, in a French-speaking tradition that actually shares most of the tenets of the republican school. It is obsessed with the common good and dignifies persons only when they are concerned with public duties, while despising them as petty when preoccupied with their day-to-day life. Most importantly, it dismisses individuals as totally unimportant in and of themselves and as beings who can find salvation only in the benevolent embrace of the state. This is the tradition of Rousseau, a thinker neglected by Pocock, Wood, Banning, and most of the others, but one who clearly is the perfect exponent of the doctrine, albeit one that, as any scholar of the period knows perfectly well, was totally unimportant for the Americans who revolted against the British Empire in the 1770s.

Jean-Jacques Rousseau should be the true hero of republicanism, instead of Machiavelli or Harrington. If there is one truly revolutionary character who tried to develop the full potential of republicanism, it is Robespierre, the devoted follower of Rousseau, and not Thomas Jefferson. It is difficult to miss the republican import of Rousseau's reflections, as for him the task of the sovereign authority was to transform "each individual, who is by himself a perfect and solitary whole, into part of a larger whole from which this individual receives, in a sense, his life and his being."[71]

Rousseau is the key thinker of Communitarians, the philosophically more sophisticated cousins of republican theorists. Alasdair MacIntyre, Michael Walzer, and Charles Taylor claim Rousseau as one of their favorite thinkers, since he did everything possible to break down the distinction between positive and negative freedom. But Rousseau is not for the timid. He could be an inspiration for political theorists who understand that government is coercion and are ready to advocate the use of state force to the fullest extent. The real enemy of human sociability, according to Rousseau, is the property owner: He is a criminal, because he destroyed the original unity among men by raising barriers—literal fences—between himself and his fellow man.

While the hardcore republican historiography is generally oblivious of this great republican thinker, this picture is gradually changing. In *Machiavellian Moment*, Pocock seems to give him full credit when he states that "Rousseau was the Machiavelli of the Eighteenth-century,"[72] but the rest of the quotations from the Geneva-born thinker are quite generic. In Wood's *Creation*, Rousseau is mentioned two times, inconsequentially and without a single direct quote. But other scholars of the same school have included him in the Olympus of republicanism. In his doctoral dissertation, Maurizio Viroli had already attempted to render Rousseau a palatable classical Republican. For him, "There is but one form of liberty: republican liberty."[73] Of course, in doing so, Viroli had to obliterate many of the Rousseauian features, which make him a fairly sinister character in the gallery of classical Republicans. Not only is the author of *Contrat Social* presented as favorable to property ownership, but Viroli ventures to make him the champion of property rights: "Private property is a sacred right grounded in the social contract. Thus any attempt to confiscate private property would be unlawful."[74]

A recent contributor to republican theory states that "[Rousseau's] definition of citizens not as mere bearers of privileges and immunities but as 'participants in the sovereign authority' already points in the republican direction."[75] And he praises what he calls "the richness of Rousseau's brand of republican liberalism."[76] However, Sandel, like most middle-of-the-road Communitarian-Republicans, believes that Rousseau gives republicanism a bad name,[77] since his ideas are on "the coercive face of soul craft."[78]

Moreover, Rousseau is inimical to differences within a republic, as he views "political community as an undifferentiated whole," and, in short, rejects a "pluralist vision"[79] of republican politics. Yet in the works of the author of *Contrat Social*, one finds patriotism, self-sacrifice, attachment to the republic, and everything that is needed to diminish the individual so that the dichotomy between the person beleaguered by civilization and the natural being is washed out, that is, more or less everything republicanism is supposed to stand for. It is indeed in the *Social Contract* that we find innumerable occurrences of virtue, continuous references to the "common good" and the "public good," whose existence is taken for granted. Of course, all these concepts are encapsulated in Rousseau's notion of the general will, and virtue becomes nothing more than the docile conformity of the individual to the general will, the will of the sovereign. It is with Rousseau that we can perfectly see the beginning of a tradition in which limitation of power is not a problem, constitutional formulas are meaningless, and, in general, all the things that are part and parcel of classical liberalism are simply inoperative.

The true liberty of men is to conform to the will of the state, and the essence of virtue in the Rousseauian community is to be ready to prostrate oneself in front of the general will. The maximum degree of republican virtue is, in fact, to follow the general will even when—and particularly when—it flows against one's private interests.

The Counterrevolution in Historiography

The republican paradigm began building up in the 1960s and 1970s as a new, distinctively wrong, but somewhat interesting way of analyzing the past. Soon, however, it tried to reshape the past, and thus merged its efforts with the communitarian critique of liberalism. It went from revisionism to revivalism. At that point, the republican synthesis became a little tedious and plainly wrong. Moreover, by now the republican school no longer can claim any sort of leadership in the scholarship of the American founding.

Asher Horowitz and Richard Matthews have stated that the debate on the Founders' ideology has now settled on "paradigmatic pluralism." The late eighteenth-century American political thought was wrapped up in many different and sometimes conflicting political discourses, of which republicanism was merely one.[80] Some other historians are willing to use the words liberal and republican not as opposite but as companion concepts. Richard Dagger engages in extreme concept twisting in order to reconcile these differing ways of thinking.[81] One thing is for sure: No one can claim today that republicanism was the only way of thinking from which the Founding Fathers could choose.

A certain irony might be detected in the fact that in the beginning it was the republican contention that Locke, liberalism, and natural rights were negligible at the founding. After the counterrevolution of scholarship, though, Republicans became the ones trying to present the two doctrines as not being in conflict. Now there is even talk of "republican liberalism." Lance Banning believes that republicanism was no more than a hypothesis, one that could live side by side with the settled convictions of previous generations of historians.

> The republican hypothesis, as I had always understood it, had never been intended to deny a central role in the Revolutionary thinking for liberal ideas—not, at least, if "liberal" means a democratic, individualistic, and contractual conception of the origins and limits of governmental power.... Rather, the republican hypothesis had always seemed to me to be an argument that Lockean or liberal ideas were only part of an inheritance, a context, or a universe of thought which could be better understood by recognizing that it was a great deal more complex than earlier interpretations had suggested.[82]

The force of the counterrevolution in historiography has been astounding. It "has been altogether successful in trimming the exclusivist claim of the synthesizers. The...dominance of the revisionist account is now merely a matter for textbooks and other venues that lag behind current scholarship."[83] And the republican school is now split: Pocock on one side and the rest on the other. The disagreement was acknowledged by no other than Lance Banning in a footnote of extreme relevance: "American historians have not ordinarily gone as far as Pocock toward discounting Locke's influence."[84] One could picture John Pocock, the scholar who has revised his revisions least often in the past decades—actually, the Johns Hopkins' professor was forced to give in on something, for instance, he does not consider anymore the American Revolution a *British* Revolution[85]—as the general of an army in total disarray. In fact, the American high-ranking officers are actually abandoning the field. "Banning now wishes to speak of something he calls 'liberal republicanism,' Michael Lienesch of a 'hybrid' between the two traditions. Wood wants to deny he ever saw republicanism and liberalism as contraries."[86]

After concessions to his critics here and there, Wood restated his position, arguing from the same perspective but reaching a quite different conclusion. The problem he addressed was how it was possible that America, this pure republican, anticommercial, self-sacrificing haven, became, in less than fifty years from the Revolution, "the most liberal, the most democratic, the most commercially minded, and the most modern"[87] country in the world.

According to Wood, "liberalism" is the fall from the republican Eden. It is nothing other than the byproduct, in itself radical, of a "betrayed revolution."[88] The conclusion of Wood's book is that democracy and corruption prevailed.

>]A new generation of democratic Americans was no longer interested in the revolutionaries' dream of building a classical republic of elitist virtue out of the inherited materials of the Old World. America, they said, would find its greatness not by emulating the states of classical antiquity, not by copying the fiscal-military powers of modern Europe and not by producing a few notable geniuses and noble souls. Instead, it would discover its greatness by creating a prosperous free society belonging to obscure people with their workaday concerns and their pecuniary pursuits of happiness— common people with their common interests in making money and getting ahead. No doubt the cost that America paid for this democracy was high—with its vulgarity, its materialism, its rootlessness, its anti-intellectualism.... The American Revolution created this democracy, and we are living with its consequences still.[89]

In any case, the Lockean counterrevolution has been very productive, as it has forced some very fine scholars to rethink and reassess the role of John Locke as the English Founding Father. After the works of Huyler, Zuckert, Dworetz, and a number of others, it will be much more difficult to dispute the diffusion, utilization, and relevance of Lockean moral philosophy in the colonies and the early republic.[90] Paul Rahe, who has devoted a great amount of energy and ink to investigating the relationship between ancient republican thought and modern America, states that "the 'civic humanism' which some purport to find in the seventeenth and eighteenth-century Britain and America is by and large a figment of the scholarly imagination."[91] More recently, Jerome Huyler—who in the volume Locke in America persuasively demonstrates how widespread was the Lockean creed in the colonial and founding period—suggests: "It is time to discard altogether the essentially misleading Lockean/republican dichotomy."[92] And the most succinct refutation of the entire intellectual republican construction is to be found in a divertissement by John Diggins, the rewriting of the Declaration using the rhetoric of republicanism. The result is so grotesque that the political universe of the signers of the actual document comes out clean of any influence of vivere civile and civic humanism.

> We hold these truths to be historically conditioned: that all men are created equal and mutually dependent; that from that equal creation they derive rights that are alienable and transferable depending on the larger question of needs, among which are the preservation of life, liberty, and the pursuit of virtue in close cooperation with all fellow citizens dedicated to the commonwealth; that to fulfill these needs government is instituted among men that derives its legitimacy from the active participation of the governed.... Whereas the very identity of Americans lies in their symbol-forming, language using nature, whereas we the colonists have no recourse to God, nature or history to guide our actions, and whereas, therefore, we must rest our case on language and its context, we hereby appeal to parliament to organize a committee of Whig historians to show us the true path to virtue.[93]

The republican interpretation in the realm of historiography will more or less suffer the same fate as did the progressive school of the earlier twentieth century (its ideological predecessor). Vanished and dismissed as a general paradigm, the school nonetheless left a permanent mark on the profession. The dichotomies created by progressive historians, "the rights of man v. the rights of persons," for instance, have not yet disappeared,[94] but the general explanation of Charles Beard and others is no longer accepted. Similarly, the stress on virtue, self-sacrifice, political participation, public happiness, and the like cannot be expected to fade away soon. But the idea that somehow the political history of the West could be rewritten using "civic humanistic" jargon—the essence of the republican revolution in historiography—will seem persuasive only to a coterie of die-hard ideologues entrenched in the most prestigious quarters of Western academia.

It is not by chance that Hannah Arendt anticipated many themes that were to become of paramount importance to republican scholars (public happiness, virtue, and so on). In particular, a peculiarly Arendtian notion of virtue is acknowledged by Pocock as being of crucial importance for his civic humanists.[95] Moreover, Arendt builds her notion about "public space" on some Jeffersonian reflections, thus aiming right at the heart of the American founding. At the beginning of the chapter "Pursuit of Happiness" in *On Revolution*, the German scholar seems to recognize the obvious and the notorious: that for Jefferson and most of the Founding Fathers, happiness was in the private realm. Arendt also refers to a famous letter in which the third president affirms that he seeks "for happiness in the lap and love of my family, in the society of my neighbors and my books, in the wholesome occupations of my farm and my affairs, in an interest or affection in every bud that opens, in every breath that blows around me, in an entire freedom of rest, of motion, of thought, owing account to myself alone of my hours and actions."[96] But she dismisses the sincerity of the claim, since such reflections "do not carry much weight," because "as far as Jefferson and the men of the American Revolution are concerned…the truth of their experience rarely came out when they spoke in generalities."[97] According to the author of *On Revolution*, to American revolutionaries, "public freedom consisted in having a share in public business,…[which] gave those who discharged [public duties] in public a feeling of happiness they could acquire nowhere else."[98] Drawing on a very free reading of Jefferson's famous letter of 1816 in which he expounds on his ward system ideal, Arendt reiterates the point about the public dimension of happiness. "The basic assumption of the ward system, *whether Jefferson knew it or not*, was that no one could be called happy without his share in public happiness, that no one could be called free without his experience in public freedom, and that no one could be called either happy or free without participating, and having a share, in public power."[99]

Another influential reading of Jefferson as a republican thinker is offered by the very founder of the republican school, John Pocock. His *Machia-vellian Moment* contains a rough sketch of the Virginian, lined up with the followers of political Aristotelism via the notion of civic humanism.[100] Later, Pocock went as far as depicting the Declaration as a document utterly devoid of Lockean influences, regarding it instead as rightly belonging to the republican fold, echoing classical and Aristotelic views.[101] "The Declaration of Independence was soon…to be considered the charter of a new American civil society; but an examination of its language shows it to have been initially a document performed in the discourse of the *jus gentium* rather than *jus civile*."[102]

That a formal act of secession belongs ipso facto to the law of the nations is self-evident. But Pocock means instead to deny the relevance of the political philosophy stated in the document. His target is the same of two decades earlier. After stating that "the Declaration is very importantly a Lockean document," in the next breath Pocock disavows his statement: "It cannot get to be seen as a Lockean politics of the relations of government to society, or a Lockean ecclesiology of religious liberty, or a Lockean political economy of individual property and rights."[103] It is enough to make one's mind spin. In which sense this is meant to be Lockean is left unsaid. Shortly after, to muddle things further, Pocock refers to "the authors of the Declaration," as if a few negligible stylistic adjustments could deny Jefferson's authorship of the document.[104]

It is important to emphasize that Pocock is not an authority on the thought of Thomas Jefferson and that his main source on this subject is Lance Banning's work. In fact, Pocock was a member of the faculty board at the Washington University when Banning was earning his Ph.D., thus a large part of his understanding of Jefferson originates from his reading of the then young historian's dissertation.[105]

Banning himself has not delved in depth into the character of Thomas Jefferson and his political thought, investigating instead the ideology of the beginnings of the Virginian's party. Specifically, Banning tries to distinguish an alleged republican influence on the Jeffersonian political doctrine, widely shared during the critical events of 1800. For this reason, his work is somewhat peripheral for any study focused on the thought of the author of the Declaration.

Banning saw "republicanism" as a thoroughly pervading influence in the Anglo-American world during the founding period—a sort of straitjacket that constrained the intellectual freedom of action of the characters of the time in a far greater degree than usually recognized. In fact, "No man's thought is altogether free. Men are born into an intellectual universe where some ideas are native and others are difficult to conceive….

In 1789 Americans lived in such a world. The heritage of classical republicanism and English opposition thought, shaped and hardened in the furnace of a great Revolution, left few men free."[106]

Banning's real "finding," upon which Pocock has repeatedly insisted, is the geographical scope, from England to revolutionary America, of the contrast between Court and Country, namely the emphasizing of the previously referenced parallelism between the political themes of the so-called opposition—the group of Whigs who continued to oppose the government even after the Glorious Revolution in England—and the Jeffersonian party. In his opinion, the party ideology that was taking root in the 1790s in America reproduced the old English contest and the themes of the classical republican tradition: the idea of the Republic as founded on the notion of common good, a Country ideology seeing a clear conflict among the interests of the people and those of the party, and a political conception radically linked to the idea of the sovereignty of the people.[107] The influence of the opposition thinkers had already been emphasized by Bernard Bailyn,[108] albeit in relation to the whole revolutionary generation. Following in the footsteps of Banning and of the republican school, the characterization based upon the opposition of Country and Court has been grafted onto American historiography and used in recent years to illustrate some rather complex relationships, as those between Federalists and Anti-Federalists.[109]

At the same time, another renowned historian of early America, Forrest McDonald, offered a premodern view of Jefferson and his followers, in a vein that, although more nuanced, was fundamentally similar to Banning's. In the opinion of McDonald,

> Though the Jeffersonians borrowed some of their ideas from James Harrington and other seventeenth-century writers and some from John Locke, their ideology was borrowed *in toto* from such oppositionists as Charles Davenant, John Trenchard, Thomas Gordon, James Burgh, and most especially Henry St. John, First Viscount Bolingbroke.... This was the Republican's ideology and the essence of their program: restore the separation of powers through the voluntary restraint of virtuous officials, cast out the monarchists and the money men, repeal the most oppressive of taxes,

slash expenses, pay off the public debt, and thus restore America to the pristine simplicity of an Arcadian past.[110]

To conclude this long historiographical note—which is, however, necessary in order to understand the terms of the wider debate in which Jeffersonian studies take place today—it is to be stressed that, however stimulating it can be to investigate the American political thought in the late 1700s, and to follow the less beaten intellectual paths, instead of sticking to the mainstream interpretation of American history, both common sense and the serious studies of the former generations of scholars cannot be dismissed lightly.

When a thinker is being revisited with the tools of the republican tradition, concerned with the notions of virtue, participation to the political life, and common good, any regard to the issues of limitation of power, and of the coercion of the individual by the government are bound to disappear. This is all the more problematic in the case of Thomas Jefferson, who spent his whole life on the reflection upon the best mechanism to curb and oppose the concentration of political power, both of governments against individuals and of the union against the states.

The whole revolutionary generation, and Jefferson in particular, were firm believers in the importance of curbing power and of the individual right to resistance—with any means available—to the usurpations of government. Jefferson asked, "What country can preserve its liberties, if its rulers are not warned from time to time, that this people preserve the spirit of resistance?"[111] Mark these words: "spirit of resistance" to governments; not exactly a request for participation in the Commonwealth.

The vision expressed in virtually every line written by the third president is one of a strictly limited role for the government in every field, with the possible exception of education,[112] where Jefferson occasionally envisaged a degree of public initiative but only by local governments. As Joyce Appleby accurately remarks, "The private came first. Instead of regarding the public arena as the locus of human fulfillment where men rose above their self-interest to serve the common good, Jefferson wanted government to offer protection to the personal realm where men could freely exercise their faculties."[113]

The true *deus absconditus* (albeit easily recognizable) presiding over the whole Jeffersonian intellectual edifice is indeed the philosophy of natural law, and his most certain and constant intellectual guide within the constellation of modern natural law is indeed John Locke, as we will see in the following chapters.

3

Jefferson on Property Rights

> Property does not exist because there are laws, but laws exist because there is property.[1]

The unifying element of the entire corpus of Jeffersonian political thought—and above all of the transition from the notion of rights of man to that of states' rights, in a continuum of reflections on political affairs and institutions—is his unreserved support for the doctrine of natural law. Jefferson believed that safeguarding the rights of man was the end (and limit) of the powers granted to government. States' rights, specifically defined as "natural" in his draft of the Kentucky Resolutions of 1798, arose from the constitutional pact and derived from the contractual nature of the American union. The same radical Lockean approach both underlies the features of his political thought and represents the logical and hermeneutic tool that gives direct insight into the heart of Jeffersonian political doctrine.

This chapter will show that Jefferson regarded property as a natural right. As will become clear, all protosocialist interpretations of his political doctrine stem from exactly the opposite assertion; that is, that Jefferson did not consider property a natural right. Thus, what Jefferson actually thought about property rights becomes of crucial consequence, since it is the only path leading to his political doctrine. If the wrong direction is taken, his political theory becomes murky and unintelligible.

The works that form part of the "revisionist" interpretation have very few textual footholds to grasp for support, as I will show. But the fact remains that they have been taken seriously in academic circles and contribute significantly to shaping the "scholars' Jefferson,"[2] a view which is far removed from the popular opinion that still recognizes the third president as a champion of limited government and individual rights.

It is germane to start with the preamble to the Declaration of Independence in the form in which it was articulated by Jefferson:

> We hold these truths to be sacred & undeniable; that all men are created equal and independent, that from that equal creation they derive rights inherent and inalienable, among which are the preservation of life, & liberty, & the pursuit of happiness; that to secure these ends, governments are instituted among men, deriving their just powers from the consent of the governed; that whenever any form of government shall become destructive of these ends, it is the right of the people to alter or to abolish it, & to institute new government laying it's foundation on such principles and organising it's powers in such forms, as to them shall seem most likely to effect their safety and happiness.[3]

Jefferson's first draft differs from the final version because "sacred & undeniable" truths became "self-evident" truths.[4] The expression "self-evident" has caught the imagination of scholars.[5] It is maintained that herein lies the entire epistemology of Jeffersonian natural law.[6]

The postulate of self-evidence is typically Lockean, as pointed out by several Jeffersonian scholars.[7] Locke addressed this issue in his 1690 work *An Essay Concerning Human Understanding*, illustrating it with a series of practical examples, and clearly delineating the meaning of these truths that can be grasped by means of intuition. Locke defined such awareness as intuitive knowledge, which consists of perceiving the truth of the principle immediately upon understanding its terms.[8] The other forms of knowledge, on the other hand, are not immediate and require proof.

Mathematics is no more than a model, and knowledge of this kind can also be obtained with regard to political and social issues. In a September 1789 letter to Madison, which we will discuss in greater detail further on, Jefferson stated, "I set out on this ground which I suppose to be self evident, that the earth belongs in usufruct to the living; that the dead have neither powers nor rights over it."[9] More than thirty years later, taking up the same concepts, he declared, fully in harmony with the Lockean view of intuitive knowledge, "These are axioms so self-evident that *no explanation can make them plainer*, for he is not to be reasoned with who says that non-existence can control existence, or that nothing can move something."[10]

Joyce Appleby is right on the mark when she asserts that "the natural rights philosophy did not represent for Jefferson...an intellectual discourse going back to the Stoics.... For Jefferson...the implementation of natural rights required radical surgery to the traditional body politic. More urgently, the dead hand of the past had to be lifted from the shoulders of the living. Liberation had to be actual, psychological, to become politically effective."[11]

As for the Revolution's historiography, it is well known, as we have seen, that various authors consider the traditional or positive rights of the Englishmen as the underlying foundation of the settlers' rebellion. But the preamble to the Declaration, with its emphasis on natural rights, not positive rights, belies this idea. In the preeminent revolutionary document, all rights, starting with the colonies' right to independence, are unequivocally prescribed by the "Laws of Nature and Nature's God."

In an 1824 letter, the third president compared England's Glorious Revolution to the American Revolution: "Our Revolution commenced on more favorable grounds. It presented us an album on which we were free to write what we pleased. We had no occasion to search into musty records, to hunt up royal parchments, or to investigate the laws and institutions of a semibarbarous ancestry. We appealed to those of nature, and found them engraved in our hearts."[12] That the Declaration contains a general philosophy of relations between political power and civil society appears indisputable. This notwithstanding, it has often been regarded by scholars as the birth certificate of a new nation, rich in striking phrases, with considerable stylistic effect and potentially evocative, destined to reverberate in citizens' hearts throughout the ages, yet virtually devoid of practical relevance save for one specific point, namely, the severance of the links between the colonies and the mother country.[13]

Jefferson firmly believed that his generation's decision represented a torch of freedom for the rest of the planet as well.

> May it [the Declaration] be to the world,...the signal of arousing men to burst the chains under which monkish ignorance and superstition had persuaded them to bind themselves, and to assume the blessings and security of self-government. That form

which we have substituted, restores the free right to the unbounded exercise of reason and freedom of opinion. All eyes are opened, or opening, to the rights of man. The general spread of the light of science has already laid open to every view the palpable truth, that the mass of mankind has not been born with saddles on their backs, nor a favored few booted and spurred, ready to ride them legitimately, by the grace of God. These are grounds of hope for others. For ourselves, let the annual return of this day forever refresh our recollections of these rights, and an undiminished devotion to them.[14]

This powerful message of emancipation embracing the whole of mankind also represents the authentic interpretation of the Declaration, inasmuch as the latter has an innovative conceptual structure and is addressed, as was customary during the Enlightenment, not only to Americans but to all men on earth. The protection of the inalienable rights of individuals, which emerges incontrovertibly from the text, is the only possible function of the government, the latter consequently being reduced to a "philosophical minimum," that is, to a very strict contract between citizens and policemen.

The Declaration is rather vague on the degree of severity of violations that would justify recourse to revolution. The reference is to "a long train of abuses." Many scholars have noted[15] that Jefferson has in mind a specific Lockean passage: "If a long train of abuses, prevarications, and artifices, all tending the same way, make the design visible to the people,…it is not to be wondered that they should then rouse themselves, and endeavour to put the rule into such hands which may secure to them the ends for which government was at first erected."[16] Jefferson does not quantify the abuses a population can tolerate before rebelling: "Prudence, indeed, will dictate that Governments long established should not be changed for light & transient causes. Accordingly all experience hath shewn, that mankind are more disposed to suffer, while evils are sufferable, than to right themselves by abolishing the forms to which they are accustomed."[17]

Again, we can compare Jefferson's language with Locke's: "Till the mischief be grown general, and the ill designs of the rulers become visible…the People, who are more disposed to suffer, than right themselves by Resistance, are not apt to stir."[18] Canadian historian Ronald Hamowy provides an elegant and correct definition of the meaning of a "just political order" (the Jeffersonian "pursuit of happiness") as it is evinced by the Declaration: "[Men] may act as they choose in their search for ease, comfort, felicity, and grace, either by owning property or not, by accumulating wealth or distributing it, by opting for material success or ascetism, in a word, by determining the path to their own earthly and heavenly salvation as they alone see fit."[19]

It is important to emphasize that the clearest confirmation of Jefferson's espousal of the principles of natural law resides in the right to "alter or to abolish" government.[20] The government—the state, according to continental terminology—is by no means a "natural given" of human society. It may be a necessary evil, or even a perfect mechanism for safeguarding the natural liberties of man, but it is not the ineluctable horizon of political communities. In a letter he wrote to James Madison from Paris, Jefferson timidly manifested an embryonic preference for a society without a state, while nevertheless revealing awareness of the impracticality of such an approach: "Societies exist under three forms, sufficiently distinguishable. 1) Without government as among our Indians.... It is a problem, not clear in my mind, that the first condition is not the best. But I believe it to be inconsistent with any great degree of population."[21]

Although he had substantial confidence in the experiment of self-government that was taking shape in America, Jefferson did not hesitate to assert that if he were called upon to decide between the two opposite poles, anarchy was preferable to despotism. "Those societies (as the Indians) which live without government enjoy in their general mass an infinitely greater degree of happiness than those who live under the European governments. Among the former, public opinion is in the place of law, & restrains morals as powerfully as laws ever did anywhere. Among the latter, under pretence of governing they have divided their nations into two classes, wolves & sheep."[22]

However, under a quite moderate light, Robert R. Faulkner notes the Jeffersonian distaste for government: "Jefferson always wrestled with an underlying conviction that government in general was a questionable imposition on natural liberty."[23] What should be particularly emphasized is that Jefferson appears to have been completely devoid of the specter of *horror vacuity* that commonly raises its ugly head whenever there is talk of absence of government. His fears were always about too much government. For Jefferson, the real political problem is that government has to be made "good and safe," tamed like a wild beast.

There is a gulf, or perhaps an abyss, that separates Jefferson's conception from the doctrine that sees "tyranny" (exploitation, prevarication, dominion, and so forth) as the natural product of social interaction, and political power as a possible solution. Indeed, one could easily argue that, for Jefferson, the possibility of systematic coercion simply cannot exist outside of the political arena. Government and freedom seem to be diametrically opposed, and the advancement of the one entails a diminishment of the other. The struggle, as he asserted in 1788, was clearly moving toward the paired terms government and tyranny. "The natural progress of things is for liberty to yield and government to gain ground."[24]

Jefferson and Locke

As pointed out by Joseph Ellis, the Declaration contains a vision of "a world in which all behavior was voluntary and therefore all coercion unnecessary."[25] The synthetic description of the state of nature, of the ends of government, and of the natural rights of individuals as expressed in the first propositions leave no doubt in this regard. The philosophical underpinning of the Declaration is the doctrine of inviolable rights of the Lockean tradition, and the influence of the English philosopher is so striking that only a lazy student or a scholar of great erudition could fail to recognize them.[26]

The influences present in the "birth certificate" of the American republic were already well known at the time. Richard Henry Lee, who had signed the motion for independence at the Continental Congress in June 1776, perhaps nursing a slight feeling of resentment toward the man who had usurped his claim to fame by drawing up the celebrated text, accused Jefferson of having copied the Declaration from John Locke's *Second Treatise on Government.*[27] And many Founding Fathers had voiced the idea that the document, which was beginning to gain so much attention, was actually nothing more than a simple synthesis of what had been discussed in those years. Jefferson, for his part, not only did not deny the charge but maintained that this was the true strong point of the text. In fact, many years later, he stated that in drafting the Declaration, he did not believe it was his task to find out new principles, or new arguments, never before thought of, not merely to say things which had never been said before; but to place before mankind the common sense of the subject, in terms so plain and firm as to command their assent.... [The Declaration] was intended to be an expression of the American mind.... All its authority rests then on the harmonizing sentiments of the day, whether expressed in conversation, in letters, printed essays, or in the elementary books of public right, as Aristotle, Cicero, Locke, Sidney, etc.[28]

Moreover, in a letter to Benjamin Rush, Jefferson mentioned those he regarded as immortal heroes in the history of mankind: Locke, Francis Bacon, and Isaac Newton.[29] Hence, Richard Matthews is mistaken when he claims: "At no time...does Jefferson claim Locke—or any other philosopher—as his guiding political theorist."[30] It is clear that Locke is Jefferson's lodestar as far as political theory goes, while Newton is the guide for natural science, and Bacon is his mentor for moral philosophy.

To the end of his life, Jefferson never tired of repeating that the author of the *Two Treatises* should be considered one of the greatest authorities to be included in the Olympus of the political concepts to which Americans most widely subscribed. "As to the general principles of liberty and the rights of man, in nature and in society, the doctrines of Locke, in his 'Essay concerning the true original extent and end of civil government,' and of Sidney in his 'Discourses on government,' may be considered as those generally approved by our fellow citizens of this [Virginia], and the United States."[31] This should be no cause for surprise. Lockean political doctrine, or at least a popular version of it, became common currency in the colonies, partly on account of *Cato's Letters*, the collection of political essays written by English pamphleteers John Trenchard and Thomas Gordon in the 1720s, and partly by virtue of the spread of works of Sir William Blackstone. While some chapters of Blackstone's *Commentaries* could be interpreted as a departure from Lockean moral philosophy, Blackstone was famous among the colonists because he considered the rights of life, liberty, and property and also the rights of preservation and self-defense as absolute. The parts of the *Commentaries* that were read and appreciated the most were in total harmony with the *Two Treatises*.

The notion that Jefferson's vision shared much with the Lockean fabric was commonplace not only among his contemporaries but also at a later period, in the second half of the nineteenth century. During the 1900s, this line of interpretation (at least in reference to Jefferson) became almost routine among scholars. In fact, some interpretations of Locke as a radical majoritarian theorist have had their impact on the scholarly literature. According to such explanations, Locke regarded civil society, acting in its full political capacity (that is, following the will of the majority), as fit to do everything it pleased with regard to property rights.[32]

This brings us to the question of Jefferson's adherence to the Lockean approach on the issue of property rights, since this appears to be of prime significance.

Jefferson against Locke?

According to Jefferson, Locke's thought was extremely influential in shaping the "harmonizing sentiments" of the revolutionary era, particularly in the drafting of the Declaration. But many scholars have felt that such an interpretation presented a largely incomplete, if not totally deceptive picture, and have sought additional sources that may have contributed to Jefferson's intellectual stance. Some have gone so far as to extirpate Locke himself from Jefferson and, thus, from the founding. As we have seen in the preceding chapter, for example, Garry Wills, in his 1978 work *Inventing America*, launched the most comprehensive, though ultimately unpersuasive, attack against the (presumed) influence of John Locke on the Declaration of Independence.[33] The author not only replaces Locke with the Scotsman Hutcheson as the primary philosophical authority whose influence can be discerned in the Declaration, he also invents an organicist, Communitarian, and anti-individualist Scottish Enlightenment about which one may legitimately harbor more than a few doubts.

In a book on Jefferson's political philosophy, Garrett Sheldon does not directly deny the Lockean roots of his thought, but proposes a looping interpretation of Jefferson's political stance. He claims that Jefferson was influenced by Locke during his early days, subsequently assuming the attitudes of a classical Republican during his maturity, only to revert to a Lockean period in his last period: "The statist [statesman] as Picasso," as Michael Zuckert comments ironically.[34]

Other scholars, while acknowledging the Lockean influence, have nevertheless argued that Jefferson was hostile to property rights, or at least that he did not regard them as natural rights. This, in effect, is tantamount to depicting his political thought as far removed from Locke's, since Locke's stature as an original political thinker is dependent on the doctrine of the legitimate origin of property in the state of nature.

Basically, then, although authoritative historians, such as Forrest McDonald, maintain that "almost to a man, Patriots were agreed that the proper ends of government were to protect people in their lives, liberty, and property,"[35] some believe that the exception, pertaining specifically to the last of these, was represented by Jefferson himself.

A fundamental element that helps to shed light on this attempt of severing or attenuating the links between Jefferson and Locke is the old distinction proposed by the "progressive school" between property rights and human rights. In truth, those who have sought to present a non-Lockean Jefferson have done so while shackled, consciously or otherwise, by the categories of the progressive school. It is necessary to offer a brief analysis of how the idea that property rights could stand in opposition to human rights arose among historians.

The scholar whose name is linked to the clearest presentation of Jefferson's as a champion of "human rights v. the rights of property" is Vernon Parrington, who wrote *Main Currents in American Thought*, the document which the generation between the two wars came to see as the classic treatise on American thought. Parrington believed that the Declaration of Independence was a "classical statement of French humanitarian democracy," whereas the Constitution was "an organic law designed to safeguard the minority under republican rule." For Parrington, it was incontestable that the two documents formed part of a "conflict between the man and the dollar" that had characterized American history ever since its origins.[36]

Parrington, though, was merely echoing ideas already expressed by Abraham Lincoln, blending them with the progressive school's theories. In an important letter in which the future president apologized for not being able to take part in Jefferson's birthday celebrations, Lincoln stated that "the Jefferson party formed upon the supposed superior devotion to the personal rights of men, holding the rights of property to be secondary only and greatly inferior."[37] On the question of his party, which he regarded as the true heir of Jeffersonism, Lincoln declared that "Republicans...are for both the man and the dollar, but in case of conflict the man before the dollar."[38]

This idea of a struggle between man and the dollar was taken up repeatedly by Parrington, who transformed Jefferson into one of the great champions of this titanic and totally far-fetched clash. In this, the Harvard scholar was unquestionably influenced by the works of J. Allen Smith, Frederick Jackson Turner, and the leading figure of the progressive school, Charles Beard.

Individual Rights and Property Rights

These early twentieth-century historians developed what has come to be known as the "conflict" interpretation of American history. Not only did they view the history of the republic as torn by bitter clashes, they also pointed to the feature that formed a constant element of these tensions: an unceasing struggle between persons and property, between democracy and aristocracy.

In his 1903 work *History of American Political Theories*, which gained considerable popularity, Charles E. Merriam launched the first attack on the Constitution, arguing that from the point of view of its fundamental inspiration, it ran counter to the revolution. The revolution, he claimed, was authentically democratic, while the Constitution was conservative, if not outright reactionary.[39]

J. Allen Smith took this line of interpretation to greater extremes four years later in *The Spirit of American Government*. Smith adopted a strongly polemical stance with a marked tendency to project present controversies into the past—the evident original flaw of the entire school. The Constitution was seen as a tool exploited by conservatives and property owners for their own defense against the "natural" rights of the numerical majority. Protection of property was the aim to which the wealthy classes conspired. In their perspective, democracy was nothing more than wool pulled over people's eyes.[40]

Charles Beard presented the most comprehensive indictment of the Constitution. Beard's fame springs precisely from having cast the conflictual element in American history in terms of "rights of persons" versus "rights of property," which he believed were incorporated in the Declaration and the Constitution, respectively.[41]

Unfortunately, this dichotomy exerted protracted influence on American research, and its effects have made themselves felt almost to the present day, miraculously surviving the intellectual bankruptcy of the progressive school. Much of the literature on the founding period is still more or less consciously, to some extent, under "progressive" influence. Moreover, today, almost a century after its crystallization, much still remains of the widely followed, though highly misleading, property versus human rights dichotomy.

Jennifer Nedelsky, in her *Private Property and the Limits of American Constitutionalism*, does not conceal her radically democratic vision and declares herself convinced that the preoccupation of the drafters of the American Constitution "with protecting property from democratic incursions...led to the greatest weakness of our system: its failure to realize its democratic potential."[42] While not providing an in-depth account of her own conception of the opposition between democracy and rights of property—indeed, this is consistently taken for granted—Nedelsky's criticism of the framers, and of Madison, in particular, nevertheless emerges quite clearly. It is based on her assumption that a greater protection awarded to property rights necessarily entails a decrease in the right of political participation. Thus, her fundamental tenet is that the Founding Fathers, when contemplating the bifurcation between property and equality, opted for defense of the former. It matters little that they never genuinely faced a political dilemma of this type. They were profoundly convinced that the protection of property and the protection of freedom were one and the same, inasmuch as property, freedom, and political participation formed an interwoven and indivisible conception of politics.

The dichotomy is both logically unfounded and historically unacceptable. None of those who took part in the Revolution believed that defense of the person and of rights of the person entailed denial of the rights of property. Although there was fervent debate on legitimately or illicitly acquired property, no one sought to utilize democracy, the extension of suffrage, and parliaments for the purpose of expropriation.

The idea that property was endowed with a characteristic that approached sacrality was closely connected with the love of freedom. As Edmund Morgan put it, "For Eighteenth-century Americans, property and liberty were one and inseparable, because property was the only foundation yet conceived for security of life and liberty: without security for his property, it was thought, no man could live or be free except at the mercy of another."[43] In a suitably peremptory tone, the well-known historian also pointed out that "we should totally abandon the assumption that those who showed the greatest concern for property rights were not devoted to human rights."[44]

There appears also to be another, more subtle way of portraying an anticapitalist third president. Recently, Claudio Katz has argued that Thomas Jefferson indeed followed John Locke in his general property rights outlook, but the former derived from it conclusions that are at odds with the latter's free-market inclinations. More specifically, "Jefferson's conception of property precludes capitalist labor arrangements...he amends the property right to proscribe economic relations that require some individuals to work under the direction of others."[45] The author of the Declaration, according to Katz, "anticipated the charge...that working for hire represented a diminished form of liberty, tantamount to 'wage slavery.'"[46] In fact, "he envisions a market economy that excludes the necessity of working for hire."[47]

Katz's argument is almost entirely based on a passage found in a letter to Dr. Thomas Cooper, written on 10 September 1814. In this letter, Jefferson allegedly proclaims that to command one's labor is tantamount to being a slave master and that "individuals forced into a lifetime of wage labor are virtually as unfree as slaves."[48] While he certainly preferred the concept of the freeholder working on his own land to the dispossessed individual of European cities, the evidence corroborating a ban on working for a wage is rather meager. In the above-mentioned letter, Jefferson compares the social conditions in England and the United States. He declares that England is composed of three social classes. "The aristocracy, comprehending the nobility, the wealthy commoners, the high grades of priesthood, and the officers of government... The laboring class.... The eleemosynary class, or paupers, who are about one-fifth of the whole."[49] Jefferson immediately identifies the real problem: "The aristocracy, which have the laws and government in their hands, have so managed them as to reduce the third description below the means of supporting life, even by labor; and to force the second, whether employed in agriculture or the arts, to the maximum of labor which the construction of the human body can endure."[50] The problem is not the division of labor and its subsequent inequality, it is the fact that the aristocrats have the government in their hands. It is a political and not social critique of the British system. On the other hand, America was blessed with a much better state of affairs: "We have no paupers.... The great mass of our population is of laborers; our rich, who can live without labor, either manual or professional, being few, and of moderate wealth."[51]

Then Jefferson resorts to what was to become the classical argument for the defense of slavery. American slaves "are better fed...warmer clothed, and labor less than the journeymen or day-laborers of England." True, slaves were subject to coercion, Jefferson admitted, "but are not the hundreds of thousands of British soldiers and seamen subject to the same...?"[52] However, he reassures his correspondent, "I am not advocating slavery.... I am at present comparing the condition and degree of suffering to which oppression has reduced the man of one color, with the condition and degree of suffering to which oppression has reduced the man of another color; equally condemning both."[53] The topic of the whole letter, it must be noted, is national defense, not slavery or wage labor. In the aftermath of the War of 1812, which had showed American military weakness, Jefferson is talking about the underclass that England was producing by political means and for political ends; the defense of the nation. This gives the British a clear advantage in world power. America, however, was blessed by the lack of such an underclass: "We can have no standing armies for defence, because we have no paupers to furnish the materials."[54] Then he proposes a military conscription for Americans, echoing the classical republican preference for the citizen soldier. "With this force properly classed, organized, trained, armed and subject to tours of a year of military duty, we have no more to fear for the defence of our country than those who have the resources of despotism and pauperism."[55]

There is no hint that Jefferson thought commanding one's labor with one's wealth is per se immoral. The political (and social) systems of the two countries were investigated in relation to their capacity for generating good soldiers and a decent army. America, for the optimistic Jefferson, enjoyed a situational advantage.

Life, Liberty, and Property

If the dichotomy between rights of property and rights of persons appears to be devoid of meaning, the attempt to separate Locke and Jefferson on the question of property rights is even more unfounded. In spite of the wealth of contemporary documents and of the political outlook plainly embodied in the Declaration, scholars of Jeffersonian thought have advanced an abundance of speculations on the status of property rights in Jefferson's political theory. Some authors maintain that Jefferson, like Robespierre, did not consider property as a natural right but as a mere convention subject to the decisions of the majority, a custom that could be regulated, compressed, or repealed at will, according to the resolutions expressed by the community.[56]

Since this line of interpretation risks becoming generally accepted, it is necessary to clarify the relation between civil rights and natural rights in the eyes of American natural rights jurists of the era. Those who contend that, for Jefferson, property may have been a civil right but not a natural right fall into an error of perspective that goes far beyond simply fitting the right of property into the wrong field. They divide the notion of rights into two fields that do not correspond to the Jeffersonian political outlook.

The idea, expressed in clear terms in the Declaration itself, is that the only legitimate end of government is that of upholding rights whose origin precedes any law written down by man. Men are already endowed with all their rights prior to entering into a state of society. The question of "civil rights," those that derive only from man's leap into "political society," is, in this framework of thought, vastly different from the facile opposition between civil rights and natural rights. For there is but one and only one civil right: It arises with the very genesis of political society, and it is the individual right to be protected in the enjoyment of one's natural rights. Individuals who have entered into political society have a "global" civil right, vis-à-vis the government; that is, the right to enjoy protection not of artificial rights—which are the fruits of changing circumstances and of the preferences of lawmakers—but of their natural rights. They are always endowed with a further natural right, which, by its very nature, cannot be the object of a contract: the right of resistance, the right to revolution, their right to protection not by the government but against the government.[57]

In *Cato's Letters*, John Trenchard and Thomas Gordon wrote about the aims of government, perfectly combining the Lockean approach with the spirit of the new Whigs. "[E]ntering into political society is so far from a departure from his natural right, that to preserve it was the sole reason why men did so; and mutual protection and assistance is the only reasonable purpose of all reasonable societies."[58] If this is the overall pattern of the relation between civil rights and natural rights for the Whigs and the

American patriots, it is particularly cogent in Jefferson. In a letter written in 1816, he reiterated, in a manner that John Locke would have appreciated, that "Our legislators are not sufficiently apprized of the rightful limits of their power; that their true office is to declare and enforce *only* our natural rights...and to take none of them from us. No man has a natural right to commit aggression on the equal rights of another; and this is all from which the laws ought to restrain him...and the idea is quite unfounded, that on entering into society we give up any natural right."[59]

The question of property rights thus becomes crucial in order to throw into sharp focus the type of system of natural rights embraced by Jefferson. We seek to pinpoint the supposed evidence, which some have seen as genuine proof, that Jefferson was opposed to viewing property rights as natural rights. But on one point it is necessary to be absolutely clear: The burden of proof lies with those who espouse the bizarre picture of a champion of Lockean natural rights—considered by his contemporaries as the most representative of the ideas of an entire generation steeped in natural law tradition—denying property as a natural right. And the clinching evidence is lacking.

Let us start by observing that if Jefferson had opposed Locke on the question of property rights, he would certainly have made this known unambiguously. For he did not generally recognize the *auctoritates*, not even those of his much-loved classical world. In fact, at the age of seventy-one, after rereading *The Republic*, he had no qualms in asserting that Plato was a thoroughly overrated thinker.[60] However, not only did he never advance any criticism against Locke, he repeatedly praised the English philosopher, to the point of stating that "Locke's little book on government is perfect as far as it goes,"[61] whereby he was conclusively referring to the *Second Treatise*, which contains the famous chapter "Of Property."

The fundamental question concerns why Jefferson, in the Declaration, replaced the Lockean triad "Life, Liberty, and Estate" with "Life, Liberty, and the Pursuit of Happiness." Vernon Parrington offers the classical formulation of the (alleged) importance of this alteration. "The substitution of 'pursuit of happiness' for 'property' marks a complete break with the Whiggish doctrine of property rights that Locke had bequeathed to the English middle class, and the substitution of a broader sociological conception; and it was this substitution that gave to the document the note of idealism which was to make its appeal so perennially human and vital."[62]

Liberty, State, & Union

It would be superfluous to dwell in any detail on the innumerable interpretations of this substitution, since most do not substantially differ from Parrington's, so it will suffice to recall only one among the many: "Substituting 'the pursuit of happiness' for Locke's right of 'property,' Jefferson attempted to extend the concept of rights for all mankind all over the globe for all times, not just property holders."[63] It is worth noting that if the congressmen had felt the replacement of the Lockean triad to be a denial of the "natural" character of the right of property, then without a shadow of doubt they would have rejected it. Whoever proposes the conception that Jefferson was soft on property rights, by adducing the famous substitution, implicitly accuses him of having duped his fellow citizens and revolutionaries. Hence, the "progressive" reading of the Declaration comprises the insertion of a bizarre conception at the very heart of the harmonizing sentiments of the Americans.

Before endorsing rash and unwarranted interpretations, such as those outlined above, it is important to analyze several issues of capital importance. First, were the two terms "happiness" and "property" opposed to one another in America at that time? And second, does the substitution point to a definitive eclipse of the Lockean triad from the horizon of Jeffersonian reflection. In other words, would he never at any time associate life, liberty, and property?

The answers to these queries are totally negative. We will illustrate this first through analysis of documents dating from the period of the Declaration and then by perusing some of the Jefferson papers—restricting ourselves to a mere selection, as they are extremely numerous—in which life, liberty, and property are presented in association, fully in line with the whole classical liberal tradition.

It has often been pointed out that many American political documents dating from that period present just such an association between property and happiness in a clearly individualist and Lockean manner. Indeed, the right to the pursuit of happiness appears to be so all-encompassing as to include the right of property. The Declaration of Rights of Virginia, drawn up by George Mason, which dates from one month prior to the Declaration of Independence, states "That all men are by nature equally free and independent and have certain inherent rights, of which, when they enter into a state of society, they cannot, by any compact, deprive or divest their posterity; namely, the enjoyment of life and liberty, with the means of acquiring and possessing property, and pursuing and obtaining happiness and safety."[64]

The Constitution of Massachusetts, drawn up in 1780, illustrates the same themes in the following manner. "All men are born free and equal, and have certain natural, essential, and unalienable rights; among which may be reckoned the right of enjoying and defending their lives and liberties; that of acquiring, possessing, and protecting property; in fine, that of seeking and obtaining their safety and happiness."[65] Likewise, the Constitution of Pennsylvania stated "That all men are born equally free and independent, and have certain natural, inherent and inalienable rights, amongst which are, the enjoying and defending life and liberty, acquiring, possessing and protecting property, and pursuing and obtaining happiness and safety."[66] And New Hampshire's 1784 constitution established that "acquiring, possessing, and protecting, property; and, in a word,…seeking and obtaining happiness" were among the natural rights of man.[67]

As is often the case in America, the question was decided by a court. In the 1906 case *Nunnemacher v. State*, the Supreme Court of Wisconsin stated that the expression "pursuit of happiness…unquestionably…[entails] the acquisition of private property."[68] The court was right, overall. It seems highly implausible to suggest that happiness and property in America could be invoked in opposition to one another. Life, liberty, property, security, and happiness are the most frequently recurring terms in all discussions on natural rights in late eighteenth-century America. It is quite reasonable to assume that Jefferson, in his search for a potentially evocative triad, resolved to utilize what he believed to be the three stylistically most attractive and least legalistic terms, since these were also terms that cast a light of "new Humanism" on the entire revolutionary upheaval.[69] According to Adrienne Koch, "there is ample evidence" that Jefferson regarded property as a natural right.[70]

In fact, as suggested by Cecelia Kenyon, the replacement may well have an ultraindividualist significance: "The idea of happiness as an end of government was firmly rooted in colonial attitudes before 1776. It was…a far more individualistic end than the protection of property. Property was a tangible, objective element, while happiness was a subjective goal depending on individual interpretation."[71] Or, as argued by William Scott, "It is tempting to conclude, but impossible to prove, that in 1776 Jefferson sensed the disparity between certain contemporary forms of private property and Locke's idealized 'natural property' and that in an effort to restore the old moral content to the concept of individual property, Jefferson substituted in its stead the more suggestive phrase 'pursuit of Happiness.'"[72]

Some might wish to contend that although happiness and property were considered *uno et idem* (one and the same) at that time, Jefferson nevertheless introduced a substitution. Thus, leaving aside the general problem of actions and omissions, an omission in a political document is certainly a fact that calls for an explanation. In this case, however, the fact in itself is rather less conclusive than it might appear at first glance. As already mentioned, Jefferson would continue to associate the terms of the Lockean triad throughout the rest of his writings, showing that the substitution by no means indicated an implicit purpose to exclude property from the catalog of natural rights. The terms "life and property," "liberty, life, and property," and "liberty and property" constantly recur throughout Jefferson's work and are used in a manner fully consistent with the typical utilization and contextualization of the entire classical liberal tradition. A few examples will suffice to demonstrate this point.

In 1775, penning one of his first official documents, Jefferson stated that it was the settlers' right "to protect from every hostile hand *our lives & our properties*."[73] Half a century later, in the last official text he proposed to the 1825 Virginia Assembly (a document that was never approved), we find clear expression of the idea that "man is capable of living in society, governing itself by laws self-imposed, and securing to its members the enjoyment of *life, liberty, property*, and peace."[74]

During this half-century span, one finds many allusions to the doctrine of natural rights that should leave the unbiased interpreter with no doubt as to Jefferson's true inclinations. In 1809, in a statement addressed to the Assembly of Virginia, after declaring his satisfaction for the considerable success and acclaim being achieved by the American experiment of self-government, Jefferson went on to declare that "in no portion of the earth were *life, liberty, and property* so securely held."[75]

His private correspondence likewise abounds in similar references. In 1823, musing on the constitutions of the various states, which undeniably presented a wide range of apparently discordant political ideas, he nevertheless was at pains to underline that "there are certain principles in which all agree, and which all cherish as vitally essential to the protection of *life, liberty, property,* and the safety of the citizen."[76]

Finally, even those with only the faintest awareness of the extent to which the author of the Declaration cherished the right to freedom of conscience cannot fail to agree that the association between rights of conscience and rights of property enunciated in a public speech surely constitutes definitive proof of this close interconnection. In 1803, as the president endeavored to explain to America what would turn out to be his greatest political success story, the Louisiana Purchase, he mentioned the necessary steps that still remained to be completed:

> With the wisdom of Congress it will rest to take those ulterior measures which may be necessary for the immediate occupation and temporary government of the country; for its incorporation into our Union; for rendering the change of government a blessing to our newly-adopted brethren; for securing to them *the rights of conscience and of property:* for confirming to the Indian inhabitants their occupancy and self-government, establishing friendly and commercial relations with them.[77]

On this point, it is germane to quote from *Cato's Letters,* which stated that freedom of expression "is so essential to free government, that the security of property, and the freedom of speech, always go together." And, so add the authors, "in those wretched countries where a man can not call his tongue his own, he can scarce call any thing else his own."[78]

The Corrections to Lafayette's Draft

As definitive evidence that Jefferson did not consider property to be a natural right, beyond his alteration of the Lockean triad in the Declaration, some have pointed to an episode that was remarked upon by Gilbert Chinard in the 1920s.[79] The account of the event has long been part of *The Papers of Thomas Jefferson,* whose excellent editorial notes should help scholars not to draw hasty conclusions. It is generally reported that Jefferson, while in Paris in July 1789, advised Lafayette to strike the right of property off the list of natural rights in the famous draft of the Declaration of Rights.

Before ascertaining whether there is any truth in this report, it should be noted that what commentators fail to emphasize is that Jefferson did not recommend that Lafayette remove from the list of natural rights the right to "la disposition entière de sa personne, de son industrie, de toutes ses facultés" ("the absolute possession of his person, of his industry, of all his faculties"), an even stronger, precise, natural, and Lockean version of property rights. As Jefferson was hardly a novice in political theory, had he really intended to strike property rights off the list of natural rights, he would have removed the cited sentence.

The Jeffersonian position on Lafayette's Draft of a Declaration of Rights on questions pertaining to "rights of property" and "defense of one's honor" is as follows:

> Tout homme naît avec des droits inaliénables; tels sont [le droit de propriété, le soin [de son honneur et] de sa vie, la disposition entière de sa personne, de son industrie, de toutes ses facultés, la recherche du bien être et de la résistance à l'oppression. (Every man is born with some inalienable rights; such as [the right of property, the care [of his honor and] of his life, the absolute possession of his person, industry, and all his faculties, the pursuit of well being and of resistance to oppression.)[80]

The editor's "Note 2" asserts that the first parenthesis was opened and never closed, and points out that in the definitive Declaration of Rights presented by Lafayette on 11 July 1789, property does not appear first on the list, but instead occupies the third position.[81] One may reasonably infer that Jefferson had no intention of advising his friend to delete property from the list of rights, but rather to move it. Why should it be moved? The reason is obvious. Throughout the Whig tradition, property comes after life and freedom (it could not be otherwise). It was William Blackstone who ultimately awarded property the place the entire school had already assigned to it: "The third absolute right, inherent in every Englishman, is that of property."[82]

The failure to close the parenthesis must also have caught the attention of Gilbert Chinard. Insistent upon portraying Jefferson as opposed to property rights, Chinard resolved to take the matter in his own hands, and, in a work that quoted the document *verbatim*, Chinard himself closed the parenthesis.[83] In this context, it cannot be overlooked that Chinard was one of the main editors and commentators of Jefferson, although it could be said that his interventions have often been philologically questionable.

It is relevant to mention that on the issue of property rights, Chinard attributed to Jefferson's hand a letter that had actually been written *to* Jefferson by Thomas Paine.[84] The letter in question seems to confirm the distinction in Jefferson's mind between natural rights and "secondary rights," the latter including property rights, but for the small detail that, far from being written by Jefferson, it was instead sent to him.[85] Realizing his appalling mistake many years later, Chinard republished the letter, claiming that those words, although written by Paine, were, in fact, a perfect representation of the thought of Thomas Jefferson. It is worth reproducing the fragment in which Chinard blithely confesses his mistake and deliberately perseveres in his error. So powerfully swayed is the French professor by his own biased paradigm that he produces a travesty of Jefferson's thought:

> In the first edition of this study was inserted at this point a document which I erroneously attributed to Jefferson, when, in fact, it came from the pen of Thomas Paine and was probably written ten years later. While expressing my regrets and apologies to the writers who have been misled by this false attribution, I still believe that it sums up so concisely the early philosophy of Thomas Jefferson that it may be not out of place to reproduce it again.[86]

Inalienable Rights and Natural Rights

Some scholars, while recognizing that the opening propositions of the Declaration are of Lockean derivation, explain the modified triad through recourse to a concept of "inalienability" which does not completely coincide with that of "naturalness." In other words, certain rights are argued to be natural, but not inalienable, and among these is the right of property. This, it is maintained, is the key to Jefferson's removal of the term from the document.[87]

Before going into these arguments in greater detail, it is perhaps appropriate to state, as a premise, that alienable natural rights do indeed exist, but only if "natural" is taken to mean those rights that men possess in the state of nature. For example, in the Lockean version of natural rights, the right to self-defense is natural in the sense that it belongs to men in the state of nature. Yet not only is this right alienable, but it must necessarily be transferred to political society during the course of the transition from the state of nature to that of civil society. This notwithstanding, the construction of the distinction between "inalienable" and "natural" rights is, to say the least, founded on a distortion. Let us examine why.

Morton White, while asserting that happiness and property cannot be considered separately (proposing Geneva philosopher Jean Jacques Burlamaqui as one of the sources of Jeffersonian thought)[88] believes that "Jefferson could hardly have regarded the right to property...as unalienable...because the idea that one may alienate what one owns is at least as old as Aristotle."[89] Although Jean Yarbrough does not acknowledge that property rights have the character of naturalness in Jeffersonian thought, she nevertheless realizes the absurdity of considering them a mere fruit of conventions. "Jefferson...believed that men entered into society to secure their property as well as their persons, and that the protection of property was a legitimate concern of society."[90] Despite this valuable insight, Yarborough subscribes to White's stance when she states, "Inalienable rights refer to that category of natural rights that we cannot give up or transfer to another.... Although all inalienable rights are natural rights, deriving their inalienability from man's inherent nature, not all natural rights are inalienable. Stable and exclusive property, being less than a natural right, cannot be inalienable."[91]

The relation between natural and inalienable rights thus becomes increasingly complicated. In an essay composed in the early 1980s, a well-known and respected scholar of Locke, John Simmons, put forward a similar line of reasoning, although his investigation did not focus specifically on Jefferson.[92] Starting out from the obvious consideration that the term "inalienable" does not appear in the *Second Treatise*—although, in my view, such a notion is plainly implied—his entire construction was designed to demonstrate the existence of natural rights that were at the same time alienable. After a tortuous explanation of the differences that can be traced within certain types of rights versus others in Lockean thought, Simmons attempts to highlight several points by recourse to illuminating examples. To demonstrate that the right of property is alienable despite being natural, Simmons offers this example: "I may decline to exercise my property rights by allowing the neighborhood children to play baseball in my yard."[93]

Despite Simmons's view that this shows alienability, surely, in this specific case, I am clearly making full use of my rights of property over the yard, inasmuch as these imply the possibility of excluding or including others as I please. Simmons further contended, "There is no oddity in the idea of a right being, for a specified period of time only, alienated (as in a contract granting temporary property rights)."[94] Of course there is not. But one may wonder what relevance this has for the issue of the "alienability" of property rights.

These reflections reveal the existence of an underlying confusion, which, were we not talking about serious and refined scholars, one might be tempted to say are ludicrous; that being, a confusion between a right and the object of a right. The right of property entails the power to alienate the goods that form the object of this right. Jefferson espoused this triviality to an Indian chief: "The lands were your property. The right to sell is one of the rights of property. To forbid you the exercise of that right would be a wrong to your nation."[95]

Individuals could conceivably never exchange a single good during the entire course of their lives and still fully enjoy the inalienable and natural right of property, on a par with the greatest investor or real estate owner in the world. This is because the right of property in no way derives from market transactions. An exchange transfers rights over things, but it does not create the right. Rather, property rights derive from the nature of human beings, primarily from their full ownership of themselves.

The real foundation of the natural right to property is not rights over things, but self-ownership. One cannot deprive oneself of self-ownership, while on the other hand, rights over tangible things are perfectly alienable. Since man cannot abjure himself and his own nature, all rights that constitute the essence of a human being are inalienable. That is, they cannot form the object of a transaction, whether voluntary or involuntary. To put it simply, "We may alienate (or destroy) the object of an inalienable right, but not the right itself."[96] As far as property rights are concerned, it is perfectly plain that the possibility to alienate property rights over things in no way entails the right to alienate the right itself or the moral capacity to be the holder of property rights.[97]

The paradox of inalienable rights, all of which are, of course, natural rights, lies precisely in the fact that no one can legitimately deprive himself of them. Or, rather, even if a person were to do so, others could not take this into account. Imagine the case of a man who abandons a monastic order, where he had taken a vow of poverty, in order to return to broader society. Can he be said to have alienated his right of property to the extent that anyone may feel entitled to take over the goods he legitimately possesses? Obviously not. Or consider the much more striking case of the inalienable and natural right to life. Can someone who has attempted suicide then be killed by anyone, given that the would-be suicide has signaled he has "alienated" his right to life? If the importance of self-ownership within the concept of human nature is not fully understood, then it becomes difficult to comprehend why property rights took on such immeasurable importance for eighteenth-century thinkers. It is the right to dispose fully and freely of one's own body, of one's own faculties, of the fruits of one's labors, and of all that is acquired without violating the rights of others.

Defining rights as "inalienable" simply means that they cannot be estranged from the subject, either by the holder of these rights or by anyone else. These are rights that cannot be disposed of by the government. In fact, government is the most typical violator of such rights. In the eighteenth century, the adjectives "natural," "inalienable," inherent," and "essential" appear as synonyms. In the case of Jefferson, for example, the rights that governments had been established among men to safeguard were defined as "intrinsic and unalienable" in the Declaration, while "freedom of religion [is] the most inalienable and sacred of all human rights."[98] The usage of the terms is admittedly less than rigorous (in a strictly logical perspective, inalienability admits of no gradations), because the doctrine to which these terms refer is clear and familiar. Inalienable simply means that no one can deprive himself (or his descendants) of these rights, not even voluntarily. But inalienability bears the imprint of nature. Nature makes certain rights inalienable by branding them with her own imprint. By creating man, the "God of Nature" has also endowed man with natural and inalienable rights. These two characteristics of the rights imprinted by nature are inseparable.

If one wished to find a means of distinguishing between these two categories, one could perhaps argue that inalienability refers directly to the "inner" space of a right, while naturalness has a bearing on the political sphere. I cannot relinquish my inalienable rights, just as the government cannot legitimately violate my natural rights. From the point of view of the government, these rights must be considered natural, while for the individual they must be considered inalienable. Consequently, the fact that a right is inalienable means that the individual cannot surrender it, and, since it is natural, the government cannot sever it from the individual.

Although such comments may appear simplistic in the eyes of sophisticated contemporary observers, these were precisely the terms and the framework the Founding Fathers had in mind when reflecting on rights. They would never have believed it possible that a right to a certain quality of life could be put forward, or a right over another person's goods, or the right to have a minimum income guaranteed through taxation. If these particular conceptions of what constitutes a right have become common currency, and, indeed, perfectly respectable within present-day social philosophy, then this is all the more reason why extreme care should be taken to restrict such conceptions to the contemporary debate.

Current interpreters generally do little justice to the fervent supporters of natural rights of many generations ago, because they do not believe—it is claimed they cannot any longer believe—that nature herself prescribes man's rights. When a building technique declines, its secrets are lost. What appeared simple to the architects of Gothic cathedrals remains a mystery for posterity. In the same manner, current debates on rights, even when conducted in the apparent attempt to reconstruct a lost world, lead to such a complicated rendering of what used to be simple and clear in the eighteenth century as to make it totally unrecognizable. We stand today in the wake of a protracted spell of juridical normativism, in which the ancient notion *Quod principi placuit legis habet vigorem* (What pleases the prince is law)[99] has been enormously refined. That this tendency has also succeeded in making it impossible for scholars to grasp the concept of an order founded not on the volition of a sovereign authority but on nature is one of its most predictable consequences.

Property over Ideas?

A hasty reading of a Jeffersonian reflection in which he considers the full right over ideas to be illegitimate, and explicitly acknowledges the utilitarian character of such a right, has led some scholars to fabricate a further piece of a mosaic to be fitted into the construction of a Jeffersonian softness on property rights.[100]

The conclusion that Jefferson was against copyright by no means allows one to deduce that he was opposed to the natural origin of the rights of property. In fact, the question of intellectual property is far from being resolved unequivocally within classical liberal doctrine of Lockean descent. Whereas a notable nineteenth-century classical liberal such as Gustave de Molinari was in favor of a perpetual intellectual right of property, conceiving ownership of ideas as perfectly analogous to ownership of a material good, other classical liberals argued in favor of the natural right of single individuals to copy and reproduce whatever is legitimately theirs. In the latter perspective, such thinkers also argue against the claim that there can exist a monopoly, even if only for a limited period of time, guaranteed by the government and consenting to the exploitation of this or that intellectual creation. Even in cases in which they have analyzed the possible alternatives between the current public safeguarding of intellectual property rights and a hypothetical free order that would require authors to internalize the costs of introducing protection against imitation (by means of contracts, technical solutions, and so forth), economists and jurists of the classical liberal tradition have not reached the same conclusions.[101]

Murray Rothbard's thoughts on government protection of property rights over ideas provide insights on public protection of copyrights in matters concerning literary production or patents. No one, according to Rothbard, can maintain that material goods, which can become exclusive property, should be regarded as equivalent to ideas that are freely circulating and are not lost at the moment when another person also comes into contact with them. This does not mean that the author of a text or the inventor of a patented device cannot find suitable strategies to exploit his own work in the most successful manner possible, while still respecting classical liberal principles. For in surrendering a literary work or the use of an invention, an author or an inventor can require a clause to be signed, whereby the purchaser is forbidden to carry out reproductions or to utilize the intellectual content incorporated in the object beyond a certain date.[102]

Rothbard does not quote Jefferson, but his arguments seem to echo those in the above-mentioned letter. The third president totally denies that inventors have any "natural and exclusive right" to their inventions. "If nature has made any one thing less susceptible than all others of exclusive property, it is the action of the thinking power called an idea.... The moment it is divulged, it forces itself into the possession of every one, and the receiver cannot dispossess himself of it."[103] What is the specific characteristic, he wonders, of an idea? "Its peculiar character...is that no one possesses the less, because every other possesses the whole of it." But the argument against exclusive possession is entirely derived from the very nature of the "good" describable as an idea.

> That ideas should freely spread from one to another over the globe, for the moral and mutual instruction of man, and improvement of his condition, seems to have been peculiarly and benevolently designed by nature, when she made them, like fire, expansible over all space, without lessening their density in any point, and like the air in which we breathe, move, and have our physical being, incapable of confinement or exclusive appropriation. Inventions then cannot, in nature, be a subject of property.[104]

As a result, all rights arising from the exploiting of one's own ideas are either contractual or customary. Indeed, it is precisely Jefferson's position, which denies the naturalness of a monopoly over the exploitation of mere ideas, that appears to be more consistent with the classical liberal and Lockean tradition.

The Sovereignty of the Present Generation

Another famous piece by Jefferson takes a position that most authors find hard to reconcile with the doctrine of property rights of Lockean lineage. The reference here is to the famous letter written during the final stage of his stay in Paris, where the French Revolution was by now in full swing. It is addressed to James Madison and dated September 1789. The contents of the letter underscore the concept that the "Earth Belongs in Usufruct to the Living."[105]

The reflections on generational sovereignty put forward by Jefferson have now become a classic of American political literature of the era, but far from being an expression of antiproperty extremism (as some have sought to claim), they are instead assertions of the idea of founding a society by "taking reason for our guide, instead of English precedent."[106] Indeed, reason has priority over any other manner of building a society, because it is the law of nature. According to John Locke, "The state of Nature has a law of Nature to govern it, which obliges every one, and reason, which is that law, teaches all mankind who will but consult it, that being all equal and independent, no one ought to harm another in his life, health, liberty or possessions."[107]

The question that Jefferson put to his friend—a problem Jefferson believed to be rather original—was that of "whether one generation of men has a right to bind another." His answer was totally to the negative: "I set out on this ground which I suppose to be self evident, that the earth belongs in usufruct to the living."[108] Because, he went on, "society and society, or generation and generation there is no municipal obligation, no umpire but the law of nature. We seem not to have perceived that, by the law of nature, one generation is to another as one independent nation to another."[109]

These thoughts have been interpreted by some scholars as a sort of momentary aberration, as Jefferson was carried on the wave of emotion arising from the events in France. Julian Boyd states without hesitation that such a vision "is irrelevant for the American situation."[110] The same opinion is also voiced by Noble Cunningham.[111] Certainly, the letter was written at a very critical time, just a few days after the National Assembly had thrown out the proposal to insert the clause Jefferson had discussed with Lafayette, referring to the right of future generations—*le droit des générations qui se succèdent*—to revise the Constitution (26 August 1789). But there is reason to believe Jefferson was not thinking only of France. The tone of his letter is very general, and the mention of the law of nature as the only yardstick in the relations among generations leaves little room for doubt: The range of application of the principles expressed is extremely wide and addressed to all human communities that have decided to live in accordance with the rules of reason.

Furthermore, Jefferson asked Madison to go ahead and make use of the letter, and the suggestions contained therein, within the framework of American legislation. "Your station in the councils of our country gives you an opportunity of producing it to public consideration.... At first blush it may be rallied as a theoretical speculation; but examination will prove it to be solid and salutary."[112] The American circumstances appeared a most promising terrain for the prompt implementation of such a principle, since "we do not owe a shilling which may not be paid with ease principal and interest, within the time of our own lives."[113]

The notion of a potentially ever-changing constitution—the one Jefferson expounds in this letter—was and still is opposed by thinkers of a conservative bent. Edmund Burke replied to the radical reformers headed by the young William Pitt, who called for a wide-ranging alteration of the British constitution as representation and suffrage, by upholding the virtues of the permanence of the constitution itself against the vagaries of opinion: "Man is a most unwise and a most wise being. The individual is foolish; the multitude, for the moment, is foolish, when they act without deliberation; but the species is wise, and, when time is given to it, as a species, it almost always acts right."[114]

The virtue of the British constitution lay indeed in its unchanging, almost organic, character. "It is a constitution made by what is ten thousand times better than choice; it is made by the peculiar circumstances, occasions, tempers, dispositions, and moral, civil, and social habitudes of the people, which disclose themselves only in a long space of time."[115] As to the independence of a generation from the preceding ones, Burke believed that "a nation is not an idea only of local extent and individual momentary aggregation, but it is an idea of continuity that extends in time as well as in numbers and in space."[116]

To be sure, Burke acknowledged the merit of the arguments based on natural law but recognized that they were completely outside a political frame of reference and went to impinge on more fundamental considerations. "They who plead an absolute right [to individual self-government] cannot be satisfied with anything short of personal representation, because all natural rights must be the rights of individuals, as by nature there is no such thing as politic or corporate personality: all these ideas are mere fictions of law, they are creatures of voluntary institutions; men as men are individuals, and nothing else."[117]

Let us focus again on the idea that "the Earth belongs in usufruct to the living." Much has been written on this concept, in some cases with startling and highly contestable interpretations.[118] Among the latter category, perhaps the most remarkable is that offered by Staughton Lynd: "The most important American reflection...about property was Jefferson's doctrine that the earth belongs to the living. It was in this form that the Revolutionary generation approached most nearly the socialist conception that living labor has claims superior to any property rights."[119]

By contrast, the Jeffersonian approach, with its powerful thrust toward sweeping away any order that is based on privilege or runs counter to reason, is truly revolutionary, even though it is predominantly grounded in the common sense of his era. And it is revolutionary, a widely held view notwithstanding, in a genuinely Lockean sense.

Given the absolutely speculative nature of Jefferson's letter/essay, totally devoid of references to possible sources, I will put forward an interpretation based on logical inferences and cogency of arguments. Let us start from Locke's *Second Treatise*, a potential background that has been unjustly uncharted in this regard.

Crawford B. Macpherson suggests repeatedly that Locke was responsible for transforming the natural right of property of the individual to the means for his subsistence into a right of illimitable appropriation, leaving nonproperty owners no choice but to sell their labor.[120] The assessment is not novel, as it moves along the same lines of the "Georgist" critique. Henry George was convinced that whoever owned the land could also reduce his fellow men to slavery. "Place one hundred men on an island from which there is no escape, and whether you make one of these men the absolute owner of the other ninety-nine, or the absolute owner of the soil of the island, will make no difference either to him or to them."[121]

However, at least in the first state of nature (the second arises with the institutionalization of money), Locke's theory of appropriation appears anything but unlimited. Quite the opposite, in fact. The limits he sets are so stringent (and probably logically unsustainable[122]) that one might even go so far as to conjecture the impossibility of private property in the Lockean state of nature. Locke's proviso and its restrictions on appropriation are discussed later in this book.

A clearer understanding of this question can be obtained by first examining some of the main points of the Lockean theory of property. In the Lockean vision, the prerequisite of natural justice is common ownership without individual appropriation. Jefferson echoed this conception almost verbatim in a note from Paris written to Rev. James Madison, head of William and Mary College and father of his considerably more renowned namesake: "The earth is given as a common stock for man to labour and live on."[123]

What Locke sought to demonstrate was that a developmental path could be traced without violating the principles of justice, starting out from the state of affairs in which the whole of the earth was given by God to all men in common and eventually leading to private property. Given the fact that God originally gave the earth to Adam and then to all of Adam's descendants, it follows that it was given to all men in common. However, Locke makes clear, what has never been held in common is self-ownership: "Though the earth and all inferior creatures be common to all men, yet every man has a 'property' in his own 'person.' This nobody has any right to but himself."[124]

A person acquires rights of property over a *res nullius* by blending his or her own labor with the object. That which previously was inert and without any utilization whatsoever, now can no longer be characterized in this manner, by virtue of human labor. That which an individual removes from the state of nature should properly be considered as his, because he has mixed his labor with matter. According to Locke, "[This] excludes the common right of other men. For this 'labour' being the unquestionable property of the labourer, no man but he can have a right to what that is once joined to."[125]

The perfect legitimacy of this process derives from the fact that every person has full title to his or her own body, faculties, and talents. By no means can this be regarded as a sort of device designed to justify the original acquisition. For Locke, consensus and communal property must be taken at face value. If a man's body and will belonged to other individuals, and not exclusively to the subject himself, he would have to ask other human beings, the true proprietors, for permission to act.

Locke adds a stringent condition for the possibility of appropriation, though, namely that there must be "at least...enough, and as good left in common for others."[126] It is this which constitutes the Lockean proviso, the meaning of which is further clarified:

> Nor was this appropriation of any parcel of land, by improving it, any prejudice to any other man, since there was still enough and as good left, and more than the yet unprovided could use.... Nobody could think himself injured by the drinking of another man, though he took a good draught, who had a whole river of the same water left him to quench his thirst. And the case of land and water, where there is enough of both, is perfectly the same.[127]

Liberty, State, & Union

The other restriction on original appropriation is that of the possibility of utilizing the appropriated products.

> As much land as a man tills, plants, improves, cultivates, and can use the product of, so much is his property.... God and his reason commanded him to subdue the earth—i.e., improve it for the benefit of life and therein lay out something upon it that was his own, his labour. He that, in obedience to this command of God, subdued, tilled, and sowed any part of it, thereby annexed to it something that was his property, which another had no title to, nor could without injury take from him.[128]

The Lockean proviso, apparently intended to be valid for all goods, actually applies most particularly to the case of land.[129] However, with the transition to the second state of nature, which comes about through the invention of money, and, above all, to political society by means of the contract, both the proviso and the limit of perishability and effective utilization of the products vanish completely.

Some scholars have argued that in the Lockean framework, with the transition to the second state of nature and then to political society, private property becomes illegitimate. Since the institutionalization of money supersedes all the natural limitations to private appropriations, the system goes back to the original premise of common ownership. As the proviso is not satisfied anymore—there is not "enough and as good" left for others— the goods once legitimately owned in private revert to common ownership.[130]

The possibility of accumulating incorruptible goods, such as gold and silver, leads to the logical disappearance of the limits, because "the exceeding of the bounds of his just property [is] not lying in the largeness of his possession, but [in] the perishing of anything uselessly in it."[131] The spread of precious metals leads to a world in which man "may, rightfully and without injury, possess more than he himself can make use of by receiving gold and silver, which may continue long in a man's possession *without decaying for the overplus.*"[132] Taken at face value, the Lockean proviso would result in a prohibition against appropriation in the state of nature. As Murray Rothbard has pointed out, "Locke's proviso may lead to the outlawry of all private ownership of land, since one can always say that the reduction of available land leaves everyone else, who could have appropriated the land, worse off."[133]

Moreover, again within the framework of the economic analysis put forward by the Austrian school, Israel Kirzner has made clear that a discovery act does not necessarily leave anybody worse off, because, prior to that discovery, the resource simply did not exist.[134]

Such an interpretation is particularly interesting inasmuch as it explicitly harkens back to the Lockean doctrine of property, while rejecting the proviso. In Rothbard's account, "The homesteader—just as the sculptor, or miner—has transformed the nature-given soil by his labor and his personality."[135] He argues, "The land communalists, who claim that the entire world population really owns the land in common, run up against the natural fact that before the homesteader, no one really used and controlled, and hence owned the land. The pioneer, or homesteader, is the man who first brings the valueless unused natural objects into production and use."[136] By contrast, Robert Nozick accepts the proviso. Indeed, he awards it a pivotal position in his analysis of justice in the acquisition of property by root of title.[137]

Thus, contemporary debate on this issue is multifaceted, but it is clear that the dismissal of the Lockean proviso comes from scholars belonging to the Austrian school of economics. It is only through elaboration of the analyses put forward by a tradition that sprang from Carl Menger, and was worked out in greater detail in the works of Ludwig von Mises, that a blatant contradiction is thrown into sharp relief. The incongruity is in considering a resource to have been nonexistent for mankind up to that specific moment, while also regarding it as unappropriable because this would worsen another individual's situation. Clearly, this theoretical option was totally absent both in the era of Locke and in Jefferson's time, for knowledge of the "discovery" mechanisms typical of a market economy was still in its infancy.

At any rate, Jefferson's assertions concerning land and the sovereignty of the present generation is nothing more than an extension of the limits on exploitation set by Locke. Putting property to good use (a prohibition against waste) and the Lockean proviso (appropriation of goods without causing a deterioration in the condition of others) are restrictions that hold in the relations between generations, and they illuminate the theoretical framework of Jeffersonian thought.

For the author of the Declaration, as we have seen, the generations stand facing one another, as do whole nations or individuals in the state of nature.[138] Therefore, the law of nature regulates their relations. It is the duty of a generation to leave land "enough and as good" for the following generations. This is evidently an extension of the proviso, because the properties are the same. One's own successors do not enjoy a generic right to unexplored lands, but to the specific property already owned by their parents. Just as the new generations have the right to get property that is not burdened with debts, so also the "others," those who do not participate in that specific appropriation, have exactly the same right to enjoy land "enough and as good" in the Lockean state of nature. Similarly, property cannot be exploited and destroyed, jeopardizing the future of the coming generations. Waste is not countenanced by the law of nature.

The sovereignty of the present generation can thus be defined as the right to receive a world in which the present has not been mortgaged by the ancestors. Every nineteen years, according to Jefferson's calculations (which were based on the mortality tables formulated by Georges Louis Leclerc, Comte de Buffon), a generation comes into the world. This generation has the right to a fresh start, whereas the one that preceded it had the duty not to destroy the world in which the present generation must live.

Jefferson enormously expands the range of action of this principle. All laws, constitutions, and personal and public debts are erased at the close of the nineteen years. "Every constitution...and every law, naturally expires at the end of 19 years. If it be enforced longer, it is an act of force and not of right."[139] However—and many commentators place excessive emphasis on the present generation, often losing sight of the meaning of the duties to which the previous generation is beholden—this idea, which in itself appears radical and revolutionary, is conservative in the etymological sense, if considered in reference to the preceding generation. Debts that extend beyond one's own generation cannot be valid. The sins of the fathers do not pass on to their children, but they are undeniably sins. We are dealing with a principle of personal and generational self-restraint that is endowed with the full force bestowed on it by virtue of its being grounded in natural law.

Jefferson imagines a sort of "permanent revolution," a constant transition between society and the state of nature, such as will maintain the criteria of justice intact. The new and "innocent" beginning that is the birthright of each generation is also a social contract by means of which everything can be thought out afresh, except for the idea that this may be possessed of extragenerational effect, or may in any other way run counter to natural law. Since laws tend over time to stray from natural law, the reiteration of the contract enables each generation to reestablish its bond with the natural order. This can be understood as a device intended to revive the identity between natural and "municipal" laws that lies at the center of Jefferson's political concerns. It would ensure a means for unfailingly restating at regular intervals that natural law and the provisions deriving from nature itself and from reason are in full force. The relations prevailing between the generations are formed by the law of nature alone, and, at every new beginning of a generation over the world, a new contract, or an explicit statement of support for the old contract, would be compulsory. Jefferson thereby sidestepped the problem of "tacit consent" that had arisen in the Lockean framework, where, by merely living in a place, the individual implicitly gave consent to the system of government in force. Instead, Jefferson moved toward a fully consensual conception of political obligation.

Madison regarded this vision with disapproval. While appreciating its principle, Madison could not fail to realize that it would severely undermine the security of property rights. The fears voiced by Madison in connection with frequent constitutional changes are well known.[140] The Jeffersonian doctrine, if applied coherently, would have involved fixed-term constitutions and laws that would be subject not merely to the possibility but rather to the certainty of revision in the space of less than two decades. In fact, it would have resulted in a situation in which it would no longer be possible for approval to be implicit. Naturally, a given generation could simply reiterate approval of all the laws passed by the previous one, but this would have required unequivocal action.

Madison replied that land could be transferred only in its natural state, devoid of the improvements ushered in by the deceased, because the present generation draws advantage from the enhancements of property that were the work of those no longer among the living. In essence, if we accept the benefits, then we are also duty bound to accept the damage that previous generations inflicted on the heritage they have handed down to posterity. Furthermore, public debts, Madison added, can also be contracted for a good cause, as had been the case for the funding of the American Revolution.

Madison's worries were indeed momentous. Jeffersonian radicalism was difficult to reconcile with the certainty of property rights. But the debate should by no means be conceived of as a contrast between a Socialist and a classical liberal. Rather, it was fully internal to the Lockean tradition of natural rights, a tradition reshaped by Jefferson into one of its most radical formulations, consistently individualistic and property based. In fact, Jeffersonian thought is twofold: There exists a sort of "normal" flow of political thought and a utopian momentum. In the latter, he forced the horizon beyond its customary limits and demonstrated that, by following the classical principles that presided over the construction of modern natural law, one can reach extremes of radicalism capable of subverting any non-natural order. One cannot but agree with Herbert Sloan, who affirms that "Jefferson is…capable of creating his own form of utopia, debt-free, beneficent, and in keeping with the teachings of natural law."[141]

Finally, a specific question must be addressed. Why was this reflection received with such embarrassment by those who see a Lockean Jefferson—a Jefferson as champion of limited government and natural rights—and with such jubilation by those who advocate a departure from this view in various ways? This can be explained by the fact that neither side appreciated the revolutionary character of classical liberal doctrine. The majority of commentators we have mentioned composed their works when, in Europe, "liberalism" had become synonymous with social conservatism, and the self-proclaimed heirs of the classical American liberal tradition had become avowedly conservative.

Jefferson, on the other hand, both in his most radical writings and in his condemnation of feudal vestige, seemed to be driven by concerns springing from that historical approach—of radical and classical liberal origin—which claimed that the feudal overlords had built up their wealth thanks to the favors granted by political power and by a system that cannot be reconciled with the natural order. Over time, these favors had been paid by the underclass, by those who had far less access to political power and, as a result, to the iniquitous means of acquiring property. Adopting Jefferson's line of reasoning, it would seem that one could envision a genuinely revolutionary program designed to expropriate the expropriators.

Justice demands respect for rules, procedures, and guarantees. Over two centuries ago, Jefferson pondered the hypothesis of striking out against those who drew advantage from an unjust system. He believed in a strong version of natural rights, in particular, property rights, legitimized on the basis of a reconstruction that included the historical framework. A person is the owner of a certain house because he has purchased it with honestly earned money, or because he won it in a lottery, or because it was donated to him, and so forth. A correct procedure, one that does not encroach on the property rights of others, legitimates ownership. But if this is true in a positive sense, it must be so in a negative sense as well. Illegitimate procedures must (should) be followed by expropriation and restitution.

In sum, Jefferson the political thinker (not, of course, Jefferson in power) was spurred by an impetus toward a radical rethinking of the whole of society and its rules, prompted by total rejection of any point of reference other than reason. This radicalism is difficult to reconcile with the concept of "liberalism" held by many historians. Consequently, those who have embarked on the project of interpreting the great Virginian as a classical liberal have done so by giving a very wide berth to his "utopias," while those who have endeavored to seriously address the most utopian aspects of his thought have ended up fabricating a collectivist, organicist, and protosocialist Jefferson. Thus, an in-depth understanding of the revolutionary character of the classical liberal theory of natural rights represents one of the necessary steps in order to do justice to Jefferson.

Jefferson on Property

As a politician and a statesman, "Jefferson consistently opposed the destruction of property rights by agents of government, even with majoritarian support."[142] Doubt has never been cast on this view, as far as I am aware. Those who would classify Jefferson in the role of a protosocialist and veritable champion of man in a nonexistent struggle between the latter and the dollar restrict themselves to speculating on his thought. As I hope to have demonstrated, the line of reasoning they espouse is deceptive.

Given the character of this analysis, it is germane to dwell in greater depth on Jefferson's support for an understanding of property rights that rigorously clings to natural law. Over time, Jefferson voiced numerous criticisms against various laws on property whenever such laws effectively guaranteed the property of certain individuals at the expense of other people's property. However, all of Jefferson's criticisms are grounded on positive laws, contending that the government, which had been established to safeguard the property of all of the people, was now being redesigned to safeguard the property of some at the expense of others.

Let us turn to some passages in which Jefferson's statements in favor of the naturalness of rights of property are crystal clear. In his discussion of state constitutions, Jefferson wrote that these were sound fundamental laws since, despite all their differences, they enshrined the concept that citizens "are entitled to freedom of person, freedom of religion, freedom of property, and freedom of the press."[143] This view mirrors other reflections he put forward elsewhere, which makes it clear that he fully endorsed a Lockean conception in an oblique yet no less significant manner. In annotations to the work by Antoine-Louis-Claude Destutt de Tracy, Jefferson wrote, "If the overgrown wealth of an individual is deemed dangerous to the State, the best corrective is the law of equal inheritance to all in equal degree; and the better, as this enforces a law of nature, while extra-taxation violates it."[144]

In addition, in another important consideration on finance and on the tools required for a sound credit system, Jefferson offered a more classical line of reasoning. "No one has a natural right to the trade of a money lender, but he who has the money to lend."[145] If a person who has money to lend has a natural right to practice the profession of money lender, then his entitlement to his own money is likewise original and natural.

A letter from Jefferson to the well-known Physiocrat and free-trade advocate Pierre Samuel Du Pont de Nemours, who lived in America, contains a statement whereby the Virginian maintains that justice, not majority rule, constitutes the foundation of society. Moreover, he openly recognizes that property is founded on the natural rights of individuals: "I believe…that a right to property is founded in our natural wants, in the means with which we are endowed to satisfy these wants, and the right to what we acquire by those means without violating the similar rights of other sensible beings."[146]

In 1816, Jefferson wrote to his friend Samuel Kercheval that "the true foundation of republican government is the equal right of every citizen, in his person and property, and in their management."[147] Therefore, the legitimacy of democracy itself derives from firm support for the principles of individualist natural law. Indeed, Jefferson reiterated that political rights are inextricably associated with natural rights and, more specifically, with rights of property: "No Englishman will pretend that a right to participate in government can be derived from any other source than a personal right, or a right of property."[148] On this point, Michael Zuckert aptly asserts that Jefferson did not reject the natural right of property in favor of a higher form of democracy, but rather derived his higher form of democracy from the right of property.[149]

It is also important to note, with regard to the closely connected theme of the redistribution of wealth, that Jefferson spoke a language that was unequivocally in harmony with classical liberal thought, ruling out that variations in the structure of the majority in the assemblies might lead to a power to legislate on questions of property. "To take from one, because it is thought that his own industry and that of his fathers has acquired too much, in order to spare to others, who, or whose fathers have not exercised equal industry and skill, is to violate arbitrarily the first principle of association, 'the guarantee to every one of a free exercise of his industry, and the fruits acquired by it.'"[150]

In his first inaugural address as president, Jefferson reiterated that he preferred a "government, which…shall leave them…free to regulate their own pursuits of industry and improvement."[151] Four years later, in his second inaugural address, he declared that the government must maintain the "state of property, equal or unequal, which results to every man from his own industry, or that of his fathers."[152]

Of prime importance is the celebrated passage from *Notes on the State of Virginia*, in which Jefferson states that the government's acts with regard to freedom of conscience are illegitimate because conscience inflicts no harm on any citizen. "The legitimate powers of government extend to such acts only as are injurious to others. But it does me no injury for my neighbour to say that there are twenty gods, or no god. It neither picks my pocket nor breaks my leg."[153]

Here, in addition to a foreshadowing of the classical theme of nineteenth-century liberalism, it is clear that Jefferson regarded property and protection against physical harm as closely correlated. In what way can one inflict injury on others? By encroaching on their natural rights. As a suitable example, Jefferson mentions picking a pocket and breaking a leg: The absolute goods to be safeguarded are one's property and freedom from physical harm. That such a conception is fully in tune with Locke's approach can clearly be seen by comparing it with the *Epistola*, "No injury is thereby done to anyone, no prejudice to another man's good."[154]

Although eclectic in his economic persuasion—a Physiocrat in his early days, subsequently converted to the teachings of Adam Smith, and then an admirer of Destutt de Tracy in his maturity—Jefferson evinced a preference for a laissez-faire regime that would allow the free operation of talents, efforts, and prior situations (e.g., inheritance, possibly impartially divided amongst all offspring) as compared to any conceivable redistribution of wealth. In a recent dictionary of American political thought, Jefferson is correctly presented as one of the early American champions of laissez-faire capitalism.[155]

This should be no cause for surprise, since Jeffersonian thought is totally devoid of that collectivist view which is conducive to the acceptance of a redistributive approach. In the above-mentioned letter on the theme of generational sovereignty, Jefferson states, "What is true of every member of the society individually, is true of them all collectively, *since the rights of the whole can be no more than the sum of the rights of individuals.*"[156] It is precisely this outlook that must be kept in mind in order to understand the true meaning of the "pursuit of happiness" in Jeffersonian doctrine; that is, the right to have a government that does not infringe on one's own natural rights, in particular, on property rights.

4

Popular Sovereignty from Locke to Jefferson

> Where the law of majority ceases to be acknowledged, there
> government ends, the law of the strongest takes its place, and life and
> property are his who can take them.[1]

In the previous chapter, we discussed at length the perfect compatibility
between Locke's arguments in favor of property and those of the Virginian.
It is now necessary to summarize the positions of the Englishman on some
crucial political-doctrinal points in order to grasp the clear Lockean
derivation of Jefferson's thinking. An analysis of the idea of civil society, of
government, consensus, and majority rule in the thought of Locke and
Jefferson will clearly show the thread that runs between the two. In
particular, it must be emphasized that John Locke, whose main doctrinal
contributions are the theory of consensus, majority rule, popular
sovereignty, and natural rights, pursued the very same line of enquiry on
the question of government as did the Virginian. Locke endeavored to
show how a legitimate government is formed, not how governments
historically rose. Just as Locke did not state that all governments arise
through a contract, but that the only legitimate governments are thus
established, Jefferson affirmed that the just powers of governments drew
their origin from the consensus of those governed. The complete lack of
historical references in Locke matches the general scorn Jefferson showed
toward past eras, to that "semibarbarous ancestry" from which America had
freed itself. For this reason, a brief illustration of Jefferson's view of history
seems an appropriate conclusion to the present chapter.

In general, the slight differences of political stance between the English
philosopher and the American thinker are mere radicalizations. Jefferson
amplifies Locke's political precepts, showing less faith in government and
political power and greater reliance on the majority and on "the people."
Indeed, the author of the Declaration was convinced that the people could
not, of their own volition, divest themselves of their natural rights (one

must make allowances; he hadn't witnessed what later generations did). Likewise, Jefferson also believed the people to be the best guardians of their own unalienable rights. In brief, he believed *inalienability* put a premium on the *naturalness* of laws. Suspicion toward government weakens, although never completely fading away, when the government is completely controlled by the people.

Let us start out with a subject that has already been touched upon: happiness.

Property and Happiness

One of the greatest oddities of the antiproperty interpretations of Jefferson, to which we have devoted extensive attention, is that the pursuit of happiness, included amongst the natural rights listed by the Declaration, has been used to suggest a non-Lockean origin of the document. As we have seen, many commentators have emphasized that the American founding act could perhaps be considered vaguely Lockean, but the mention of the pursuit of happiness, it is claimed, imparts a completely different character upon it, thereby disconnecting the Declaration from the Whig tradition. Quite the opposite is true, though. The document's firm roots in Lockean ground should be seen precisely in the right of the pursuit of happiness.

John Locke is one of the greatest theorists of happiness. Happiness, its pursuit, and its relation with the legal framework and with natural rights are constant themes throughout his works. Happiness is the supreme value that dominates man's and even God's actions: "God Almighty himself is under the necessity of being happy."[2] According to Walter Euchner, "The true meaning of the Lockean theory of happiness lies…in that Locke enunciated it…in the form of a theory of human action."[3]

The almost hedonistic features of this pursuit of happiness have been noticed by numerous authors, and Leo Strauss detailed his vision of a veritable right to happiness that could incontrovertibly be inferred from Locke's philosophy.[4] There appears to be, in any case, a constant shifting in Locke from eudemonism to hedonism because of the changing concepts of happiness, often defined as mere absence of pain. A few examples will suffice.

In the *Essays on the Laws of Nature* (written in 1664, but only published in 1954), in the course of an investigation of the different notions of that which is good and that which is just in various nations in various eras,

Locke writes, "how to reach happiness, that is, about the law of nature."[5] The Englishman awards to the pursuit of happiness pride of place in his doctrinal analysis. Naturally, as has been widely noted, the specific expression "pursuit of happiness" recurs frequently in the *Essay Concerning Human Understanding*, a work that had a great influence on the young Jefferson. In a paragraph entitled "The necessity of pursuing true happiness the foundation of Liberty," Locke states,

> As therefore the highest perfection of intellectual nature lies in a careful and constant pursuit of true and solid happiness; so the care of ourselves, that we mistake not imaginary for real happiness, is the necessary foundation of our liberty. The stronger ties we have to an unalterable pursuit of happiness in general, which is our greatest good...the more are we free from any necessary determination of our will to any particular action.[6]

The pursuit of happiness is the supreme good that endows man's will and actions with freedom. The more steadily man keeps to the path toward happiness, the greater his freedom. And this steadiness springs from correct perception of the goal.

In the *Reasonableness of Christianity* (1695), one of Jefferson's favorite essays, from which he undoubtedly built up his own view on religious tolerance (together with *Letters Concerning Toleration* [1689])[7] Locke emphasizes, "Mankind, who are and must be allowed to pursue their happiness," feel little obligation to follow orders that appear in contrast with "their chief end, happiness."[8] The individual pursuit of happiness is essentially an insuperable limit for any religious, social, or juridical rule. Any laws conflicting with this goal would not be merely immoral but indeed quite pointless.

It is in some minor and unfinished essays, though, that the goal of the pursuit of happiness appears even more clear, as instrumental, hedonistic, a principle of pleasure that naturally drives individuals to behave in one way or another. In fact, "happiness consists in what delights and contents the mind; misery, in what disturbs, discomposes, or torments it."[9] Basically, Locke states, "the business of men [is] to be happy in this world by the enjoyment of the things of nature subservient to life, health, ease and pleasure." For "his mind and faculties were given him...to procure him the happiness which this world is capable of." As a result, mankind should "[direct] their thoughts to the improvements of such arts and inventions, engines and utensils as might best contribute to their continuation in [this world] with conveniency and delight."[10] How does one find happiness? "Morality is the rule of Man's actions for the attaining happiness," given that "happiness...being their end the means of attaining it can be alone the rule of action."[11] But happiness is also one of the firm foundations upon which the edifice of private property stands, since, although the holding of property in common is not unwarranted per se, Locke nevertheless states, "If all things be left in common, want rapine and force will unavoidably follow in which state, as is evident, happiness cannot be had which cannot consist without plenty and security."[12]

So what must the government do to promote the happiness of its citizens? The government's duty is to act against those who abuse the natural order to restore safety, the precondition for the pursuit of happiness, and nothing more. No public happiness exists that can be achieved by simply enacting some legislation. At best, it is possible to remove the impediments to the free pursuit of happiness, namely the fear that others may behave in a way harmful to our own natural rights. Beyond the very complex problem of whether an early philosophy of laissez faire can be perceived in Locke, it is clearly true that no positive governmental act has ever been enacted to promote the happiness of individuals. The entire analysis of happiness eludes the politician's classifications, and it is no coincidence if Locke's most important political work features the term "happiness" itself only occasionally and not univocally.[13]

A view of happiness as the absence of government interference is also apparent in many pages of Jefferson's writings. Perhaps the following passage, written in 1802 during his first presidential term, is one of the most important for a proper understanding of the role of government in Jefferson's political doctrine. "The path we have to pursue is so quiet that we have nothing scarcely to propose to our Legislature. A noiseless course, not meddling with the affairs of others, unattractive of notice, is a mark that society is going on in happiness. If we can prevent the government from wasting the labors of the people, under the pretence of taking care of them, they must become happy."[14]

In fact, the pursuit of happiness is, for Jefferson, exactly what property is for Locke. Note that Locke does not use this last term univocally in the

Second Treatise. While it is often synonymous with estate, very often it becomes a cover term for all of man's natural rights. "Man...hath by nature a power not only to preserve his property—that is, his life, liberty, and estate, against the injuries and attempts of other men."[15] This broad notion of property, not restricted to physical goods, is what men aim to protect by establishing government. The political implications of the term "property" are extremely clear in Locke. One finds both the idea of the natural origin of property and that of the supreme end of government, namely the protection of property. Property is the code for Life, Liberty, and Estate, or rather of freedom and natural rights. Vis-à-vis the state, the individual must demand recognition of his own rights that are anterior to the establishment of any civil government. Vis-à-vis the individual, the state must ensure that the individual fully enjoys all of his natural rights. Thus, for Locke, society (synonymous with government) is preferable to the state of nature only under certain conditions. The natural state "is a state of limited safety and considerable uncertainty, a state of significant but not desperate 'inconveniences,' a state to which only certain limited forms of political society will be preferable."[16]

As early as 1664, Locke had identified the central point of his own political investigation: property and the law of nature. "The strongest protection of each Man's private property is the law of nature, without the observation of which it is impossible for anybody to be master of his own property and to pursue his own advantage."[17] In Locke, the concept of property is entirely political and tends to be confused with the implications of the social contract. Indeed, the supreme end of government is the defense of property.[18] It does not concern a sort of "obsession with property," since, as Martin Seliger correctly observes, "Locke's emphasis on the right of property seems to stem from his awareness that life and liberty may mainly be jeopardized through the violation of property rights."[19]

The Englishman thus believed that government arose for the protection of property, and, in a similar vein, Jefferson believed that it was established to permit men to pursue their own happiness without coercion. That is to say, the government's only purpose is to allow men their freedom and to afford them the same protection they would provide for themselves if only they were able. Otherwise put, "a wise and frugal government, which shall restrain men from injuring one another, which shall leave them otherwise free to regulate their own pursuits of industry and improvement, and shall not take from the mouth of labor the bread it has earned. This is the sum of good government, and this is necessary to close the circle of our felicities."[20]

Property and Consensus: Locke in America

Locke's doctrine, as we have emphasized, is a revolutionary approach destined to release its potential more in America than in his home country. By means of a complex theory based on the idea that "mixing" labor with inert matter gave the individual the right to possession of the land and its fruit, Locke justified the original acquisition of property. All this, of course, was envisioned as occurring in the state of nature, before any sort of stable political society had become established. The author of the *Two Treatises* thus added a crucial adjunct to the modes of legitimate acquisition of property: Whereas up until his time, voluntary exchange, bequest, and inheritance were the accepted ways to acquire property, from Locke onwards, the idea of legitimate original appropriation entered permanently into the debate on property and was destined to change it to a great extent.

Only the inconveniences of the state of nature—first and foremost the difficulty in maintaining law and order; the fact that the only way of resolving controversies was that of self-defense—drove men to enter, by means of a contract, into a state of society. "I easily grant that civil government is the proper remedy for the inconveniences of the state of Nature, which must certainly be great where men may be judges in their own case, since it is easy to be imagined that he who was so unjust as to do his brother an injury will scarce be so just as to condemn himself for it."[21]

The principle that no one should be able to judge when he is a party involved in a case (*nemo judex in re sua*) accounts for the birth of government. It is important to note that with the transition to society through a unanimous contract, men did not forgo their natural rights but only the right to take the law into their own hands. The contract therefore implies relinquishing the right of self-defense (a price compensated for by security in enjoying one's own rights), but not the forfeiture of natural rights, since according to Locke's doctrine, such rights are unalienable.

Nevertheless, the emergence of the contract (unanimously agreed) and the extremely limited ends of government are insufficient to protect individuals against the government's inclination to overstep its bounds. To complete his system, Locke introduces that very same right to resistance that the scholastic tradition and the seventeenth-century English Monarchomachs had already theorized: the appeal to Heaven. Thus, not only was political power to be extremely limited, it was also liable to arouse a "legitimate revolution" in case it acted in a way contrary to the ends for which it was established.

As already noted, Locke was considered an aside in the history of the political thought of English-speaking peoples to the historians belonging to the republican school. Some authors go as far as to deny that the *Two Treatises* had achieved any significant circulation in colonial America. Among these, John Dunn[22] states that the *Second Treatise* "was only one...among a large group of other works which expounded the Whig theory of the revolution, and all its preeminence within this group is not noticeable until well after the general outlines of the interpretation had become consolidated."[23] This does not seem a conclusive argument. The assertion that in America "the book was of no great popularity before 1750"[24] proves little or nothing. In actual fact, although Locke's ideas became widespread in the 1760s and 1770s,[25] the meeting between the author of the *Two Treatises* and America had already occurred both on the doctrinal and empirical level.

The colonies could already boast a political tradition founded on a compact, on the consensus of the governed, and on self-government. In 1639, the charter of Connecticut (Fundamental Orders of Connecticut),[26] considered the first authentic constitution of the American settlers, and which remained in force for 179 years, was based on the concept of "popular sovereignty," a political idea that Locke himself would develop many decades later. In short, the notion of sovereignty in America was first born in the minds of the people, not of the king's mentors, thereby making the American polity receptive to Locke's ideas. In some ways, the climate was more favorable in America than in England. From the institutional perspective, seventeenth-century England certainly knew the concept of "parliamentary sovereignty," while that of "popular sovereignty" was only sporadically mentioned and debated, for the most part, in the doctrinal field.[27]

Indeed, Donald Lutz is right when he observes that "many of the principles and assumptions of American constitutionalism were operative before Locke published his *Second Treatise on Civil Government.* In temporal terms, it makes more sense to call Locke an American than it does to call America Lockean."[28] As far as the revolutionary generation is concerned, there is no doubt that "the conception of the state which prevailed in the Revolutionary period was very largely that which we find in the political writings of John Locke."[29]

Moreover, what clearly associates Locke with the Atlantic colonies is the political theme of the "American land," a land of milk and honey, richer and more fertile than any other part of the world. It is not just Locke's followers in America who popularized the myth of their own land as a paradise ripe for appropriation. It was Locke himself who interpreted the potential of the new continent: "In the beginning, all the World was *America*."[30] In this way, Locke could establish a link between his own theories on original appropriation in an ancestral past and a well-defined present, also setting the theoretical premises for the revolutionary future of the colonies of European origin.

Of course, it should be noted that in actual fact, America was never the Lockean Eden of popular myth. The land policy implemented by the colonial governments (first the British, later the American) favored large private companies, awarding them a monopoly over the settlement of vast areas of free land, and allowing the most blatant speculations. By Jefferson's time, for example, it was practically impossible for settlers to obtain land by root of title. A similar system of government-granted monopoly existed throughout the nineteenth century, in particular with the enormous federal concessions granted to the railroad companies.[31]

All this notwithstanding, the settlers' vision of perfect property was usually in tune with that advanced by the *Second Treatise*.[32] Americans seemed very keen to welcome any argument advanced on behalf of property and expressed in Lockean terms, enduring well into the future. In an essay written a few decades ago, Robert Dahl, the eminent scholar of the radical democratic school, opted not to attack Locke's ideas on property, holding it wiser instead to ridicule those who think they can apply such notions to modern corporations. As Dahl stated, in order to understand the nature of the new property relations, we should "abandon the absurdities of extending Locke on private property to ownership or control of the modern business corporation."[33] Of course, the remedy advocated by Dahl to remove the impediments to democracy is a well-known tool called socialism all over the world. But since this term is rather unpopular in the American political culture, he resorts, in most of his writings, to a number of cunning theoretical and semantic devices in order to avoid disclosing his political leanings.

In any case, it was not merely the sense of justice pervading Locke's ideas that appeared convincing to the Americans. In his works, in fact, was investigated the principle on which a just society could be built in full harmony with the entire colonial institutional history.

Consensus as a foundation of government, the right to self-government of each community, and the derivation of this arrangement from man's natural rights (clearly inscribed in the book of nature) make Locke's doctrinal-political system a sophisticated construction of the most widespread political ideas among American settlers. America was "Lockean" well before becoming acquainted with his ideas, as mentioned earlier, and it was precisely for this reason that the English philosopher became known and venerated by all the exponents of the revolutionary generation. Furthermore, the fact that, according to Locke, the "public good" could only be achieved by the free pursuit of individual "private goods," makes him both the forerunner of traditional liberalism and the champion of laissez faire capitalism. This would ultimately inform the rhetoric of the American political discourse—and, in an altogether lesser degree, the actual practice of society—right up to the beginning of the last century.

It was fashionable until a few decades ago to advance interpretations that depicted Locke as a zealous advocate of majority rule, proclaiming self-preservation as the supreme value.[34] Yet the prevailing and most convincing view remains—as an outstanding opponent of Locke and his doctrine recalls—that of the "theorist of the liberal state, of constitutional or limited government...of government conditional on the consent of the governed, or the majority rule qualified by individual rights."[35]

It should never be forgotten that everything in Locke proceeds from the notion of property, and his political ideas cannot be grasped without clarifying the legitimacy of the acquisition of property. One of Locke's greatest contributions to the doctrine of property, and, therefore, to modern political thought, is his having posited the nonconsensual origin of property. The decision about what is mine and what is yours does not take place on the basis of expectations and agreements, but is grounded instead on natural law and, therefore, on laws dictated by nature to man.

While accepting Hugo Grotius's and Samuel Pufendorf's premises on the originally shared possession of nature, Locke drew completely different conclusions. The division of property into many different lots takes place in full compliance with the law of God and nature and not according to an agreement among men. In *De jure belli ac pacis* (1625), Grotius affirmed that the transition from shared possession to individual must be based upon some form of consent, tacit or expressed: "It must have been generally agreed, that whatever any one had occupied should be accounted his own."[36] Likewise, Samuel Pufendorf, in his *De jure naturae et gentium* (1672), devoted a whole chapter to the subject of the origin of property, reaching similar conclusions. For the German thinker, there must be an agreement that excludes common possession when faced with appropriation by someone. The accord is "that what any person had seiz'd out of the Common Store of Things, or out of the Fruits of them, with design to apply to his Private Occasions, none else should rob him of."[37]

It is only in Locke that one finds a theoretical investigation of the natural right to property in connection with the notion of a government founded on consensus. In this perspective, as the doctrine of the origin of property gradually gave way to the political history of property, consensus materialized and took permanent root in the Lockean construction. Property is independent of any agreement among men, and yet consensus, from which political society legitimately arises, is based on property. When compared to the previous century's tradition, this Lockean reversal of the relationship between property and consensus embodies a fundamental passage that makes clear the revolutionary character of the political beliefs held by the author of the *Two Treatises*.

First, society is established on the foundation of natural rights, rather than rights being themselves the by-product of society and agreement. The only fact that justifies society's existence is man's complete, unconditional possession of all his natural rights. For no one could take part in the birth of political society were he not in full possession of his faculties of judgment and his rights.

Property, in its political unfolding, becomes something other than the "right to property." Locke defines property as that element "the nature whereof is, that, without a Man's own consent, it cannot be taken from him."[38] Political relations imply a consensual forfeiture of property in the form of taxation, and very solid arguments could be adduced to show that the most important political obligation in the modern state is, precisely, taxation. Politics, though, and the ensuing obligations, tend to be encompassed within a very different order from that theorized by all the thinkers in the Machiavelli-Bodin-Hobbes strand of theory. In fact, the political order envisioned by Locke is a genuine twin of that of the market. What is the nature of market relations? It is the voluntary character of every individual transaction, since where there is coercion, there is no market. If one constructs a political obligation based on consensus, if each transaction can be traced back to an agreement, then coercion is no longer the essential feature of political power. Many a scholar has perceived the innermost driving force of the Lockean system to be the effort to define the conceptual categories of a veritable oxymoron—that is to say, a nonsovereign government, or at the very least, a noncoercive political system. As the famous English Socialist Harold Laski recalled many years ago, "It is not an accident which makes him [Locke] construct a non-sovereign state."[39] Although a nonsovereign state is nothing but a contradiction in terms, Locke's political thought revolves around and is nurtured by this contradiction.

In Locke, there is a general dissolution of the very concept of sovereignty, not a simple shift of attributes from the body of the sovereign to that of the community. While it is partially true that "in Locke's theory, sovereignty can exist nowhere except in the community as a whole,"[40] on the contrary, it cannot validly be claimed that "this is the original and supreme will which organizes the government and defines its just powers."[41] For the criteria of legitimacy of the government as well as the definition of the scope and limits of its powers were all decided *ab origine*, well before the formation of the political community that sprang from the contract.

Locke and Jefferson: Political Majorities and Natural Rights

At this point, it is important to note how the idea of majority rule is grafted onto this structure, because this very same concept would subsequently be, albeit less methodically, espoused by Thomas Jefferson throughout his life.

We have mentioned the strict limits on government action, but the problem remains of how power should operate under normal conditions. Locke has no doubt that unanimity should be the preferred criterion, and yet, given the technical impracticality of this solution, he concludes that the principle of the majority must be considered a "natural law," dictated by "right and just reason" and acting as the vehicle by means of which society functions, changes, and develops. By appealing to majority rule, man can decide the best form of government for his own political community, as well as the actions of "routine administration," such as elections of citizens to public office. In the *Second Treatise*, Locke gives a clear explanation of the concept of majority as a general rule for the functioning of a society. The majority enjoys the power to act and make decisions as if it were the whole. "When any number of men have so consented to make one community or government, they are thereby presently incorporated, and make one body politic, wherein the majority have a right to act and conclude the rest."[42] Thus, while the setting up of the body politic itself requires unanimity, a majority is sufficient for its decisions. "For, when any number of men have, by the consent of every individual, made a community, they have thereby made that community one body, with a power to act as one body, which is only by the will and determination of the majority."[43]

It can be inferred from this statement that only unanimity may make political societies arise to create "one body politick," yet once this has occurred, a simple majority becomes the will of the political group. However, this takes place according to a "law of nature" and does not in any way represent a "natural right." In fact, how could it be otherwise? Locke's views on natural rights are, first and foremost, those which man enjoys in the state of nature. In such a state, there is no body politic, nor contract, and therefore no one could claim the right for some decisions to be taken by majority rule. Locke explains how he arrives at such a conclusion with reference to the mechanics of social groups:

> For that which acts any community, being only the *consent of the individuals* of it, and it being one body, must move one way, it is necessary the body should move that way whither the greater force carries it, which is the consent of the majority, or else it is impossible it should act or continue one body...and so every one is bound by that consent to be concluded by the majority. And therefore...the act of the majority passes for the act of the whole, and of course determines as having, by the law of Nature and reason, the power of the whole.[44]

The very same definition can be found in Jefferson. Reason and nature, it is stated, are in agreement, in that they both point to the majority of members as the key element that should lead the community. Nevertheless, it must not be forgotten that the arguments adduced are also of a utilitarian nature: "For where the majority cannot conclude the rest, there they [the community] cannot act as one body, and consequently will be immediately dissolved again."[45] In effect, Locke defends majority government with utilitarian justifications. Without it, civil society could not survive for long.

From a superficial reading of the quoted passages, Willmoore Kendall and many commentators before and after him have evinced the omnipotence of majorities in the Lockean community. The most succinct, if not the first account of these ideas, is owed to Charles Vaughan: "Locke's statement on the power of the majority amounts to a blank cheque drawn in favor of 'the majority,' and eventually filled up either by the tens or millions, as fortune may decide."[46] Yet these interpretations are utterly misleading. The check is not completely blank; on the contrary, it is almost completely filled in, so that the majority, for all intents and purposes, merely endorse it or put upon it their "seal of approval."

If one can say anything of significance about the majority in Locke's system, it is that his vision is constructed in such a limited way as to make difficult to enlist the English philosopher to the ranks of the theorists of democracy. In fact, when men join together in society, "[They] must be understood to give up all the power necessary to the ends for which they unite into society to the majority of the community."[47] Yet Locke has established precisely these aims, which we have already broadly analyzed.

The legitimacy of the government proceeds from "the consent of any number of Freemen capable of majority, to unite and incorporate into such a Society."[48] But no legitimate government can act against the purposes for which civil society was formed (security in enjoyment of the individual's natural rights). Locke makes an inseparable connection between consensus and right of property. Obviously, the "good" that is known as protection— the specific reason for the establishment of government among men—is expensive and must be paid for, but everything must occur through consensus. "The consent of the majority, giving it either by themselves or their representatives chosen by them; for if any one shall claim a power to lay and levy taxes on the people by his own authority, and without such consent of the people, he thereby invades the fundamental law of property, and subverts the end of government. For what property have I in that which another may by right take when he pleases to himself?"[49]

If government is a device created by man for the protection of property, or, rather, of life, property, and liberty, then in no instance—neither by majority nor consensus—shall it act against the purposes for which it was adopted. In short, in order for a government to be considered legitimate, it must be subjected to a twofold restriction. It must protect the individual's natural rights and have their consensus to do so. To be legitimate a government must respect both the general aims of the polity and the initial conditions of the political obligation, namely, consensus. What is true for the individual is also true for the collective. "Men being…by nature all free, equal, and independent, no one can be put out of this estate and subjected to the political power of another without his own consent."[50] An authoritative political obligation obviously proceeds from consensus, but this observation does not necessarily mean that such consensus is also the basis of political society. Rather, it is simply its modus operandi.

Locke reiterates his conception of the state in the *Epistola de Tolerantia*. "The commonwealth seems to me to be a society of men constituted only for procuring, preserving, and advancing their own civil interests. Civil interests I call life, liberty, health, and indolency of body; and the possession of outward things, such as money, lands, houses, furniture, and the like."[51] The framework of government in Locke is clear: It arises in order to protect values (rights) that stand above government itself. So it is not the latter, but rather the values that are to be protected, and which constitute the focal point of politics. In the Lockean viewpoint, it is clear that government is completely subordinated to the goods that are essential for the very individual that government itself is duty bound to protect. So it is apparent that Locke sets man's natural rights far above majority decisions; indeed, man's rights are placed outside the scope of action of the majority.

It is now germane to attempt to establish how much of this systematic theory was accepted and expanded by Jefferson into a permanent fixture of the America political tradition. The Jeffersonian position on majority rule emerges in his various works and manifests itself in apparently divergent form over time, yet it has an internal coherence that derives directly from its specific Lockean roots.

The perpetual fascination that emanates from Jefferson's political doctrine, and especially the fact that it has survived the passage of time (though often misinterpreted and modified in some essential points), springs from his faith in the people. It is, to be sure, the fountainhead of a peculiar delusion, that of Jefferson as the theorist of liberal democracy. But this is precisely why the issue should be addressed carefully: "I know of no safe depository of the ultimate power of the society but the people themselves, and if we think them not enlightened enough to exercise their control with a wholesome discretion, the remedy is not to take it from them, but to inform their discretion by education."[52]

Just as the individual was the best judge of the means of achieving his or her happiness, so the people, to be construed as nothing more than a group of individuals, were certainly capable of defending their natural rights better than anyone else. In Jefferson, the "democratic" and republican decision, in favor of popular control over the institutions, comes from his unconditional adhesion to the doctrine of natural law. What more stalwart champion of their rights than the people? And if they should turn out to be ready to exchange their own natural rights for safety or economic welfare, then the remedy would consist in their education.

In effect, Jefferson firmly believed in the self-evidence of the truth proclaimed in the Declaration and was convinced that the improvement of knowledge would reveal to everyone once and for all that man's rights must be the foundation of proper political institutions. Just as he was convinced of the truth promulgated by reason and nature, he also believed that the majority should always prevail. "Every Man's reason...[is] his own rightful umpire. This principle, with that of acquiescence in the will of the majority, will preserve us free and prosperous as long as they are sacredly observed."[53]

It should also be said that the Virginian always distinguished between an honest, unbiased majority and the one which results from corruption. One of the principles of his "republicanism" was that "the will of the majority *honestly expressed* should give law."[54] But a majority instigated by corruption lost all rights to pass laws and its decisions must be considered devoid of any legal effect.

Jefferson gives some of his earliest reflections on his ideas on representation with regard to the Constitution of Virginia. The approved document was far from his constitutional canons. In *Notes on Virginia*, Jefferson had some choice words to say about the Constitution of Virginia of 1776, even though the cause of such a disgrace was to be found in the inexperience, rather than in the treachery, of his fellow citizens: "This constitution was formed when we were new and unexperienced in the science of government. It was the first too which was formed in the whole United States. No wonder then that time and trial have discovered very capital defects in it."[55]

Republicanism, Jefferson was to write many years later, is that type of government in which there is the implementation of "government by the people, acting not in person but by representations chosen by themselves— that is to say, by every Man of ripe years and sane mind who either contributes with his purse or person to the support of his country."[56] Unmistakably, Jefferson had a Lockean view of who should have the right to vote. Whoever fights for his country and pays his country's taxes must be given the chance to have his say in public matters. Therefore, he went on in his criticism of the Constitution of Virginia, it was hard to see why "the majority of the men in the state, who pay and fight for its support, are unrepresented in the legislature, the roll of freeholders intitled to vote, not including generally the half of those on the roll of the militia, or of the tax-gatherers."[57] And even among those who actually exercise political rights, "the shares are very unequal."[58] Moreover, "The senate is, by its constitution, too homogeneous with the house of delegates. Being chosen by the same electors, at the same time, and out of the same subjects, the choice falls of course on men of the same description. The purpose of establishing different houses of legislation is to introduce the influence of different interests or different principles."[59]

Another worrying anomaly was the question "that the ordinary legislature may alter the constitution itself."[60] But perhaps the gravest issue was the concentration of powers in the legislature. "All the powers of government, legislative, executive, and judiciary, result to the legislature. The concentrating these in the same hands is precisely the definition of despotic government. It will be no alleviation that these powers will be exercised by a plurality of hands, and not by a single one. 173 despots would surely be as oppressive as one.... An elective despotism was not the government we fought for."[61]

Jefferson showed himself to be anything but enthusiastic toward the unhampered powers of the assembly, since such an arrangement might conceivably be conducive to a sort of tyranny. For Jefferson, as for many political thinkers of the Enlightenment, democracy was essentially construed as republicanism, understood as the people's control over their own government and over their elected representatives. In an important letter written to John Taylor in 1816, Jefferson openly tackled these great questions. "Besides much other good matter, it [the book that Taylor had not long before published, *Enquiry into the Principles of our Government*] settles unanswerably the right of instructing representations, and their duty to obey."[62] The type of representation Jefferson advocated manifestly had nothing to do with the system that was gaining ground in Europe. Jefferson conceived of representatives as an instrument of the people, ready to execute promptly their will, and there was no room at all for Old World notions, such as the "representative of the country" without any constraints on his mandate.[63]

The restriction exists and it is very strong: The people's representatives are only designated because of the impracticality of the people themselves to assemble and decide on each matter, and representatives are not entitled to decide in place of and possibly against the wishes of those who have elected them.

There is no country to be represented, no abstract idea onto which to graft the very same notions informing the monarchy of divine right, but only the will of the voting citizens to be executed immediately. In his own words, Jefferson believed that "the mass of the citizens is the safest depository of their own rights and especially, that the evils flowing from the duperies of the people are less injurious than those from the egoism of their agents."[64] Republicanism in a pure form "would be where the powers of the government, being divided, should be exercised each by representations chosen either *pro hac vice* (for the occasion), or for such short terms as should render secure the duty of expressing the will of their constituents."[65] He was convinced that "proximate choice and power of removal is the best security which experience has sanctioned for ensuring an honest conduct in the functionaries of society."[66]

The basic republican tenet is direct popular control. Although "the term republic is of very vague application in every language,"[67] Jefferson attempted to define it more clearly. "Purely and simply, it means a government by its citizens in mass, acting directly and personally, according to rules established by the majority; and that every other government is more or less republican, in proportion as it has in its composition more or less of this ingredient of the direct action of the citizens."[68] This element measures the degree of republicanism in the political arrangements of a country: "The further the departure from direct and constant control by the citizens, the less has the government of the ingredient of republicanism."[69] The view, therefore, of representation as a simple mirror of an elected member that *non agit sed agitur* (that is, does not act but is acted upon) is extremely important and must be emphasized, lest one run the risk of misunderstanding the entire Jeffersonian edifice, placing it alongside other constructions that are light-years away from his thinking. In Jefferson, there is no trace of the presumed unity of the represented body, namely the people (always seen as a group of separate individuals), which opens the door to theoretical speculations based on organicistic metaphors such as nation, society, or class.

Regarding the thorny issue of the optimal dimensions of a republic, Jefferson maintained a certain ambiguity. In 1816, having reiterated that "action by the citizens in person, in affairs within their reach and competence, and in all others by representations, chosen immediately, and removable by themselves, constitutes the essence of a republic,"[70] Jefferson declared himself convinced "that a government by representation is capable of extension over a greater surface of country than one of any other form."[71] Yet in the above-cited letter to John Taylor, he expressed himself in a rather different manner. A genuine republican government "is evidently restrained to very narrow limits of space and population. I doubt if it would be practicable beyond the extent of a New England township."[72] Here, he was following the entire line of classical, modern, and Anti-Federalist political thought in considering a republic equivalent to pure democracy, whose political deliberation was wholly unmediated, whereas a month before he had seemed to accept the famous arguments put forward by Madison in *Federalist*.

If state constitutions were not fully republican, this must be ascribed "not to any want of republican dispositions in those who formed these

Constitutions, but to a submission of true principle to European authorities, to speculators on government, whose fears of the people have been inspired by the populace of their own great cities."[73] One can thus trace an anti-urban element in Jefferson's thought, whereby European populations were conceived as a degenerate mass, partly because the large cities of the Old World degraded them. This strand of thought developed during his period in France and integrated well with his moderate agrarianism. Citizens allowed to have voice in the political process should most definitely not be the dispossessed, indolent masses he had seen in Paris, ready to become the *clientes* of the politicians of the day, but freeholders, so independent as to succeed in making the political class an instrument for their own use.

In what may be considered an essay on the Constitution of Virginia and popular sovereignty, Jefferson wrote the Virginian writer Samuel Kercheval, explaining his ideas about majority rule and consensus as the basis of legitimate political society. At the beginning of the revolutionary adventure, when the Constitution of Virginia was approved, "We had not yet penetrated to the mother principle, that 'governments are republican only in proportion as they embody the will of their people, and execute it.' Hence, our first constitutions had really no leading principles in them."[74]

Jefferson established the ground for debate, setting out some clear points: "Let it be agreed that a government is republican in proportion as every member composing it has his equal voice in the direction of its concerns (not indeed in person, which would be impracticable beyond the limits of a city, or small township) but by representations chosen by himself, and responsible to him at short periods."[75] Jefferson was anxious to prevent the emergence of a professional political caste; the shortness of the terms of elected representatives was instrumental to achieve his vision. Now, the Virginian constitution envisaged a chamber of representatives elected by half of the population and a senate elected by even fewer citizens and enjoying a term of office that was far too long. Moreover, the cabinet had a governor at its head who was not even chosen by the citizens and whom they could not remove. The judicial power vested in the state's Supreme Court was completely independent of popular opinion and the court itself enjoyed the privilege of being governed by a body of their peers, while the judges in the lower courts were appointed for life and had the power of selecting the members of the jury.[76]

So how could it be, Jefferson mused, that despite all this, Virginia had a fairly acceptable form of government? For Jefferson, this was attributable to the quality of the population. "Where then is our republicanism to be found? Not in our Constitution certainly, but merely in the spirit of our people. That would oblige even a despot to govern us republicanly. Owing to this spirit, and to nothing in the form of our Constitution, all things have gone well."[77] The fact that everything had gone relatively well "is not the fruit of our Constitution, but has prevailed in spite of it."[78] So the author of the Declaration set forth a scheme to reform the Constitution, starting out from a doctrinally precise recognition (mentioned earlier in another context): "The true foundation of republican government is the equal right of every citizen, in his person and property, and in their management."[79] The counties were very badly organized and it was necessary to do the following:

> Divide the counties into wards of such size as that every citizen can attend, when called on, and act in person. Ascribe to them the government of their wards in all things relating to themselves exclusively. A justice, chosen by themselves, in each, a constable, a military company, a patrol, a school, the care of their own poor, their own portion of the public roads, the choice of one or more jurors to serve in some court, and the delivery, within their own wards, of their own votes for all elective officers of higher sphere, will relieve the county administration of nearly all its business, will have it better done, and by making every citizen an acting member of the government, and in the offices nearest and most interesting to him, will attach him by his strongest feelings to the independence of his country, and its republican Constitution.[80]

Jefferson then turned his attention beyond Virginia and sketched out this plan of government for the entire union:

> 1, the general federal republic, for all concerns foreign and federal; 2, that of the State, for what relates to our own citizens exclusively; 3, the county republics, for the duties and concerns of the county ; and 4, the ward republics, for the small, and yet numerous and interesting concerns of the neighborhood; and in

government, as well as in every other business of life, it is by division and subdivision of duties alone, that all matters, great and small, can be managed to perfection. And the whole is cemented by giving to every citizen, personally, a part in the administration of the public affairs.[81]

The force of Jefferson's reasoning was equal only to his ability to make his ideas known, even when simply describing them to a friend. Jeffersonian criticism became common currency and, in fact, the Constitution of Virginia was altered shortly thereafter. The new document largely adopted the amendments proposed by the Virginian—although not going as far as the establishment of "ward" levels of government—particularly with regard to the popular election of all the judges.

On a different note, it is important to investigate the link between taxation and despotism. For Jefferson, political power had such specific, restricted tasks that any increase in taxation could hardly be justified on the basis of a widening of the scope of governmental action. Moreover, he was convinced—and on this point, history has shown him to have been spectacularly wrong—that, far from increasing government powers, popular control would curb government excesses. Consequently, in his eyes the greatest danger came from the possibility of legislators plunging citizens into debt. "We must not let our rulers load us with perpetual debt. We must make our election between economy and liberty, or profusion and servitude."[82]

Jefferson believed there was nothing truly innocent or neutral in the power that a group of men exercised over other men. The absence of law and order did not necessarily entail a Hobbesian state of unrestricted warfare among individuals. On the contrary, government abuses were the element that triggered such a situation, elicited by the conflicting interests of different groups and their struggle to take over control of the government. In short, it is in the political arena and not in the state of nature that the *bellum omnia contra omnes* where everyone fights everyone else takes place. When speculative interests on public debt are set in motion, "begins, indeed, the bellum *omnium in omnia*, which some philosophers observing to be so general in this world, have mistaken it for the natural, instead of the abusive state of man. And the fore horse of this frightful team is public debt. Taxation follows that, and in its train wretchedness and oppression."[83]

In this context, Jefferson reintroduced his idea of "expiry-date" constitutions and of the generational pace of politics that had already been advanced in the famous letter to Madison in 1789. "Let us provide in our Constitution for its revision at stated periods."[84] "It is now forty years since the constitution of Virginia was formed,"[85] and given that two-thirds of the living population have died since then, "have then the remaining third, even if they had the wish, the right to hold in obedience to their will, and to laws heretofore made by them, the other two-thirds, who, with themselves, compose the present mass of adults? If they have not, who has? The dead? But the dead have no rights."[86]

It is therefore the majority of the living, at every given moment, who have full sovereignty over their own political systems. But how is the majority formed, or, rather, how can its voice be recorded? Here was the real problem for Jefferson, who was continually concerned about popular opinions being expressed honestly. The opinion of the people must be sounded by resorting to the wards system: "The mayor of every ward...would call his ward together, take the simple yea or nay of its members, convey these to the county court, who would hand on those of all its wards to the proper general authority; and the voice of the whole people would be thus fairly, fully, and peaceably expressed, discussed, and decided by the common reason of the society."[87] It is clear that the common deliberation of society is deemed to be nothing more than an empirical fact, namely the sum total of individual votes, and does not partake of the more or less transcendent qualities of Rousseau's "general will." It is further evidence that the repeated attempt of finding some common ground between Jefferson and Rousseau is wholly unwarranted. The Virginian and the philosopher from Geneva are the flag bearers of two altogether different political traditions—classical liberalism and radical democracy, respectively—which are, and remain, diametrically opposed in spite of all the fusion history has forced.

This said, it is to be noted that Jefferson entertained some reservations on the matter of majority rule. On his return to America after five years spent as minister to France, Jefferson illustrated to his fellow countrymen the relationship between self-government, reason, and majority rule. "It rests now with ourselves alone to enjoy in peace and concord the blessings of self-government, so long denied to mankind: to shew by example the sufficiency of human reason for the care of human affairs and that the will of the majority, the Natural law of every society, is the only sure guardian of the rights of man. Perhaps even this may sometimes err. But it's errors are honest, solitary and short-lived."[88] Majority rule was, for Jefferson, the manner in which "the general reason of the society" was expressed.[89] And he immediately added, "We are safe with that, even in it's deviations, for it soon returns again to the right way."[90]

It is important to see how majority rule was considered to be the natural law of societies. It might safeguard man's rights, but it was by no means a natural right. If anything, it was an instrument to implement a natural law, that of self-government. The fact that Jefferson used terminology that is clearly identical to Locke's to identify the majority (the Englishman referred to "Law of nature and reason," the Virginian to "natural law" and "general reason of the society") is very important and reveals his position. Rights belong to the individual, while a natural law may be valid as much for individuals as for human societies. It is the fact of being nothing other than the sum of the single individual reasons that confers a special power on the majority. The number prevails not because of some transcendental characteristic of the social body but because it is made up of many individuals. Such a scheme is also deemed to be the greatest technical and legal bulwark against brute force. "The first principle of republicanism is, that the *lex majoris partis* (majority rule) is the fundamental law of every society of individuals of equal rights; to consider the will of the society enounced by the majority of a single vote, as sacred as if unanimous, is the first of all lessons in importance, yet the last which is thoroughly learnt. This law once disregarded, no other remains but that of force, which ends necessarily in military despotism."[91] In short, the old maxim that it is better to count heads to settle a problem than smash them has truth in it.

In a well-known, oft-quoted letter written to the French Physiocrat Dupont De Nemours, Jefferson explains that not majority but "justice is the fundamental law of society...the majority, oppressing an individual, is guilty of a crime, abuses its strength, and by acting on the law of the strongest, breaks up the foundations of society."[92] As early as 1801, referring to the battle won against the Federalists, he stated in his first inaugural speech that the country had spoken and that the majority had settled the dispute. He then added, "All, too, will bear in mind this sacred principle, that though the will of the majority is in all cases to prevail, that will, to be rightful, must be reasonable; that the minority possess their equal rights, which equal laws must protect, and to violate which would be oppression."[93]

Jefferson's constant attention to the infringement of rights and coercive orders has pointed some commentators in the right direction: His ideas are not easily reconciled with the concepts that presided over the development of the modern state. Germane to this issue is the observation of a certain inability on the part of Jefferson to appreciate the notion of state and its conceptual typologies. It does not escape notice, though, that this observation is not infrequently made with polemical intent, as if the state and its categories should be the ultimate goal of political thought. Gordon Wood, for example, states that "not only did Jefferson thus refuse to recognize the structure and institutions of a modern state, he scarcely accepted the basic premise of a state, that is, its presumed monopoly of legitimate control over a prescribed territory."[94] Locke and Jefferson shared an aversion to the state that lay much farther back in time. In particular, both rejected that feature of modern politics represented by the two different moral universes that form the setting for the actions of "simple" individuals and of those who act in the name of, and on behalf of, the state.

As is well known, the split between morals and politics (or rather between the morals of politics and the morals of the citizens) began with Machiavelli's *Prince* (1532) and became widely accepted in later works, especially Giovanni Botero's *La Ragion di Stato* (1589), in which the political and moral underpinnings of the state were clearly expressed. For the sake of the state, men may carry out deeds that otherwise would be considered crimes. Locke and Jefferson hold society to be, instead, a whole, with the standards of morality as universally valid. If anything, public immorality constitutes an aggravation. This is exemplified in a passage where Locke considers public and private crimes to be equivalent: "The injury and the crime is equal, whether committed by the wearer of a crown or some petty villain. The title of the offender and the number of his followers make no difference in the offence, unless it be to aggravate it."[95]

No appeal to the safeguarding of the state may justify the crime. If no peaceful redress appears possible, "If God has taken away all means of seeking remedy, there is nothing left but patience."[96] The abuse does not in any way lessen the validity of the rights of the aggrieved party; it will be the duty of his descendants, if anything, to restore them to the legitimate owner. However, there may also be cases where there is no court for appeal.

> [With] no court—no arbitrator on earth to appeal to. Then they may appeal...to Heaven, and repeat their appeal till they have recovered the native right of their ancestors.... If it be objected this would cause endless trouble, I answer, no more than justice does, where she lies open to all that appeal to her. He that troubles his neighbour without a cause is punished for it by the justice of the court he appeals to. And he that appeals to Heaven must be sure he has right on his side, and a right, too, that is worth the trouble and cost of the appeal, as he will answer at a tribunal that cannot be deceived.... From whence it is plain that he that conquers in an unjust war can thereby have no title to the subjection and obedience of the conquered.[97]

Jefferson is less forbearing: Political power must be subjected to frequent popular revolts, not merely to the threat of rebellion. There is no public end that can justify oppression and injustice, and acquiescence to a tyrannical power is considerably more dangerous than a hasty revolt. The spirit of resistance to the government is the foundation of liberties:

> *Malo periculosam libertatem quam quietam servitutem.* Even this evil is productive of good. It prevents the degeneracy of government, and nourishes a general attention to the public affairs. I hold it that a little rebellion now and then is a good thing, and as necessary in the political world as storms in the physical.... This...should render honest republican governors so mild in their punishment of rebellions, as not to discourage them too much. It is a medicine necessary for the sound health of government.[98]

An extremely important point that Locke and Jefferson have in common is their (near) silence regarding the traditional problem of the "tyranny of the majority." Although the subject matter of a masterly analysis by Alexis de Tocqueville some ten years after Jefferson's death, it was already well known, both in the seventeenth and eighteenth century. Manifestly, this issue is closely connected to the right to resistance.

Notwithstanding the claims put forward by some interpreters, Locke attributes this right both to society and to individuals. "And where the body of the people, or *any single man*, are deprived of their right, or are under the exercise of a power without right, having no appeal on earth they have a liberty to appeal to Heaven whenever they judge the cause of sufficient moment."[99] Simmons, one of the most gifted Lockean scholars, correctly observes that had Locke "*not* affirm[ed] an individual right of resistance…it would make no sense at all for him to twice assure his readers that individuals' having such rights is not a threat to the order of society…Locke tries to make acceptable to a nervous audience a quite radical doctrine of lawful individual resistance, contending that anarchic consequences will not follow from general acceptance of the doctrine."[100]

The appeal to Heaven is obviously justifiable even against majorities if the latter violate natural rights. Thus, Jefferson, in full accord with the Lockean scheme, had no need to draw up an inventory of the decisions that could be taken by majority rule. Indeed, his entire thinking is aimed at reserving the least space possible to politics. Man's natural rights are as inviolable by political power as by an omnipotent majority. As discussed in the previous chapter, they are beyond the reach of individuals, as untouchable by the holders of power as by the person entitled to these rights. Since legislators are bound to enact laws that do not in any way oppose these rights, it becomes clear that majority rule has a very restricted scope. In brief, man's representatives are elected by majority vote, and the representatives are then under a binding obligation to respect man's natural rights, because, as legislators, "their true office is to declare and enforce *only* our natural rights."[101]

If one can legitimately speak about Jeffersonian "democratic radicalism," it is in the sense that every public office must be elective, every power consecrated by consensus. The power granted to a majority may appear extensive, especially in its generational structure and compared with previous generations, but it is, on the contrary, strictly bound to the protection and respect of the natural rights of the individual. "A generation may bind itself as long as its majority continues in life; when that has disappeared, another majority is in place, holds all the rights and powers their predecessors once held, and may change their laws and institutions to suit themselves. *Nothing then is unchangeable but the inherent and unalienable rights of man.*"[102]

The recognition that majorities are nothing more than occasional coalitions of minorities (down to the smallest one, namely the minority of one individual) also underpins the ethical preference for a federal system built up from concentric circles, ranging from the individual to larger governmental units. This system was to represent the ultimate synthesis between republicanism, democracy, and the rights of man.

The recognition that in the formation of a majority there is leeway for the coercion of individuals urged Jefferson to devise a system to make every voice heard, a system much more complex and stringent than the one envisaged by the American Constitution. The later Jeffersonian political reflection is a vision of a "republic of republics," built on the true guardian of the polity, namely the propertied individual, jealous of his own rights and ready to "let the heart be torn out of his body sooner than his power be wrested from him by a Caesar or a Bonaparte."[103] We will investigate the ward-republic in chapter 6.

Adams and Jefferson: Between History and Reason

The book fated to draw the lines of the intellectual battle on the assessment of the French Revolution, Edmund Burke's *Reflections on the French Revolution*, appeared in 1790. It immediately caused a stir in America as well. Burke's thesis, setting the Glorious Revolution in opposition to the French events, was that "the Revolution was made to preserve our ancient, indisputable laws and liberties and that ancient constitution of government which is our only security for law and liberty." He concluded, "The very idea of the fabrication of a new government is enough to fill us with disgust and horror. We wished at the period of the Revolution, and do now wish, to derive all we possess as an inheritance from our forefathers."[104]

In 1791, *The Rights of Man*, Thomas Paine's polemical rejoinder to Burke's work, broadened the dispute about the relative merits of the English system of government compared with the French (and, in Paine's opinion, also American) revolutionary paradigms. After a cursory reading, Thomas Jefferson proposed an American edition of the pamphlet, and he enclosed a short letter together with the book. Paine's work, Jefferson declared, would be a real antidote "against the political heresies which have sprung up among us."[105] Trumpeted in a blaze of publicity by the press of the day, Jefferson's opinion was actually meant for the vice president, John Adams,[106] whose partiality for the English system was well known.

Soon, a heated debated ensued in the papers of the time, to which Jefferson and Adams, at the time secretary of state and vice president, did not take part directly, although their looming presence was clear for all to see.[107] Adams was depicted as the defender of the rights of the past, of an English system for the most part rejected by the people, of a hereditary monarchy and aristocracy, whereas Jefferson was seen as the champion of human rights and reason. This characterization has been enduring, such that Michael Lienesch states that the peculiarity of American political ideas of the origins is that "in essence, for every Adams there is a Jefferson."[108]

Jefferson's opinion of John Adams and his works was, in truth, very questionable. So questionable that the latter challenged his friend/rival to quote him the exact passages in which he had allegedly defended the English monarchic and aristocratic system, but was never satisfied. Over time, though, Jefferson was able to capitalize enormously on the political standing he had acquired from the publicity surrounding his endorsement of Paine's work. Thus, it was in the early 1790s that the author of the Declaration became the champion of the "spirit of 1776," the defender of the American Revolution against the perceived tendency toward backsliding and lapsing into old ways.

In a letter written many years later, Jefferson clarified exactly what it was that distinguished him from Adams. He stated that "Mr. Adams' system of orders…[implied] opening the mantle of republicanism to every government of laws, whether consistent or not with natural right."[109] This opinion seems to echo Anne Robert Jacques Turgot, who, in a famous letter that was to provide Adams with the polemical inspiration for his Defence[110] of the constitutions of the American states, argued about "the falshood [sic] of that thread–bare sentiment of the greatest class of even the most republican writers, *that liberty consists in being subject only to laws*, as if a Man oppressed by an unjust law, was free."[111]

It must be noted, in passing, that Jefferson was always quite intolerant of notions of liberty based upon respect for the laws, as if these were not manmade artifacts but prescriptions coming directly from above. In 1819, he wrote, "Liberty…is unobstructed action according to our will. But rightful liberty is unobstructed action according to our will, within the limits drawn around us by the equal rights of others. I do not add 'within the limits of the law,' because law is often but the tyrant's will and always so when it violates the right of an individual."[112]

Significant concordances of opinion can be found between Turgot and Jefferson. Among the various criticisms leveled at the constitutions of the American states, the most important, in Turgot's eyes, was that "instead of bringing all the authorities into one, that of the nation, they have established different bodies."[113] On the issue of the earliest attempts at confederation, he declared that "in the general union of the states, I do not see a coalition, a melting of all the parts together, so as to make the body *one* and homogeneous."[114] It was precisely this belief that in the political sphere everything tends inevitably toward unity—the fetish even of the best classical French liberals—that was at the heart of Adams's countercriticisms in the *Defence*.

Moreover, the accusation against Adams is difficult to uphold in the specific terms put forward by Jefferson. Thus, while it is true that Adams's preference, obsessively reiterated in his works, was for a government of laws, not of men, he had nevertheless declared in the *Defence* that the American constitutions "exhibited, perhaps the first example of governments erected on the simple principles of nature."[115]

It is perhaps more interesting to observe that there were indeed some marked divergences between the two, and that wherever they differed, it was inevitably within the scope of the controversy launched by Burke and Paine. While Adams had always greatly admired the English past and the history of freedom that embodied the quintessence of the institutions of that country, Jefferson did not acknowledge that history was imbued with any specific authority, much less the history of England. As early as in the *Notes on Virginia*, he had expressed a less than flattering opinion of England: "The sun of her glory is fast descending to the horizon. Her philosophy has crossed the Channel, her freedom the Atlantic."[116] His assessment of the political history and current situation of England could not have been more clear or more peremptory. "It is not in the history of modern England or among the advocates of the principles or practices of her government, that the friend of freedom, or of political morality, is to seek instruction."[117] By now, "the vital principle of the English constitution is corruption, its practices the natural results of that principle, and their consequences a pampered aristocracy, annihilation of the substantial middle class, a degraded populace, oppressive taxes, general pauperism, and national bankruptcy."[118]

Adams, on the other hand, in *A Dissertation on the Canon and the Feudal Law* (1765), which was written in the aftermath of the Stamp Act with the purpose of reawakening the spirit of freedom in his fellow countrymen, maintained that Americans should "search into the spirit of the British constitution; read the histories of ancient ages; contemplate the great examples of Greece and Rome."[119] This love of history, this pride in the English heritage, and the conviction that the English tradition held the keys to a free future never abandoned him. By the same token, in his subsequent choice of the seventeenth-century Italian historian Enrico Caterino Davila, author of the *Historia delle guerre civili di Francia* (1630), as his ideal interlocutor, Adams showed a love for the past and erudition that stands in sharp contrast to Jefferson's tastes.

Jefferson's indifference to experience and "the rights of history" make him an anti-Burkean *par excellence*. In 1799, he wrote to Elbridge Gerry, in a letter that sounds like a veritable profession of political faith,

> I am for encouraging the progress of science in all it's branches; and not for raising a hue and cry against the sacred name of philosophy; for awing the human mind by stories of rawhead & bloody bones to a distrust of its own vision, & to repose implicitly on that of others; to go backwards instead of forwards to look for improvement; to believe that government, religion, morality, & every other science were in the highest perfection in ages of the darkest ignorance, and that nothing can ever be devised more perfect than what was established by our forefathers.[120]

The following year, he reiterated the idea to Joseph Priestley: "The Gothic idea that we are to look backwards instead of forwards for the improvement of the human mind...is worthy of those bigots in religion and government, by whom it has been recommended, and whose purpose it would answer."[121]

When a friend happened to ask him for advice about the most suitable readings in every field, Jefferson offered his most deeply felt view of history, before launching into one of his usual attacks on David Hume. "History, in general, only informs us what bad government is. But as we have employed some of the best materials of the British constitution in the construction of our own government, a knolege [*sic*] of British history becomes useful to the American politician."[122] One cannot fail to note the full consonance with that view of history as "the drainpipe of the most barbarous centuries," a typical Enlightenment view. His habitual disdain for the political doctrines current in Europe is likewise well known. At the end of his life, he maintained that the adverse influence European doctrinal influences on America had almost compromised its revolution. This effect, he contended, was responsible for the reemerging conservatism of the age:

> The fact is, that at the formation of our government, many had formed their political opinions on European writings and practices, believing the experience of old countries, and especially of England, abusive as it was, to be a safer guide than mere theory. The doctrines of Europe were, that men in numerous associations cannot be restrained within the limits of order and justice, but by forces physical and moral, wielded over them by authorities independent of their will.[123]

Jefferson was well aware that the doctrinal development of natural law and popular sovereignty came from Europe, but he was perhaps not wrong in refusing to consider this the theoretical and practical core of European politics. The political categories worked out by absolutism in Europe had resulted in a legacy that was difficult to overcome, and it was almost with irritation that Jefferson noticed the tendency for "European" proclivities to persist in a revolutionary country that had—and had done battle on the field to achieve—all the rights to a new dawn that would look to "reason for...guide, instead of English precedent."[124]

If Jefferson did not consider history as an infallible guide for the present times, he was nonetheless well grounded in it, particularly in the Whig historiographical tradition, exemplified by Paul de Rapin's *History of England*. The influence of the Whig tradition—with its emphasis on the Saxon origins of English freedom and its belief that the Norman invaders had dealt them a death blow—most certainly played a fundamental role in the development of the political ideas that became the hallmark of Jefferson and the Founding Fathers. According to Jefferson, English political divisions were founded on the following principle: "It has ever appeared to me, that the difference between the Whig and the Tory of England is, that the Whig deduces his rights from the Anglo-Saxon source, and the Tory from the Norman."[125]

The so-called "Saxon myth" consisted in number of notions typically associated with the Old Whig tradition. These ideas had gained credence in various ways and they were actually far more useful as the foundations of a specific political ideology than as tools of careful historical research. History is full of myths of this kind, such as the *Magna Charta* (1215) as being the foundation of English freedom, a myth propounded by Edward Coke,[126] and it makes little sense to judge the myths of the past with one's gaze directed toward present-day scientific/historical research.

The Jeffersonian work where the Saxon myth emanates the full force of its political implication is the *Summary View of the Rights of British America*, the short essay written in 1774 that placed him at the head of the radical revolutionary movement. Jefferson stated that the relation between England and the colonies was the same as that between England and Scotland before the 1707 Act of Union. That is to say, these were recognized as two different countries that happened to have the same executive but no other political connection. From a careful reading of Whig historians, Jefferson had become convinced that feudalism in England was imposed by the Norman conquest, which had drowned in blood the traditional English liberties. Jefferson saw an analogy with the attempts by the King of England to impose on America the feudal concessions and arbitrary taxes of French ancestry.

In Jefferson's opinion, the real body of common law was Saxon, since the Norman Conquest marked the beginning of its decline in favor of written law. In short, the only way to safeguard English liberty lay in the rediscovery of Saxon roots and in the eradication of the Norman encrustations.

Much of Jefferson's effort against English dominion in America, against feudalism in Virginia, and for separation of the church from the state should be read as part of a wider "work for a realization of his Saxon 'heavenly city.'"[127] Similarly, one can hardly fail to sense the Enlightenment echoes reverberating through the mythicized pre-Norman or prefeudal past cherished by Jefferson. The Saxon period is assumed to have been happy, because in that time men lived in harmony with nature and reason. But these are indeed Enlightenment ideas, projected into a bygone time which, far from becoming the center of gravity of metahistorical reflection, is, in effect, the appendix to an intensely theoretical investigation in which the focal points are nature, the individual, and reason.

5

Jefferson and American Constitutionalism

Were we directed from Washington when to sow
and when to reap, we should soon want bread.[1]

We will now investigate the problem of Jefferson's proper place within the political constellation that had taken shape in America during the period 1787–1789, while he was minister to France. Undoubtedly, Jefferson had been lucky to escape the need to take sides in the bitter political struggle of that time. Yet this problem cannot be eluded if one is to proceed to a proper historical reconstruction of his thoughts on federalism. It must also be addressed in order to understand the political-constitutional doctrine he expounded in the Kentucky Resolution, which we will dwell on in considerable depth in the next chapter.

Despite the rivers of ink written to show the alleged endorsement by Jefferson of the Constitution, it can be stated with a fair degree of certainty that he was not particularly happy at the idea of it actually coming into force. In fact, for many months his approach was to support its approval and then to call for a new convention to mend some of its most egregious flaws. Yet it must be admitted that, excepting some moments of heated frustration, Jefferson was relatively lenient in his appraisal of the constitutional instrument (which Adams, Washington, and Madison had sent to him in Paris shortly after its approval on 17 September 1787), and he further mitigated his criticism over the course of time. Still, Jefferson was far away from the scene at the time, and he did not wish to become embroiled in a controversy about which he had only secondhand information. Thus, a gradual change can be seen in his approach to the Constitution, whereby his initially critical attitude underwent a gradual shift toward a slightly more favorable, albeit lukewarm, judgment, with a subsequent shift to almost wholehearted acceptance once the outcome was clear.

Some authors have seen this changing attitude as reflecting Jefferson's opportunism and lack of intellectual integrity. They claim that Jefferson subtly and shrewdly modified his judgment in direct proportion to the apparent likelihood that the Constitution would be adopted, as far as he could judge on the basis of news reaching him from America. Franco Venturi, a great Italian student of the 1700s, although no specialist in American history, went as far as to assert that Jefferson "immediately thrust İhimself into a feisty political controversy against the draft of a new Constitution, forcefully rejecting it, and declaring himself to be an Anti-federalist even before having had time and leisure to become a Federalist," only to change position as the opposite view seemed to prevail. "As soon as the reports coming from America seemed to show the Federalist party being in the ascendance, he began to show a considerable degree of caution."[2]

But let us start from the beginning. As far as the regime produced by the Articles of Confederation was concerned, Jefferson had already expressed a very flattering appraisal of the government established under the Confederacy. He had taken part in the early congressional debates on representation (in which both the larger and the smaller states had immediately started to express conflicting views on the subject), and he was fairly skeptical about the possibility of successfully building a *plan of union*, as Congress avowedly intended to do. In spring 1777, a letter by Jefferson—which could be regarded as the first of a memorable correspondence—conveyed to John Adams his concern about the fact that "the great and small colonies are bitterly determined not to cede"[3] on the issue of representation. In effect, his suggestion prefigured the solution that would be adopted in Philadelphia ten years later: "Any proposition might be negatived by the representatives of a majority of the people of America, or of a majority of the colonies of America."[4] Therefore, the majority of the population and that of the colonies should both be considered legitimate.

The opinion voiced by Adams was that under the Articles of Confederation, Congress was little more than a diplomatic assembly. Strongly opposed to this view, Jefferson forcefully argued that by decision of the courts "the Confederation is part of the law of the land, and superior in authority to the ordinary laws, because it cannot be altered by the legislature of any one state."[5] Or better, that clause mistakenly referred to as "federal supremacy"—which would later be incorporated in Article 6 of the Constitution—was already implied in the logic of developments taking shape during the confederacy period. The truth is, Jefferson maintained,

120   *Liberty, State, & Union*

that if the clauses of an agreement, whether federal or confederal, did not have precedence over the ordinary laws (of the member states or of the confederacy itself), then there simply would not exist any agreement. On the other hand, not even the Anti-Federalists, and much less Jefferson himself, labored under the delusion that the times of the Confederation were a gilded age.

This notwithstanding, Jefferson harbored no illusion that the current arrangement was flawless. We have somewhat accurate information on his views, since in 1786 he assisted Jean-Nicolas Démeunier in drawing up the article on the United States for the *Encyclopédie Méthodique*. His aim was to help to elucidate a situation—the state of affairs in America—with regard to which there reigned great confusion in Europe. This misappraisal was, to a considerable extent, the work of the Abbot Guillaume Thomas François Raynal, whose rambling and long-winded tome *Histoire philosophique et politique des Etablissements et du commerce des Europeéns dans les deux Indes* (1770), bristling with factual mistakes, had become surprisingly popular in nonscientific circles.[6]

In response to a specific question by Démeunier, Jefferson began by praising the first constitutional instrument of the United States but did not omit to highlight its deficiencies as well. He believed it to be flawed by three basic imperfections. First, the lack of a "general rule for the admission of new states into the Union." Second, "the Confederation in it's eighth article, decides that the quota of money to be contributed [to the Union's coffers] by the several states shall be proportioned to the value of landed property in the state. Experience has shown it impracticable to come at this value." Finally, "the Confederation forbids the states individually to enter into treaties of commerce, or of any other nature, with foreign nations: and it authorizes Congress to establish such treaties." So when there existed no treaty stipulated by Congress, the states could do as they pleased. This area ought to have been more sensibly regulated.

Jefferson also added a gloss that history would shortly thereafter totally disprove, a circumstance that reveals how far he was losing touch with developing events in America as a result of his absence from the country. "These are the only alterations proposed to the confederation, and the last of them is the only additional power which Congress is thought to need."[7] For, in actual fact, there were powerful forces at work pushing toward a substantial change in the federal agreement, in order to refashion the government itself of the United States, and not only for the purpose of endowing Congress with a few extra powers.

On the issue of the alleged lack of strength of the federal and state governments, Jefferson was evidently not of the same opinion as the framers of the Philadelphia scheme:

> It has been said too that our governments both federal and particular want energy; that it is difficult to restrain both individuals & states from committing wrong. This is true, & it is an inconvenience. On the other hand that energy which absolute governments derive from an armed force, which is the effect of the bayonet constantly held at the breast of every citizen, and which resembles very much the stillness of the grave, must be admitted also to have it's inconveniences. We weigh the two together, and like best to submit to the former. Compare the number of wrongs committed with impunity by citizens among us, with those committed by the sovereign in other countries, and the last will be found most numerous, most oppressive on the mind, and most degrading of the dignity of man.[8]

Some time earlier, Jefferson had written to the Welsh scientist and economist Richard Price, the author of the essay *Observations on the Importance of the American Revolution*, published in 1785.[9] Price had voiced his unease at the feebleness of federal power under the Articles of Confederation: "The want of power in the federal head was early perceived, and foreseen to be the flaw in our constitution which might endanger its destruction. I have the pleasure to inform you that when I left America in July [1784] the people were becoming universally sensible of this, and a spirit to enlarge the powers of Congress was becoming general."[10]

However, after the ratification process had been concluded, Jefferson revealed to Price, with a scarcely veiled tone of pique and disappointment, that "our new Constitution…has succeeded beyond what I apprehended it would have done. I did not at first believe that eleven States out of thirteen would have consented to a plan consolidating them as much into one."[11] Yet he took these developments in his stride, bowing to what the states had accepted and acknowledging it as a fait accompli: "A federal government which could walk upon its own legs, without leaning for support on the State legislatures."[12]

Many years later, in 1795, Jefferson would once again voice great admiration for the Articles, as he prepared a few notes for a rejoinder to Christoph Daniel Ebeling, a professor in Hamburg and one of the first "Americanists" of the Old Continent. In Jefferson's words, "Our first federal constitution, or confederation as it was called, was framed in the first moments of our separation from England, in the highest point of our jealousies of independance as to her & as to each other."[13] He expressed some doubts about its adoption: "It is still doubted by some whether a majority of the people of the U.S. were not against adopting it."[14]

In effect, Jefferson's judgment on the Articles of Confederation was a stance he shared with the overwhelming majority of the Anti-Federalists. He was firmly convinced that the Articles were in need of revision, but he proceeded with extreme caution in suggesting any substantial alterations, a position which was essentially irreconcilable with that of the Federalists.

Jefferson's inclinations toward the Anti-Federalists is corroborated by the lavish praise he heaped upon the Articles of Confederation, as illustrated by his letter to Démeunier, in which he stated that "the Confederation is a wonderfully perfect instrument, considering the circumstances under which it was formed."[15] Furthermore, when, in November 1787, he confessed his qualms to John Adams, he did not fail to refer yet again to the ancient and venerable frame of government, namely the Articles.

> There are things in it [the new constitution] which stagger all my disposition to subscribe to what such an assembly has proposed. The house of federal representatives will not be adequate to the management of affairs either foreign or federal. *Their* President seems a bad edition of a Polish king.... All the good of this new constitution might have been couched in three or four new articles to be added to the good, old and venerable fabrick, which should have been preserved even as a religious relique.[16]

Well informed about the most recent developments back at home, thanks to the news conveyed by his trusted friends, Jefferson confided to a Virginian friend in summer 1787, "I confess, I do not go as far in the reforms thought necessary as some of my correspondents in America."

Further, expressing in a nutshell what would become the core of the Anti-Federalist position, "My general plan would be, to make the States one as to everything connected with foreign nations, and several as to everything purely domestic."[17]

Before the Philadelphia Convention, Jefferson wrote to Madison, "To make us one nation as to foreign concerns, and keep us distinct in domestic ones, gives the outline of the proper division of powers between the general and particular governments."[18] The concept was reiterated over and over again, to each and every correspondent. "My idea is that we should be made one nation in every case concerning foreign affairs, and separate ones in whatever is merely domestic."[19]

In actual fact, Jefferson consistently upheld this conception of the relations between states and the federation, not eschewing it even after the passing of the Constitution, so much so that he was later to assert, during his presidential campaign in 1800, that

> The true theory of our constitution is surely the wisest and best, that the States are independent as to everything within themselves, and united as to everything respecting foreign nations. Let the general government be reduced to foreign concerns only, and let our affairs be disentangled from those of all other nations, except as to commerce, which the merchants will manage the better, the more they are left free to manage for themselves, and our general government may be reduced to a very simple organization, and a very inexpensive one; a few plain duties to be performed by a few servants.[20]

This passage also embodies the core of Jefferson's theory of limited government, which is based on the federal division of powers. Jefferson subsequently reiterated the same idea at the close of his political career, in a comment to Destutt de Tracy:

> Seventeen distinct States, amalgamated into one as to their foreign concerns, but single and independent as to their internal administration, regularly organized with legislature and governor resting on the choice of the people, and enlightened by a free press, can never be so fascinated by the arts of one man, as to submit

voluntarily to his usurpation. Nor can they be constrained to it by any force he can possess.[21]

Again, many years later, in 1824, Jefferson stated that "the best general key for the solution of questions of power between our governments, is the fact that 'every foreign and federal power is given to the federal government, and to the States every power purely domestic.'...The federal is, in truth, our foreign government, which department alone is taken from the sovereignty of the separate States."[22]

This aspect of the Jeffersonian federal philosophy has been emphasized because it underlines his staunch belief in one of the pivotal elements of the Anti-Federalist vision, which appears truly perfect and constant over time. But let us now turn to a closer examination of the actual criticisms leveled by Jefferson against the constitutional project.

Jefferson had immediately expressed his anger against the way matters had been prepared, in the utmost secrecy, by the assembled representatives. As he wrote to John Adams in summer 1787, "I am sorry they began their deliberations by so abominable a precedent as that of tying up the tongues of their members. Nothing can justify this example, but the innocence of their intentions, and ignorance of the value of public discussions."[23] Although he was not raising the unlikely specter of a conspiracy, here, too, he was fairly close to the positions embraced by the Anti-Federalists. Abraham Yates stated, "If we take a retrospective view of the measures of Congress...we can scarcely entertain a doubt but that a plan has long since been framed to subvert the confederation."[24]

Overall, Jefferson was convinced that public opinion should be freely and promptly provided with information by an independent press. Indeed, "the press [is] the only tocsin of a nation."[25] Naturally, after many years of presidency and having been the target of some base allegations in the gutter press, Jefferson found himself compelled to claim that the press was committing suicide "by it's abandoned prostitution to falsehood. Nothing can now be believed which is seen in a newspaper. Truth itself becomes suspicious by being put into that polluted vehicle."[26]

In a very frank and sober tone, Jefferson had outlined to Madison his feelings concerning the way matters had been handled by the Philadelphia delegates. His most severe remonstration was reserved for the lack of a Bill of Rights, but he was also extremely concerned about the possibility that public figures could be reelected to office, particularly the presidency.[27] After praising what he could, he exposed his objections.

> First the omission of a bill of rights providing clearly & without the aid of sophisms for freedom of religion, freedom of the press, protection against standing armies, restriction against monopolies, the eternal & unremitting force of the habeas corpus laws, and trials by jury in all matters of fact triable by the laws of the land & not by the law of nations...a bill of rights is what the people are entitled to against every government on earth, general or particular, & what no just government should refuse, or rest on inferences.[28]

This was not the full extent of his disapproval. The regular alternation of public offices was one of the mainstays of Jeffersonian constitutional thought. "The second feature I dislike, and greatly dislike, is the abandonment in every instance of the necessity of rotation in office, and most particularly in the case of the President. Experience concurs with reason in concluding that the first magistrate will always be reelected if the Constitution permits it. He is then an officer for life."[29] He foretold, with great prescience, "The election of a President of America some years hence will be much more interesting to certain nations of Europe than ever the election of a king of Poland was."[30]

The question of an energetic government was a classic of debate in America during those years (suffice it to note how frequently the expression occurs in the *Federalist*), and it had become a mantra which, if repeated often enough, was liable to induce the peoples of the various states to accept the notion of centralization. On this point, Jefferson offered a crisp repartee: "I am not a friend to a very energetic government. It is always oppressive."[31]

His final argument in favor of adoption appears prudential, to those who are familiar with Jefferson's attention to the mood of the majority. "After all, it is my principle that the will of the majority should always prevail. If they approve the proposed Convention in all it's parts, I shall concur in it chearfully, in hopes that they will amend it whenever they shall find it work wrong."[32] This should by no means be seen as a blind endorsement of the will of the majority, but rather as a precept which— although deeply embedded in his thinking—he was not to render explicit until a number of years later, during his presidency. It then became a sort of maxim suitable for any democratic statesman: "He who would do his country the most good he can must go quietly with the prejudices of the majority until he can lead them into reason."[33]

Yet on this point, as Hoffert rather appropriately pointed out, there is a tinge of irony. "His ultimate support for the ratification of the Constitution of 1787…was based on a majoritarian theory antithetical to the theory of majority restraint at the heart of that document."[34] For the Constitution was conceived as a strong remedy against the overweening majorities that may arise in the country and could then be reflected in Congress. In this sense, because of the rigid division of powers and of political representation divided between House and Senate, the Constitution does not allow the rule of (simple) majority to prevail.

Be that as it may, it was the presidential office that gave the Virginian the greatest cause for concern. A "monocratic" summit of federal executive power immediately struck him as being dangerous, an outcome of the demand for law and order that had been one of the consequences of the recent unrest in Massachusetts.

One of the factors that weighed heavily on the summoning of the Philadelphia constitutional convention had been the widespread fears of strife engendered by Shays' Rebellion.[35] Although the revolt was quashed by 1787, it spread a climate of fear that contributed to creating a general swing in favor of the centralization of power. Commenting on and *commending* Shays' uprising, Jefferson wrote some of the most radical statements of his entire doctrinal reflection. "What country can preserve it's liberties if their rulers are not warned from time to time that their people preserve the spirit of resistance? Let them take arms…. What signify a few lives lost in a century or two? The tree of liberty must be refreshed from time to time with the blood of patriots and tyrants. It is it's natural manure."[36]

Many Jeffersonian biographers have attributed this language to the prevailing climate of opinion in France in the years immediately preceding the Revolution. In other words, it is claimed that Jefferson's feelings in this regard were projections of the effervescent French political atmosphere reverberating over the American scene, as if the author of the Declaration, having fallen prey to some strange derangement of his mental faculties, were no longer capable of distinguishing clearly between a disintegrating absolute monarchy and his then free republic.[37]

A truer picture of his frustration at the turn that events were taking at home is to be found in his political radicalism, which developed in parallel with the news reaching him from home—and not in relation with the course of affairs in France. Jefferson had immediately grasped the connection between the fears fostered by Shays' Rebellion and the new constitution. On the same day that he drafted his reply to Smith, Jefferson received a rather alarmed letter from John Jay, who was foreign minister at the time, with regard to the Massachusetts rebellion. Jay's alarm was motivated both by the event itself and by its possible repercussions. He saw in the revolt "a spirit of licentiousness...[a] reluctance to taxes, an impatience of government."[38] But the real problem lay in the influence this would have on law-abiding citizens. "If faction should long bear down law and government, tyranny may raise its head, or the more sober part of the people may even think of a king."[39]

Jefferson found the letter extremely disquieting, and he resolved to gain a more precise idea of the nature of the rebellion. His comments were generally fairly moderate. Not only had the rebels caused no damage to the lives and property of their fellow citizens, but the reasons underlying their rebellion resided in the excessive taxation imposed by the Massachusetts assembly in the attempt to clear its debts.[40] Furthermore, he urged that the leaders of the revolt should not be subjected to unduly harsh punishment:

> I am persuaded myself that the good sense of the people will always be found to be the best army. They may be led astray for a moment, but will soon correct themselves. The people are the only censors of their governors; and even their errors will tend to keep these to the true principles of their institution. To punish these errors too severely would be to suppress the only safeguard of the public liberty.[41]

Rather than violently attacking the constitutional document, Jefferson made recourse to all his eloquence in making allowances for the revolt, in tones that made a dramatic impression on subsequent commentators and certainly could not have been easy for the readers of his own day to understand. In that same period, he also wrote to John Adams's wife with expressions that must surely have sounded disturbing to the New England aristocracy. In fact, it cannot be ruled out that there may, at least in this case, have been a certain desire to *épater le bourgeois*, as if to emphasize his revolutionary zeal. Jefferson's words appeared to embody an inclination toward leniency with regard to the rebels associated with exalting resistance against the tyranny of power. "I hope they pardoned them. The spirit of resistance to government is so valuable on certain occasions, that I wish it to be always kept alive. It will often be exercised when wrong, but better so than not to be exercised at all. I like a little rebellion now and then. It is like a storm in the atmosphere."[42]

In the above-cited letter to William Smith, which contains what is perhaps the most forceful expression in the entire body of Jefferson's letters, the link between the constitutional project and the Massachusetts insurrection becomes palpable. The very office of the presidency itself (and not only indefinite reeligibility) struck him as particularly unpalatable. Here, he saw an immediate connection: "Our Convention has been too much impressed by the insurrection of Massachusetts: and in the spur of the moment they are setting up a kite to keep the hen-yard in order."[43] Now it is perfectly obvious that the "kite in the hen-yard" is the president, or rather the entire federal government. The context of the letter clearly suggests the highest offices of the executive power, but a more extensive interpretation may not be out of place.

Jefferson's friend Filippo Mazzei, who was under less of an obligation to be diplomatic, launched a direct attack on Madison with a quasi-invective in Italian (it should be recalled that the first four American presidents, as befitted well-educated gentleman of their age, were all well versed both in written and spoken French and Italian). "How could you assent to the proposed Constitution of several articles, the harbinger of lethal bolts against poor liberty? Do you fancy Washington to be immortal?... I hope you are not infected by the faith, alas far too ubiquitous, in checks and balances in matters of government."[44] As an aside, the letter was written in Paris, and the reference to the strategy correctly attributed to Jefferson (namely, to ratify the Constitution expressing reservations, and proceed immediately to amend it to fix its numerous flaws) leaves no doubt that Mazzei discussed the issue with his friend and that in this occasion he was unusually exercised by their shared concern.

Madison responded with an irritated rebuttal. "Experience has proved that the real danger to America & to liberty lies in the defect of *energy & stability* in the present establishments of the United States.... In your closet at Paris and with the evils resulting from too much Government all over Europe fully in your view, it is natural for you to run into criticisms dictated by an extreme on that side."[45]

Yet the fact remains that despite the more or less direct criticism of the proposed constitution, Jefferson eventually praised and accepted it. Without going as far as to indulge in the excesses displayed in the letter sent to the writer David Humphreys, in which he defined the Constitution as the "wisest ever yet presented to men,"[46] he had already disclosed his thoughts to George Washington. Well aware how great a store the president of the Philadelphia Convention set by the good outcome of the ratification process, Jefferson stated in his comment to the general, "I have seen, with infinite pleasure, our new constitution accepted by 11. states, not rejected by the 12th. and that the 13th. happens to be a state of the least importance."[47] Yet he added that "the minorities in most of the accepting states have been very respectable, so much so as to render it prudent, were it not otherwise reasonable, to make some sacrifice to them."[48] All things considered, one might perhaps satisfy them with a fine bill of rights, which in any case all his correspondents took for granted, since this would sweep the carpet away from under the feet of the dissidents. "The annexation of the bill of rights to the constitution will alone draw over so great a proportion of the minorities, as to leave little danger in the opposition of the residue."[49]

Furthermore, during the debate in Virginia on the subject of ratification, Jefferson's bitter foe Patrick Henry had quoted a letter in which Jefferson expressed himself in favor of a conditional adoption by the first nine states and for the remaining four to withhold their ratification, in order to obtain the acceptance of a bill of rights, and this had certainly been no source of pleasure for the author of the Declaration. "This illustrious citizen advises you to reject this government till it be amended.... Let us follow the sage advice of this common friend of our happiness."[50] Henry, however, not only sought to exploit Jefferson's suggestion, but he also misinterpreted it, given that the then minister to France had written, "I wish with all my soul, that the nine first conventions may accept the new constitution, because this will secure to us the good it contains, which I think great and important. But equally wish, that the four latest conventions, which ever they be, may refuse to accede to it, till a declaration of rights be annexed."[51] This would actually have implied, given the stage the process had reached, that Virginia should ratify the Constitution. But the prospect of being deliberately misunderstood and ridiculed—worse still, by none other than his adversaries—in a battle he did not feel to be his and about which he did not consider himself at all well informed was surely not a very agreeable one.

These feelings clearly come to the fore in the famous letter where Jefferson declared, "I am neither Federalist, nor Anti-Federalist," prompted by an explicit request from Francis Hopkinson, who urged him to clarify his position.

> I am not a Federalist, because I never submitted the whole system of my opinions to the creed of any party of men whatever in religion, in philosophy, in politics, or in anything else where I was capable of thinking for myself.... If I could not go to heaven but with a party, I would not go there at all.... I protest to you I am not of the party of federalists. But I am much farther from that of the Antifederalists. Approved, from the first moment, of the great mass of what is in the new constitution.... What disapproved from the first moment also was the want of a bill of rights to guard liberty against the legislative as well as executive branches of the government.... I disapproved also the perpetual reeligibility of the President. To these points of disapprobation I adhere.[52]

Nevertheless, Jefferson did explain to his friend that he agreed there should be no further discussion, back in America, about his position in relation to this matter. "My great wish is to go on in a strict but silent performance of my duty; to avoid attracting notice & to keep my name out of newspapers."[53] One has the impression that he did not wish to become embroiled in a controversy while thousands of miles away, especially since the length of time required for communications to be conveyed back and forth meant that his name and his prestige might be exploited by the parties at odds with one another without the slightest chance for him to spell out his true position.

The Political Theory of Thomas Jefferson

A more thoughtful explanation can also be advanced as to why Jefferson was not particularly vocal in his opposition to a constitution that he had accepted at first only with great caution, and indeed had often openly criticized. The explanation lies in the nature itself of the constitutional instrument created in Philadelphia. Jefferson's final approval is also explained as the reverse image to that of his great rival of the 1790s, Alexander Hamilton. Briefly, Jefferson and Hamilton, although certainly both harboring serious reservations about the Constitution, were to find themselves publicly praising a document that lay half way between centralization and noncentralization for two opposite reasons. The former believed it would be possible to tip the balance of power toward the states, the latter toward the union.

History was to show that Hamilton was right, but only in the short- and then in the very long-term. The legislation that was to definitively sanction the victory of the Hamiltonian mercantilist and command-directed system was actually a byproduct of the Civil War. The two National Bank acts of 1863 and 1864, the State Bank Note acts of 1865 and 1866, and the Federal Reserve Act of 1913 changed forever the power relations between the states and the federal government. In addition, it was in 1913 that two constitutional amendments were approved that closed the circle of centralization: the Sixteenth Amendment, which endowed Congress with the power to tax the income of American citizens without the obligation of apportioning the tax revenue among the states, and the Seventeenth Amendment, which introduced popular direct election of senators, substantially changing the structure of federal representation. Prior to that time, senators had been chosen by the state legislatures and were genuinely "ambassadors" of their own state within the federal government, but from that moment on, they became national political figures, their association with their own state becoming increasingly tenuous.

To better understand Jefferson's position with respect to the Constitution, it is necessary to analyze his approach in parallel with that of his great rival.

Alexander Hamilton and the Constitution

Alexander Hamilton, secretary of the treasury during the first American administration and an eminent political thinker in his own right, is a rather controversial figure to historians of American political thought, one who has consistently sparked intense debate among scholars working in this field.[54] Hamilton was the most important champion of the claims of the modern state in the European continental mold in the struggle to overthrow the natural law and classical liberal framework then prevailing in the newly independent colonies. His stance is emblematic of what was felt to be the requirements of the modern nation-state (that is, the modern state in the European continental mold) stemming from a decidedly continental background. Hamilton was the mouthpiece of those who sought to impose these aspects on the fabric of natural rights and classical liberal thought that was dominant in the independent colonies.

A staunch believer in full and absolute centralization for the American union—to the point where he left the Philadelphia Constitutional Convention on 19 June 1787 as soon as it became clear that there would be no move to sweep away the states—he "was described by contemporaries as a monarchist who hated republican government and feared democracy."[55] Four famous reports bear his name. Written between 1790 and 1791 (*Report on National Bank*, *Mint*, *Public Credit*, and *Manufactures*),[56] they outline a vision of the national economy that would be widely acclaimed in the twentieth century, although it was rather distant from the most commonly held American views of the time.

Paradoxically, though, over the past few decades Hamilton has come to be seen as one of the major thinkers shaping the philosophy of American conservatives. Ironically, the champion of a strong centralized government has become a reference point for conservatives, whereas one of the staunchest defenders of limited government has been enlisted in the ranks of Franklin Delano Roosevelt and his party.

The great American constitutionalist Edward Corwin observed that according to Hamiltonian theory, "The national government...is within the range of these [enumerated] powers a truly sovereign government, and so is under no constitutional compulsion, either in the selection of means whereby to make its powers effective or in the selection of objects to be attained by their exercise, to take account of the coexistence of the states or to concern itself to preserve any particular relationship of power between itself and the states."[57]

An overriding inclination toward the unity of the body politic, subordinating all particular interests to the general welfare emerges throughout Hamilton's writings and speeches. Indeed, it is no coincidence that Hamilton was one of the few early American thinkers to insistently refer to the notion of "the common good," "national interest," and so forth. His conflict with Jefferson was characterized by a profound divergence of a doctrinal character: "As far as politics were concerned, Jefferson thought man should pursue his happiness; Hamilton thought he should seek the national interest. One called for egoistic behavior, the other for altruistic. It was Hamilton that was the greater idealist, Jefferson the greater realist."[58]

Cecelia Kenyon's definition of Hamilton as the "Rousseau of the right" is extremely perceptive. For it is undeniable that he presented a blend of elements of twentieth-century social planning theories with aristocratic conservative leanings. Hamilton's thought lies at the roots of that collusion between Big Government and Big Business that is the concern of Western democracies and which was almost unthinkable during the foundation period of the American Republic. His impassioned and at times unprincipled search for the personal interests (of the ruling classes), which could then be leveraged in order to pursue the national interest, sets him in a peculiarly solitary place within the framework of American political thought.

Among the articles that appeared in the *Federalist*, Publius-Hamilton upheld a specific constitutional project submitted to the judgment of his fellow citizens in the state of New York. And yet, as is well known, Hamilton played no role in the drafting of the constitutional document. In Jefferson's judgment, Hamilton's support of the Constitution was not due to the positive elements it contained; instead, Hamilton was simply exploiting it as a springboard to achieve a different goal. Namely, the faction Jefferson called the monarchical federalists, of whom Hamilton was the recognized leader, had acted "for the new government merely as a stepping stone to monarchy."[59] The judgment of Karl-Friedrich Walling is probably not far from the mark: "Because he was more concerned with unleashing than restraining national power [in the 1790s, Hamilton] came close to establishing by legal construction [by the courts] what he had failed to obtain at the federal Convention: congressional authority to make all laws whatsoever for the safety and welfare of the Union."[60]

The Hamiltonian contribution to the delicate question of the Constitution cannot be understood unless it is seen in relation to his controversial relationship with the Convention. Hamilton had had the privilege of representing his own state at the Philadelphia Convention, which he had strongly supported as a means of mending the flaws of the confederation. The other two New York delegates, Robert Yates and John Lansing, Jr., did not vote the same way as Hamilton. Indeed, it was quite surprising that he was effectively nominated by the New York State convention as its own representative.

Hamilton's "active participation" at the Philadelphia Convention was essentially limited to a memorable almost six-hour-long speech he delivered on the morning of 18 June 1787, amid the dismay and admiration of his peers. Dismay at the audacity of his bold statements and admiration because it was perfectly clear that he had genuinely spoken from the heart and stated his true beliefs. On that morning, there were eleven states represented, while discussion had been in progress for almost a week on the amended plans put forward by New Jersey (small state plan) and Virginia (big state plan), which Hamilton regarded as totally inadequate to address the problems facing the country. He thus proposed his own plan for a national government,[61] which, however, had no bearing on the constitutional project that was later approved. His plan can be summarized as follows:

(1) a supreme legislative authority of the United States: two Houses, an Assembly elected every three years, and a Senate whose members would be chosen for life by indirect election;

(2) a supreme executive authority of the United States, endowed with wide-ranging powers; such authority would be vested in an elected governor (elected, for life, by an electoral college);

(2.1) almost all the powers of government were to be divided between the Senate and the governor; i.e., between a life executive and an assembly of senators who were also elected for life;

(3) a supreme judicial authority, with both original and ultimate appeal jurisdiction, vested in a body composed of ten justices;

(4) relations with the various state assemblies: the governor or the president of each state was to be appointed by the government of the United States, with a general right of veto over all state laws. No state was allowed to have an armed militia.

This framework was designed to create a uniform centralized power, with the balance totally tipped toward the executive, the latter endowed with an overarching power over the states and a declared enemy of their existence as free and independent polities. Had Hamilton's plan been approved—although, as Russell Kirk rightly observed, "such centralization would have been impossible to attain in America, even by force of arms"[62]—the United States would have become a mere decentralized republic and, in a few years, "one and indivisible," almost two centuries earlier than it actually did.

The emphasis on executive power was deliberate. Hamilton believed that the United States should have a strong government, which would lead the country toward rapid industrialization, on the lines of the British model. He had very little trust either in the invisible hand of the market— his polemic against Adam Smith is notorious[63]—or in man's capacity for self-government, and he was more inclined toward a commercial and oligarchic republic. Consequently, the executive logically became the center and the engine of the system. As John Koritansky has pointed out, "For Hamilton...only the executive had the requisite degree of unity that could generate the energy and the rationality...that is necessary for sound public policy."[64] For this reason, Daniel Elazar is quite justified in depicting Hamilton as a solitary figure against the backdrop of the political doctrines of the Founding Fathers, one who in many ways prefigured the "managerialist" school that became popular in America during the last century. Elazar goes as far as to say that "Hamilton's political thought [is]...more worthy of exploration for its contemporary implications than for elucidating his role at the founding."[65] Similarly, analyzing the various contemporary theories on the ends of the public administration, Elazar points out the modern and centralistic, top-down character of the New Yorker's thought: "Alexander Hamilton comes closest to being the classic spokesman for the national uniformity theory."[66]

But let us return to Hamilton's speech at the Convention. One can hardly fail to share the judgment expressed by the popular historian Cathrine Drinker Bowen:

> That Hamilton was not interrupted seems extraordinary, considering the tenor of his remarks, their boldness, the growing unpopularity of this "British example." *Annihilate state distinctions and state operations?* In the whole gathering, perhaps only Read of Delaware and Butler of South Carolina would have agreed. *A single*

executive, elected for life? It came closer to monarchy. Paradoxically, Hamilton's idea of a lower house elected directly by the people went beyond what most delegates were ready to concede to "democracy." Even Madison was against it. *A general and national government, completely sovereign?* Nothing less, Hamilton had argued, could establish American power at home and American prestige abroad.[67]

On the following day, 19 June 1787, Hamilton expressed his views concerning the role of the states even more clearly. According to the notes taken by Madison, on the question of the states, "He thought they ought to be abolished.... By an abolition of the States, he meant that no boundary could be drawn between the National & State Legislatures; that the former must therefore have indefinite authority."[68] Besides, he was firmly convinced that "two Sovereignties can not co-exist within the same limits."[69]

Shortly after such a revelation of his opinions on "federalism," Hamilton abandoned the Convention, reasonably convinced that the climate was not particularly propitious for such a far-reaching project. However, unlike his codelegates from the state of New York (who left the Convention roughly six weeks after the beginning of proceedings, precisely because they feared it would culminate in an excessively centralist plan), Hamilton returned to Independence Hall from time to time, and in September he took upon himself the responsibility of signing the constitutional proposal against the opinion of his own state.

Setting aside the hypothesis that Hamilton was mercurial in his opinions, scholars face an interpretive problem: Why on earth did he put his signature to, and then fiercely defend, a constitution that was certainly far removed from his ideals of government? In order to gain insight into this conundrum, we need to shift the time scale somewhat later.

According to Madison, the Philadelphia constitutional Convention had shaped a project in which two parallel universes had been outlined, each sovereign in its respective sphere, and each destined never to enter into conflict with the other: the federal government and the federated states. From the earliest years of the republic onwards, this theory—which survived right up to the 1930s with the name of dual federalism as a juridical definition of the American system of government—was shown to be a sort of constitutional daydream. Far from proceeding along parallel tracks, with clear and distinct demarcations, the states and the federal government clashed more or less straightaway and found themselves on a collision course on almost every issue. The Constitution had by no means resolved once and for all the question of relations between the states and the federal government; rather, it opened another natural battleground concerning the interpretation of the constitutional instrument itself.

In 1791, during Washington's first term of presidency, Hamilton and Jefferson were the most popular politicians in America, and they were both members of the administration. The former, a sort of "shadow Prime Minister," was the powerful secretary of the treasury, as well as the leader of the majority party in Congress, that is, the Federalist Party. The latter was the secretary of state and was beginning to organize the opposition to the centralist plan. The conflict between the two men, which dominated the political scene at the end of the eighteenth century, was inevitable and, despite conciliatory overtures by George Washington, it turned into an irreconcilable rivalry once Hamilton's bill for the institution of a federal bank obtained the majority of votes in Congress. Jefferson hoped to convince the president to reject it on the basis of its blatant unconstitutionality, but Washington, after considering the opinion of the two contenders, signed the Bank Bill, thereby yielding to Hamilton's arguments.

As early as summer 1780, Hamilton had begun to mull over the establishment of a federal central bank, provided with mixed private and public capital, and endowed with the authority of issuing bonds to finance the federal debt and enable the federal government to provide for all the country's needs, both at war and in peacetime. In 1781, the Continental Congress had created the Bank of North America, vesting it with fairly limited powers, but subsequently its statutes were repealed by the Pennsylvania assembly in 1785. The bank was reestablished in 1788, with even more limited capital, prestige, and duration.[70]

Interestingly, it may be noted here that the collaboration of Jefferson and James Madison, as well as the break of the latter with Hamilton, were occasioned by the battle against the incorporation of the bank. The two Virginians, Jefferson in the administration, Madison in Congress, failed in the attempt to thwart the designs of Hamilton. In Madison's view, the central point was the strict construction of the Constitution, as opposed to the looser reading suggested by the Hamiltonian party. In fact, the party in power did not very much care for constitutional issue. The Federalist zealot Fisher Ames "laughed at the objection deduced from the Constitution." In his view, any regard for the letter of the document and for the intent of the framers was absolutely out of place, for the simple reason that the bank was helpful to commerce and needed to confront the public debt.[71]

Once the federal constitution had been approved, the problem of the bank also became a question of constitutional interpretation. In the Hamiltonian proposal, the Bank of the United States was intended to serve as a means of repaying the debt. What Hamilton proposed was to forge a close connection between the lifetime of the bank and that of the public debt; note that he saw the latter as the driving thrust of economic growth. He manifestly wished for both the bank and the debt to be perpetual. However, awarding federal power such a sweeping mandate over the debt and over the methods of its financing, let alone a tendency to a monopoly over the issuing of money, might be regarded as a step in the wrong direction, overstepping the boundaries of the Constitution and undermining its rigorous demarcation of spheres of authority between the states and the federation.

Jefferson had realized that only a strict construction of the Constitution would save the states from having to submit to a central power. Hamilton, by the same token, was well aware that only by allowing an elastic interpretation of the constitutional provisions could the powers of the federal government be reinforced, so as to introduce at the very heart of the national political life the controversial clause referring to the absolute supremacy of federal power—the clause the states were so reluctant to accept (and on which they could not reach an agreement in Philadelphia).[72]

The opinions voiced by the two antagonists on the question of the central bank, in their report to the president, were therefore to have momentous importance. For on the one hand, they made clear the rift between those who believed the Constitution could be modified only through amendments (strict construction) versus those who argued it could be modified through interpretation (loose construction). This division was to surface again and again, in each and every American constitutional debate. On the other hand, they emphasized that the political struggle in America was to be centered on the issue of centralization and states' rights. Incidentally, it should also be noted that every fundamental change in the political and institutional makeup of America, from the Civil War to the New Deal, to desegregation, and the "Reagan revolution," has occasioned a reoccurrence of the first great American debate, the debate on federalism.

Very briefly, the two statesmen offered President Washington the following views. Jefferson started out from the Tenth Amendment ("The powers not delegated to the United States by the Constitution, nor prohibited by it to the States, are reserved to the States respectively, or to the people.") to assert that "to take a single step beyond the boundaries thus specially drawn around the powers of Congress, is to take possession of a boundless field of power, no longer susceptible of any definition."[73]

Hamilton, in contrast, aware that he had fewer textual footholds to prop himself up,[74] prepared his speech with the most painstaking attention to every minute detail,[75] and for the first time in American history, he set forth the so-called "implied powers" theory: "Every power vested in a Government is in its nature *sovereign*, and includes by *force* of the *term*, a right to employ all the *means* requisite, and fairly *applicable* to the attainment of the *ends* of such power;...there are *implied*, as well as *express* powers, and that the former are as effectually delegated as the latter."[76]

As Hamilton saw it, the constitutionality of a law should not be judged simply by looking at the specific powers vested in the federal government by the Constitution. Rather, the assessment should be conducted on the basis of a clearly specified question, namely "Does the proposed measure abridge a preexisting right of any State, or of any individual? If it does not, there is a strong presumption in favour of its constitutionality."[77]

Admittedly, the constitutional text on this point seems clear. In order to act, the federal government must be able to point to something in the letter of the Constitution that permits it to do so; and this differs sharply from the situation affecting the states, which may encounter prohibitions but have a sort of "general political competence." For Hamilton, on the contrary, a general presumption of constitutionality existed in the action of the federal government. The powers of the federal government, in his understanding, became those expressly stated by the constitutional text, those implicitly derived from the granting of the aforementioned powers, and those that did not have the effect of abridging the rights of the states or of the individuals. Within such a framework, the boundaries established by the Constitution became so blurred as to make it fairly impossible to define *a priori* where the federal sphere of authority ended and where the states' began.

As early as his contribution to the *Federalist*, Hamilton had shown himself loath to accept the limitations on federal government activity. In his own words, "These powers ought to exist without limitation, *because it is impossible to foresee or define the extent and variety of national exigencies, or the correspondent extent and variety of the means which may be necessary to satisfy them.*"[78] Shortly afterward, he added, in what has to be considered as an anticipation of the doctrine of implied powers, albeit in such generic terms that it could hardly raise serious objections: "The *means* ought to be proportioned to the *end*; the persons, from whose agency the attainment of any *end* is expected, ought to possess the *means* by which it is to be attained."[79] In this regard, a scholar who held the New Yorker in very high esteem commented, "Hamilton believed that in the final analysis the federal government and particularly the executive branch must have whatever power was needed to protect the safety and well being of the republic."[80]

The doctrine of implied powers was subsequently embraced and perfected by the third chief justice of the Supreme Court, the Federalist, John Marshall, who headed the court during the first crucial thirty years of the nineteenth century, from 1801 to his death, and who was the real *dominus* of the legal system of the young republic. With Marshall, the Supreme Court became the center of the Federalist resurgence after Jefferson's victory in the 1800 presidential election. In *Fletcher v. Peck* (1810), Marshall annulled an act approved by the assembly of Georgia, informing the state that Georgia was only "a part of a larger empire…a member of the American union…which opposes limits to the legislatures of the several states."[81] This was followed by the sentence of *Mc Cullough v. Maryland*, 1819, in which the Chief Justice crushed the attempt by a state to tax an agency of the federal government. The same year saw the Dartmouth College case, in which Marshall declared a law of the New Hampshire assembly to be null and void, thereby breaching the statutes guaranteed to the university under English rule. The centralist-Hamiltonian interpretation had found its most powerful ally in the Supreme Court—and precisely during the years of republican-Jeffersonian ascendancy. In the future, there would no longer be any need to seek arguments to persuade the president or Congress of the constitutionality of a law in contrast with the Tenth Amendment.

Here lay the real core of dispute, the deepest roots of the hostility between Jefferson and Hamilton. The dispute ran the entire gamut of issues on which they found themselves championing opposite sides: all the way from foreign policy (Jefferson was a Francophile while Hamilton was an Anglophile) to the overall political vision of the just society and of the "good life" (wary of governmental coercion and agrarian in Jefferson's position, interventionist and commercial for Hamilton). But the central point was always the institutionalization of power and of states' rights. Such ideas were anathema to Hamilton, a veritable juridical monstrosity (he regarded the state as an *imperium in imperio*), while in Jefferson's perspective these constituted the one and only true barrier against the concentration of power.[82]

Thus, in September 1787, Hamilton resolved to vigorously support a constitution about which he harbored more than a few doubts. His support was motivated by the fact that he felt it represented a step—the only step that appeared at all feasible at that moment—toward the centralization of power in America. At the same time, however, he immediately set about bringing the power and political arrangements in America closer to the vision he had extolled in his speech on 18 June 1787. Years after his death, Gouverneur Morris would recall,

> General Hamilton...had little share in forming the Constitution. He disliked it, believing all republican government to be radically defective.... General Hamilton hated republican government, because he confounded it with democratical government; and he detested the latter, because he believed it must end in despotism, and, be in the mean time, destructive to public morality.... He heartily assented, nevertheless, to the Constitution, because he considered it as a band [*sic*] which might hold us together for some time, and he knew that national sentiment is the offspring of national existence.[83]

In the course of the same piece of correspondence, Morris claimed that Hamilton hoped the United States would over time be lucky enough to be dragged into a war, "which might strengthen our union and nerve the Executive."[84]

A letter sent by Hamilton to Morris himself, dated 1802, shows Hamilton confessing he had never had confidence in the Constitution; he had only settled to working at it, he added, "and contrary to all my anticipations of its fate, as you know from the very beginning, I am still laboring to prop the frail and worthless fabric."[85] Hamilton then appended a disconsolate remark, "every day proves to me more and more, that this American world was not made for me."[86]

What is clear, at any rate, is that no particular logical inferences need be adduced to elucidate this point. Hamilton was perfectly explicit about his intentions. In a conversation with Jefferson, he quite candidly confessed "that the present government is not that which will answer the ends of society, by giving stability and protection to its rights, and that it will probably be found expedient to go into the British form. However, since we have undertaken the experiment, I am for giving it a fair course, whatever my expectations may be."[87]

Jefferson bequeathed to posterity a post-mortem judgment on Hamilton that is a tribute to the New Yorker's personal qualities, and he attributes most of his flaws to a single cause, specifically, his preference for the English model: "Hamilton was indeed a singular character. Of acute understanding, disinterested, honest, and honorable in all private transactions, amiable in society, and duly valuing virtue in private life, yet so bewitched & perverted by the British example, as to be under thoro' conviction that corruption was essential to the government of a nation."[88]

Hamilton's love for England and its social and political system was such common knowledge that the young English ambassador George Hammond, who had been sent in the 1790s to restore diplomatic relations between the two countries, praised Hamilton for his "just and liberal way of thinking" and reassured the government that the statesman in question belonged to the "party of the English interest."[89] Still, perhaps, George Will's smart remark certainly has the sound of truth: "There is an elegant memorial in Washington to Jefferson, but none to Hamilton. However, if you seek Hamilton's monument, look around. You are living in it. We honor Jefferson, but live in Hamilton's country."[90]

The establishment of the first Bank of the United States was but the beginning of the Hamiltonian system. Indeed, the system was still in its infancy. On 4 November 1791, the secretary of the treasury presented his *Report on Manufactures*, which proposed extending federal powers through a system of excise duties designed to favor the establishment of a manufacturing industry. When listing the advantages of the factory system, he noted, with remarkable cynicism, that it allowed "the employment of persons who would otherwise be idle (and in many cases a burthen on the community)...in general, women and Children are rendered more useful and the latter more early useful by manufacturing establishments, than they would otherwise be."[91] Again, and with an eye to his model of political and social development, Hamilton asserted that one of the motives that clearly pointed to the factory system as desirable and helpful was that "of the number of persons employed in the Cotton Manufactories of Great Britain, it is computed that 4/7 nearly are women and children; of whom the greatest proportion are children and many of them of a very tender age."[92]

What clearly emerges from a reading of the well-known Hamiltonian reports of the early 1790s is the vision of an economy designed more or less exclusively to serve the purposes of the national interests, according to a radicalization of the English model. In particular, the idea of utilizing the public debt to increase the power and influence of the federal government was one of the cardinal points of the political action of the secretary of the treasury. John Maynard Keynes could hardly have put it in a simpler and more effective manner, as Hamilton told financier Robert Morris in 1781: "A national debt, if it is not excessive, will be to us a national blessing." Further, keeping his eye fixed on the centralization of power, "It will be a powerful cement for our union. It will also create a necessity for keeping up taxation to a degree which, without being oppressive, will be a spur to industry."[93] How taxation could be considered a tool of economic development at the end of the eighteenth century in America is hard to understand, and the aspects that were most strongly pervaded with neomercantilist (or protoprotectionist) leanings aroused very little interest, even among his own supporters, as laissez faire was still the most widely shared social ideology. This is made clear by the fact that the opening phrase of the *Report on Manufactures*, "The expediency of encouraging manufactures in the United States, which was not long since deemed very questionable, appears at this time to be pretty generally admitted,"[94] seems little more than a rhetorical device.

Jefferson was fully aware of the consequences of such a political stance. "As the doctrine is that a public debt is a public blessing, so they think a perpetual one is a perpetual blessing, and therefore wish to make it so large that we can never pay it off."[95] The crucial feature was the shouldering of the debts of the states by the federal government. This was a point on which Jefferson, shortly after his return from Paris and still poorly versed in postconstitutional American politics, allowed himself to be wrong-footed by Hamilton, to the point that he later viewed this as one of his major political mistakes. Hamilton had proposed that the government shoulder the debts accumulated by the states during the Revolution, with the establishment of an entirely federal public debt specifically for this purpose. Such a proposal was extremely favorable to the financiers and speculators of New England and New York, who had acquired the bonds of the original debtors at the enormously devalued wartime price and who would now have a chance to amass tremendous profits by having them redeemed by the federal government at their nominal value. Hamilton's scheme for the federal government to take on the debts of the Northern states was rejected by the Southern states, who had already repaid their own debts. The tension between the two sections heightened to the point that Jefferson, fearing for the solidity of the union, reached a compromise with his adversary.

Some time later, Jefferson claimed he had been conned by Hamilton, and complained he had not clearly realized Hamilton's aims.[96] As he wrote in a letter to James Monroe in June 1790, those who opposed the shouldering of the debt (of whom there were more than a few, since a number of states had practically already settled their debt with their own means) were basically in the right, since "Congress should always prefer letting the States raise money in their own way, where it can be done. But in the present instance, I see the necessity of yielding to the cries of the creditors in certain parts of the Union; for the sake of union, and to save us from the greatest of all calamities, the total extinction of our credit in Europe."[97] Furthermore, the exchange proposed by the secretary of the Treasury was between the shouldering of the debt and the transfer of the capital to the shores of the Potomac, a proposal that was particularly dear to Southerners and to Jefferson in particular.[98] He was undoubtedly convinced by Hamilton's arguments, while Hamilton, for his part, was wont to voice fears of all kinds—especially of rivalry and wars among the states—if American policies should fail to follow the course he had charted.

In spring 1792, the secretary of state appealed to the highest political and moral authority of the country, George Washington, with the aim of opposing Hamilton's plans and trying to convince the president the real fulcrum of their disagreement. According to Jefferson, "A public debt...has been artificially created,...[and] this accumulation of debt has taken for ever out of our power those easy sources of revenue,"[99] because the entire amount of taxation should be utilized for repaying, or more exactly, for servicing the debt. And, of course, the interest was likely to become an ever greater burden. "We are already obliged to strain the *impost* till it produces clamour, and will produce evasion, & war on our own citizens."[100] Moreover, the capital utilized for speculation on the public debt was bound to become unfruitful and a source of corruption, since it was going to be diverted from any productive activities. "All the capital employed in paper speculation is barren & useless,...and is withdrawn from commerce & agriculture where it would have produced addition to the common mass...it nourishes in our citizens habits of vice and idleness instead of industry & morality."[101] In addition, this system concealed a calamity that was far more serious from a political perspective, namely, the end of the territorial division of powers in America.

> This corrupt squadron...have manifested their dispositions to get rid of the limitations imposed by the constitution on the general legislature, limitations, on the faith of which, the states acceded to that instrument...the ultimate object of all this is to prepare the way for a change, from the present republican form of government, to that of a monarchy, of which the English constitution is to be the model. That this was contemplated in the Convention is no secret, because it's partisans have made none of it.[102]

Hamilton truly intended to make his public debt perpetual. This he had expressly declared in his *Report*. His scheme involved earmarking a reserve fund in the budget to pay the interest, and a purely hypothetical possibility of repaying the entire debt; taxation would surely act as the source for guaranteeing the yearly interest. What the system envisaged, in a nutshell, was a debt—a single, consolidated debt for the states and the federation—that would be constantly refinanced. The interest on this debt would be paid by means of taxation, and the American bank would be guarantor of the debt and a source of credibility for public commitments. Interestingly, the scheme that more directly influenced Hamilton's plans was the one devised by the Englishman Charles Montagu in 1694. From a theoretical perspective, however, a clear dependence can be discerned from the financial theories of the French Jacques Necker, whose renowned three-volume *De L'Administration des finances de la France*, published in 1784, was immediately translated into English. The future secretary of the treasury had acquired a copy already in 1786.[103]

From the very beginning, Jefferson believed that the essence of the economic and political system proposed by Hamilton could be seen as consisting in the attempt to abolish "the sacred…line which has been drawn between"[104] the federal government and the state governments. When Jefferson surveyed the policy pursued by the secretary of the treasury, who liked to act as if he were a prime minister in the British fashion, he "discerned nothing less than a settled Federalist design to anglicize American society and create a monarchical form of government along British lines."[105]

Undoubtedly, there were a number of moral considerations that played a role in kindling Jefferson's scorn for the Hamiltonian economic social regime. As he complained to Washington in a private conversation, "A system had…been contrived…for withdrawing our citizens from the pursuits…of useful industry, to occupy themselves and their capitals in a species of gambling, destructive of morality, and which had introduced it's poison into the government itself."[106]

However, Jefferson's was not a distrust of financial matters born out of an agrarian mindset, as many scholars have concluded. A clear distinction must be made between Jefferson's conception of the "good life" and his political ideas. While he did indeed believe free landowners and farmers were "the chosen people of God, if ever he had a chosen people, whose breasts he has made his peculiar deposit for substantial and genuine virtue,"[107] he had no intention of forcing men to choose one particular profession as opposed to another. Likewise, Jefferson certainly did not contemplate the recourse to governmental coercion to give a preferential treatment to agriculture. In his view, political power existed merely to ensure that the natural rights of man were protected.

Accordingly, there is in Jefferson no political bias against trade and commerce or finance. Many years later, in 1813, Jefferson wrote a letter which, prompted by the contingent circumstances though it may have been, sounded like a general reflection on the entire political problem raised by the Hamiltonian system in the early 1790s. He pointed out that the golden rule for public debts should be "Never to borrow a dollar without laying a tax in the same instant for paying the interest annually, and the principal within a given term; and to consider that tax as pledged to the creditors on the public faith."[108] In this case, what are the limits on government action, and what can render the attempt to create a perpetual debt null and void? The answer is clear, and it is in tune with the arguments the Virginian had consistently put forward ever since 1789: "The laws of nature…. The earth belongs to the living, not to the dead. The will and the power of man expire with his life, by nature's law…. Each generation has the usufruct of the earth during the period of its continuance. When it ceases to exist, the usufruct passes on to the succeeding generation, free and unincumbered, and so on, successively, from one generation to another forever."[109]

After summarizing the principles he had set forth in his letter to Madison dating from twenty-four years earlier, Jefferson clarified his thought on the legitimacy of the banking system. "Every one knows, that although not literally, it is nearly true, that every paper dollar emitted banishes a silver one from the circulation."[110] Naturally, though, this need not imply that one should jettison the concept of banks. "Are merchants and others to be deprived of the resource of short accommodations, found so convenient? I answer, let us have banks."[111] But care should be taken to respect natural law: "No one has a natural right to the trade of a money lender, but he who has the money to lend. Let those then among us, who have a monied capital, and who prefer employing it in loans rather than otherwise, set up banks, and give cash or national bills for the notes they discount."[112] That is to say, private individuals can, in effect, choose what they deem to be the best manner of utilizing their resources and have every right to do so, but the government cannot grant speculative monopolies to private financiers. The judgment of immorality was not meant to be directed against finance and trade per se, but rather against such activities carried out with money not belonging to those who actually brokered deals, protected by the favor and the power of the government.

148   *Liberty, State, & Union*

In this respect, it is very easy to agree with Joyce Appleby when she states that emphasizing the Virginian agrarian outlook "points Jefferson and his party in the wrong direction.... [In fact] the agrarian myth makes him a traditional, republican visionary, socially radical perhaps, but economically conservative." In short, "Jefferson's enthusiasm for agriculture has long been misinterpreted as an attachment to the past."[113]

Jefferson himself supplied an explanation of his agrarianism, together with an admission that it was by now unviable, in an important letter dating from 1816. The problem the Virginian had sought to address since the very beginning concerned the division of labor. He had mistakenly thought that America could live off the land within a system of worldwide division of labor. At the time he wrote his *Notes on the State of Virginia* (1783–85), "The question seemed legitimate, whether, with such an immensity of unimproved land, courting the hand of husbandry, the industry of agriculture, or that of manufactures, would add most to the national wealth."[114]

If this query appears Smithian in nature, founded, as it was, on the efficiency of the division of labor, Jefferson's opinions were still shaped by the influence of the Physiocratic school. He was convinced of the existence of "spontaneous energies of the earth...[and that] one grain of wheat committed to the earth,...renders twenty, thirty, and even fifty fold, whereas to the labor of the manufacturer nothing is added."[115] But since the publication of *Notes*, everything had changed. The seas and trade had been closed off by the rapaciousness of the English and the French, who had disregarded all moral laws "established by the Author of nature between nation and nation."[116] America had been cut off from trade with other nations, so "to be independent for the comforts of life we must fabricate them ourselves. We must now place the manufacturer by the side of the agriculturist.... [He] who is now against domestic manufacture, must be for reducing us either to dependence on that foreign nation, or to be clothed in skins, and to live like wild beasts in dens and caverns. I am not one of these."[117] In sum, "Experience has taught me that manufactures are now as necessary to our independence as to our comfort."[118] In any case, Jefferson now felt that the choice between agriculture and manufactures was a technical issue that did not involve moral judgments on the different trades, "For in so complicated a science as political economy, no one axiom can be laid down as wise and expedient for all times and circumstances, and for their contraries."[119]

But let us return to the early 1790s. Jefferson was so dismayed by the Hamiltonian intrigues that he tried to devise a way to put an end, once and for all, to any plans of this kind.[120] At the same time, however, the Virginian's apprehensions and his political charisma were already producing their first effects on Congress, albeit dominated as it was by the Federalists.

In spring 1792, the question of the debt became public knowledge and was raucously debated in the House. Hamilton's *Report on the Public Credit* was prepared in January 1792 and was a direct consequence of the petitions presented to Congress by a number of creditors.[121] Hamilton suggested suspending payments until a new debt had been agreed (a sort of refinancing). Only then would the old government bonds be exchanged for the new ones, at parity. The scheme for settling the debt was a ten-year plan, which led his adversaries to fear it constituted some sort of maneuver designed to make the bonds unredeemable. It was on this occasion that the Jeffersonian ideas began to gain currency in Congress, winning over a part of the elected members and building the base for opposition to the secretary of the treasury's maneuvers.

The Hamiltonian policy, as John Taylor warned, would likely create a financial class bound to become a sort of aristocracy of the land.[122] William Findley asserted unequivocally that the proposed system was turning out to be a veritable calamity. By no means had it "increased the specie, or circulating medium, or raised the value of the lands, or promoted the manufactures or industry of the country." Quite the opposite. "Credit between man and man is lessened; extravagance and immorality have spread their baneful influence."[123] Further, Findley used a line of reasoning thoroughly typical of Jeffersonian thought: arguing against the unredeemability of the debt, Findley "denied the right of one Congress to say that another shall not provide for paying off the whole of the debt, or of any part of it."[124] Not only could the generations not mortgage the properties and decisions of others, but the legislative assemblies had the same limitations. Following John Taylor, who was certainly the Jeffersonian of greatest theoretical standing, Findley and John Francis Mercer built up a line of argument against Hamilton and his proposal to make the debt perpetual. They contended that the perpetual public debt deprived the people of sovereignty. Mercer's statements, in particular, can be seen as one of the first stirrings of political Jeffersonism in America. Quite some time before there existed an organized party inspired, if not formally led, by Jefferson, his ideas began to circulate in opposition to the designs of the secretary of the treasury.[125] The concept of transferring the debt from one generation to another, Mercer contended, also implied destroying the equality between any given Congress and those that succeeded it. "If a preceding session could make laws which a subsequent session could not repeal, the Legislative power would be gradually abridged...and eventually annihilated."[126] As he saw it, the proposed system for financing the debt was "in violation of natural right, and of the Constitution of the United States."[127]

The independence of each assembly was embodied in the power to repeal any previous law. "The power to repeal is the renewing principle essential to [Congress's] existence."[128] The exercise of popular sovereignty through elections would become devoid of meaning, and all form of self-government would cease, if the new representatives were unable to abrogate the laws enacted by their predecessors. Since his thinking still seemed unclear to several of his colleagues, Mercer went over Jefferson's letter almost word for word, carefully examining his ideas concerning the Earth, which was held in usufruct by the living, as discussed in chapter 3. Mercer further referred to Buffon's calculations in order to estimate the active span of a single generation. On some points, however, his analysis departed from Jefferson's, as in the rejection of the analogy of an individual bequeathing an inheritance burdened by heavy debts and the issue of the public debt. Nevertheless, Mercer laid great emphasis on generational sovereignty, in tones clearly echoing Jeffersonian thought. "The God of Nature has given the earth to the living. That He will make our children and our children's children as free as He made us, is what no parent, I trust, will deny...we cannot deprive posterity of their natural rights...we have a right to the fruits of our own industry—they to theirs."[129] He then went on to say, "Different generations of men bear no relation to each other but by natural law and the terms of the constitution they adopt, and even this last is limited by the former."[130]

Furthermore, it was argued that the public debt would generate a class of parasites, who invested neither in land nor in manufactures and who speculated on the vicissitudes of government. "At the first appearance of danger, they sell out, and sink your credit at the moment it becomes essential."[131] The debt is a "cancer in the body politic,"[132] to be extirpated without delay. In conclusion, "The debt is to be deplored, but it must be paid...and as fast as possible."[133] Contracted by this generation for a just cause, that being the Revolution, it ought to be repaid within the lapse of time defined by this same generation.

The Precipitation of the Conflict: States and Union

If the debt was the nerve system of the Hamiltonian system and the fountainhead of the strength of the federal government, enabling it to expand its supremacy over the states, the motives for the conflict between Jefferson and the Federalists lay even deeper, involving no less than the ultimate principles of government. While the Jeffersonian affinities with Anti-Federalist thought and positions have been documented, it is appropriate at this point to analyze how his political and doctrinal "realignment" took shape as a result of his increasing realization of the illiberal character of Hamilton's intent. It reflects how Jefferson's thought turned into a coherent system, a clear-cut political doctrine in the American context.

In the historical reconstruction of the debate on the adoption of the Constitution, Jefferson began to enlist *ex-post* the Anti-Federalists among the Republicans. The enemies of the plan of government devised in Philadelphia, both within and without the Convention, became those whose efforts accounted for the failure of the centralizing party—namely the Federalists—to achieve a complete victory. Prior to that time, the divisions, following the English Old Whig framework, were between supporters of natural rights, of limited government, and of popular sovereignty on one side and the enemies of all these notions on the other. In contrast, after the doctrinal realignment occasioned by the Constitution of the United States, things changed both in form and substance. In America, Whigs and Tories had found a new battleground, the states and the union. A strong federal power, potentially capable of being the only judge of its own powers, as in the Hamiltonian interpretation, was the Tories' new rallying point. This had to be opposed by a political grouping founded on states' rights, stemming from the fact that the latter had created the federal government merely as their agent for all common affairs.

It is important to take note of this new theoretical path of Jeffersonian thinking, since it later becomes crucial in dividing the fray between the advocates of a free and voluntary pact with the states and the champions of the consolidation of federal power. In a Jeffersonian definition, the latter now appeared as the new guise under which the ancient notion of tyranny once more reared its head (tyranny was seen as the concentration of powers in a center represented by absolute monarchy during the eighteenth century). This contrast, which had already surfaced during the first Continental Congress and persisted with even greater intensity in the constitutional ratification battle, became, under the leadership of Jefferson, the permanent character of American politics.

Moreover, the political and doctrinal cleavage was overlaid with a geographical one. The states of New England were openly Federalist, while the Southern states were increasingly siding with the party of Jefferson and Madison. It was thus easy to predict that the concurrence of the political and the geographical schism could lead the two sides to part ways. As Jefferson wrote in May 1792 to President Washington, "The division of sentiment & interest happens unfortunately to be so geographical, that no mortal can say that what is most wise & temperate would prevail against what is most easy & obvious."[134] Naturally, he also added, "I can scarcely contemplate a more incalculable evil than the breaking of the union into two or more parts."[135] When meditating on these issues, Jefferson had many a sleepless night.

> When we review the mass which opposed the original coalescence, when we consider that it lay chiefly in the Southern quarter, that...whenever Northern & Southern prejudices have come into conflict, the latter have been sacrificed & the former soothed; that the owners of the debt are in the Southern & the holders of it in the Northern division; that the Anti-federal champions are now strengthened in argument by the fulfillment of their predictions.[136]

Only Washington himself could change the course of events, by agreeing to be reelected president. "Your being at the helm, will be more than an answer to every argument which can be used to alarm & lead the people in any quarter into violence or secession."[137]

Jefferson's greatest concern was the prospect of political factions and the divisions the Federalists were inspiring in the country. Yet it was precisely during his battle against them that he underwent a change of heart and came round to adopt the view of the "naturalness" of a "party system," accepting the essentially positive nature of differences of opinion on political matters within a democratic system.[138] Thus, while in 1788 Jefferson maintained that parties were a source of corruption of principles, he later swung round to acceptance of factions and political clashes, although he never had any doubt about the rights and wrongs of matters: "Men by their constitutions are naturally divided into two parties: 1. Those who fear and distrust the people, and wish to draw all powers from them into the hands of the higher classes. 2. Those who identify themselves with the people, have confidence in them, cherish and consider them as the most honest and safe, although not the most wise depository of the public interests."[139]

Whigs and Tories were thus seen as the "natural parties" of humankind, which emerge with different likeness in every representative system. "Men have differed in opinion, and been divided into parties by these opinions, from the first origin of societies, and in all governments where they have been permitted freely to think and to speak. The same political parties which now agitate the U.S. have existed thro' all time."[140]

As he moved toward old age, Jefferson seemed increasingly willing to accept party divisions. This can be noted, for instance, in a letter to Lafayette written in 1823.

> The line of division now is the preservation of State rights as reserved in the constitution, or by strained constructions of that instrument, to merge all into a consolidated government. The Tories are for strengthening the executive and general Government; the Whigs cherish the representative branch, and the rights reserved by the States, as the bulwark against consolidation, which must immediately generate monarchy.[141]

Jefferson felt that the perspective he was sketching was not only consistent with the Constitution, but also the most realistic one possible in the American political framework. During his period as a wise and prudent observer of American politics, Jefferson addressed several rhetorical questions to an epistolary acquaintance with the intent of explaining that the states would never accept a centralization comparable to that advocated earlier by Hamilton himself and in 1823 by Hamilton's followers. He wondered "if a single State of the Union would have agreed to the constitution, had it given all powers to the General Government?... If there is any reason to believe the States more disposed now than then, to acquiesce in this general surrender of all their rights and powers to a consolidated government, one and undivided?"[142]

But when he had written to Lafayette, thirty years before and at the height of the political struggle, Jefferson had expressed himself in a far more alarmed tone: "A sect has shewn itself among us, who declare they espoused our new constitution, not as a good & sufficient thing itself, but only as a step to an English constitution, the only thing good & sufficient in itself, in their eye."[143] Despite this, his trust in the people, and in their rightful political feelings and republican convictions, never wavered, as witnessed by the following words. "It is happy for us that these are preachers without followers, and that our people are firm & constant in their republican purity."[144]

Many years later, when contesting the statement made by John Melish, who argued that both factions were faithful to the Constitution, Jefferson claimed that the division between the two parties resided in "a real and radical difference of political principle."[145] In actual fact, though, the "question of preference between monarchy and republicanism, which has so long divided mankind elsewhere, threatens [to become] a permanent division here."[146] The faction headed by Alexander Hamilton was essentially working toward one major goal, namely that the English system of government should be imported into America, "and only accepted and held fast, at first, to the present constitution, as a stepping-stone to the final establishment of their favorite model."[147] On the other hand, "The party called republican is steadily for the support of the present constitution [since] they obtained at its commencement, all the amendments to it they desired."[148] Jefferson was never in any doubt that the Anti-Federalists represented the first germ of the Republican Party; indeed, it was they who demanded and obtained the amendments to the Constitution. Furthermore, Jefferson insisted, had it been a mere clash between different factions grappling for power, but founded on a common feeling with regard to the republican principles of government, then there would never have "been a moment of my life in which I should have relinquished for it the enjoyments of my family, my farm, my friends and books."[149]. As expressed, Jefferson had been forced to abandon his pastoral life of letters and books in order to save the American republic from its Thermidor.

In a few notes taken in 1795 in order to answer questions raised by a German correspondent, Jefferson ventured even further toward an absolute identification between the Anti-Federalists and the Republicans in his battle about ratification.

> [S]ome of the monocrats got elected [at the Philadelphia Convention], with a hope of introducing an English constitution, when they found that the great body of the delegates were strongly for adhering to republicanism, & for giving due strength to their government under that form, they then directed their efforts to the assimilation of all the parts of the new government to the English constitution as nearly as was attainable. In this they were not altogether without success; insomuch that the monarchical features of the new constitution produced a violent opposition to it from the *most zealous republicans* in the several states.[150]

As soon as they had come to power, the Federalists "pressed forward the plan therefore of strengthening all the features of the government which gave it resemblance to an English constitution."[151] Furthermore, when Jefferson passed to record the groups which formed the base of the two parties, he devised no fewer than seven categories to describe the Federalists but no more than two or three for the Republicans (the former were composed of old Tories, English merchants on American soil, American merchants dependent on English capital, speculators manipulating public bonds, federal government personnel, job seekers, and persons with a weak and indolent character, as opposed to the Republicans, encompassing all landholders, farmers, and craftsmen). Despite being the majority in the country—probably 500 to one, Jefferson hazarded a guess—the Republicans were dispersed, whereas those backing the opposite party were all city dwellers, they had their own newspapers, and they had amassed an immense wealth.[152]

A few years later, the Constitution had, as he saw it, come to stand for "a mixed aspect of monarchy and republicanism," so much so, indeed, that the citizens "will naturally divide into two classes of sentiments," which would drive them "to wish to strengthen either the monarchical or the republican features of the constitution."[153] In other words, the Constitution and its ambiguities underlay the formation of the political majorities in the country. This is why the Constitution, which the two battling parties upheld mainly as a tool to stake out their positions, had to be given a clear interpretation that was in conformity with the political principles of states' rights and of limited government.

What had happened? Recall the critical, yet considerably more cautious, judgments described above. How did it come about that, once returned home, Jefferson reached this conclusion about the constitutional battle? One possible explanation is to be found in a conversation Jefferson had with George Mason in 1792. The elderly Virginian confided to him that two weeks prior to the end of the proceedings of the Convention, the plan was actually far better than the version which eventually was approved. The executive was to have a seven-year term, it could not be reelected twice in a row, there was to be rotation of offices, especially in the Senate, and, above all, super-majorities of two-thirds were to be required for the enactment of many laws, particularly those for commercial restrictions. But South Carolina, which had lost many slaves during the war with England and had enormous interest in reopening the international slave trade, entered into a pact with New England and exchanged twenty years of free slave trading against the requirement of a simple majority on matters concerning commerce. A bridge having thus been spanned between North and South, the entire construction began to shake, and with this bizarre coalition, "the great principles of the Constitution were changed in the last days of the Convention."[154]

It was also Mason who confided to Jefferson that Hamilton, held in check by Yates and Lansing, the other delegates from New York, had returned to Philadelphia to approve the definitive text but only once the deed had been done, as it were. Jefferson needed no further prompting. He immediately grasped that what was at stake was not just a matter of financial interests, but that Hamilton's propensity to corrupt people masked far more dangerous intentions. From that moment on, Jefferson became convinced of the existence of a veritable conspiracy of a "monarchical" or "monocratic" type (these were his favorite terms) which was determined to put an end to the American experiment in self-government. In order to counter such diabolical machinations, nothing could be left to chance.

In the mid-1790s, Jefferson wrote an important letter to his Italian friend Filippo Mazzei, which held an outpouring of emotions and concerns for the fate of freedom in the young republic dominated by the Federalists. Based on the contents of the message—having been made known to the American public after various convoluted activities and no fewer than three translations[155]—the letter earned him serious problems back at home.[156] Jefferson began by stating that "in place of that noble love of liberty and republican government which carried us triumphantly through the war, an Anglican monarchical aristocratical party has sprung up, whose avowed object is to draw over us the substance as they have already done the forms of the British government." A few lines later, he added, "To preserve the liberty we have obtained...we have only to awake and snap the Lilliputian cords with which they [the Federalists] have been entangling us during the first sleep which succeeded our labours."[157] These "cords" could refer to the Constitution itself, or at least to its Hamiltonian and federalist interpretation, while the labors of freedom had produced the Declaration and the Articles of Confederation.

To oppose the Federalist Party's goal of the centralization of powers, Jefferson's line of defense would, as we will see in greater detail in the following chapter, pursue a strategy of opposition whose fulcrum was in the states. The plan was well thought out and had been inchoately looming ever since the early 1790s. As Jefferson saw it, it could easily be foreseen that "the encroachments of the state governments will tend to an excess of liberty which will correct itself...while those of the general government will tend to monarchy, which will fortify itself from day to day,...as all experience shews."[158] Jefferson's line of defense had been clear since as early as 1791: "It is important to strengthen the state governments: and as this cannot be done by any change in the federal constitution...it must be done by the states themselves, erecting such barriers at the constitutional line as cannot be surmounted either by themselves or by the general government."[159]

Of course, states and union were but the specifically American terms of a much broader problem, that being whether government or freedom—in the sense of absence of coercion—was to act as the guide of society. Joyce Appleby offers a very perceptive analysis of the deeper causes behind the conflict between Jeffersonians and Federalists during the 1790s. She argues that the concept of nature, together with the nascent science of economics and the new role the economy was beginning to play in the lives of Americans, had resulted in new and divergent conceptions of society.

> Classical theory asserted the predominance of politics over all other aspects of social life. This predominance reflected and perpetuated the subordinate position of all other social institutions.... The political whole was not only greater than the sum of the parts; it alone possessed sufficient unity for a history.... From the 1620s...to the 1776 publication of Adam Smith's master synthesis, men thought about economy in ways that incessantly impinged upon politics.... Writers decomposed old meanings about civil order and recomposed the elements of time, citizenship and the distribution of authority. Outside the polity, they constructed a model of economic life that borrowed its order from nature—the newly conceptualized nature of predictable regularity. As this economy absorbed more and more of the attention of men and women it supplied a new identity for them. By the end of the eighteenth century the individual with wide-ranging needs and abstract rights appeared to challenge the citizen with concrete obligations and prescribed privileges.... In the 1790s when the Jeffersonian Republicans and Federalists confronted each other, the battle lines had been drawn around opposing conceptions of civil society.[160]

These divergent visions of society—a world that essentially proceeds entirely by itself or which had to be guided by the firm, albeit conceivably fatherly hand of government—were none other than an outgrowth and the ideological crystallization of the clash of opinions characterizing American political debate of a few years earlier. Even though it was the Jay Treaty and the ensuing protest that marked the definitive birth of the first American party system, the Democratic-Republican Party, headed by Jefferson and Madison, arose in the wake of the opposition to the Hamiltonian system that came to the fore in the very early 1790s.[161] Still, it would never have become a popular political force had it not been able to appeal to the deep-seated feelings profoundly rooted in the country, first and foremost of anti-federalism. As stated by two eminent historians, "The Democratic-Republicans elaborated many of the same themes opponents of the

Constitution had invoked during the ratification debates."[162] Furthermore, it can hardly escape notice that the "1800 revolution," that is, the Jeffersonian victory, was, from an electoral point of view, the fruit of the agreement between Virginia and New York, the two great bulwarks of anti-federalism.[163]

Jefferson's feelings were profoundly in tune with all the classical themes of the Anti-Federalists: the superiority of local over "national" interests, self-government, the close connection between localism and freedom, the direct responsibility of elected representatives, and the geographical bond between the latter and their electors. And the Anti-Federalists had been predominantly Jeffersonians—without being fully aware of it, so to speak—in their declared preference for laissez faire and for a government limited to safeguarding life, freedom, and property. When classical liberalism in the Lockean mold joined forces with the American experience of self-government, it developed into a new political ideology. Thomas Jefferson's credo now represented the cement of the coalition that opposed the party in power.

It is no coincidence that in the early years of turmoil in the political life of the young republic, Jefferson formulated a doctrine on the nature of the union that was effectively nothing less than a rationalized and constitutional version of anti-federalism. His attempt to see the Constitution as a voluntary pact—which allowed individual states the possibility of asserting their own sovereignty by invalidating federal legislation, with effects limited to within their own territorial boundaries—is one of the first chapters of that entrenched persistence of anti-federalism in American political thought, an enduring feature which has in recent years begun to attract the attention of scholars.[164] Saul Cornell, for instance, investigates the political ideas of James Madison, John Taylor, Tunis Wortman, and St. George Tucker in addition to the views held by Jefferson himself. Cornell points to the fact that far from disappearing, the ideas cherished by the Anti-Federalists were incorporated after the ratification process as part of the body of ideas of the Jeffersonian-Republican Party, to the point of blending into a persistent tradition founded on a "dissenting public discourse about politics and constitutionalism."[165]

The Jeffersonian endeavor to interpret the American Constitution as if its ratification had in no way encroached on the sovereignty of the states will be the object of analysis in the following chapter.

6

The Nature of the American Union: Jefferson and States' Rights

> God bless you, and all our rulers, and give them the wisdom, as I
> am sure they have the will, to fortify us against the degeneracy of our
> government, and the concentration of all it's powers in the hands of
> the one, the few, the well-born or but the many.[1]

While the investigation of Jefferson's thought on the themes of property,
natural law, and limited government has necessarily been conducted by
inference (albeit, one hopes, well founded), given the fragmentary nature of
Jefferson's reflections on these issues, fate has looked more favorably upon
the scholar as regards the question of federalism. For Thomas Jefferson has
left us something absolutely certain and sound on which to found our
investigations: an entire document of almost 3,000 words, which, at a careful
reading, contains the whole of his theory of the federal union. Of course, I
am referring to the Kentucky Resolutions of 1798.

This is in many ways an explosive document, fated to be long regarded
as the fountainhead of states' rights doctrine. Above all, it is a deeply
embarrassing piece of evidence for those scholars keen on creating the
image of a Jefferson who loved the union just as much as or even more than
Abraham Lincoln. The major Jeffersonian biographers tend to pass it off as
worthy of no more than a few pages among thousands; as, perhaps, a jarring
note of marginal importance in the work of an otherwise clear lifetime, to
be brushed aside like a bothersome fly that threatens to light on a tasty
morsel. Just to mention a few significant examples, the most important
biographer of Jefferson, Dumas Malone, only allocates to the Kentucky
Resolutions six pages of his monumental six-volume work on the life and
times of the author of the Declaration. Likewise, Merrill Peterson, the
author of the best single-volume Jeffersonian biography, deems this
"business" to be only worth four or five pages in more than 1,000.[2] In more
recent times, it seems quite amazing that a legal scholar such as R. B.

Bernstein, in what is said to be "the best short biography" on Jefferson, devotes only about a quarter of a page to the Kentucky Resolutions.[3] Conflicting as they are with his image of a Jefferson single-mindedly striving to achieve an ever stronger and solid union, the Kentucky Resolutions are mentioned only in passing also by Peter Onuf in a book that collects a decade of the distinguished professor's research on the works and thought of the third president of the Unites States.[4]

The Kentucky Resolutions are not only underestimated by the Jefferson scholars—mostly for ideological reasons—they appear also to be little appreciated by historians at large. Bernard Weisberger managed to write a book on the crucial election of 1800 and the political battles prior to it, mentioning the document in one single sentence.[5] Even a very sympathetic treatment of the Jeffersonian side of the struggle, such as Susan Dunn's volume on the same crucial years, devotes no more than four pages to the topic.[6]

Nevertheless, the resolutions can be deemed to be the core of Jefferson's federal idea, and they embody, in a nutshell, the whole of his constitutional doctrine.[7] The influence of the resolutions and of the writings published to explain and defend the principles that underpinned them (foremost among them, Madison's *Virginia Report*) is paramount.

In the early national period, the Principles of 1798 gained acceptance throughout the United States. During conflicts between state and national authority, reports and resolutions adopted by state legislatures, messages from state chief executives, opinions of state appellate courts, and speeches of leading citizens all ring with the words of the Kentucky and Virginia Resolutions. The Resolutions, of course, were not the first American statement of the compact theory, the locus of ultimate sovereignty, or the division of legislative sovereignty. But the Resolutions were perhaps the most lucid and succinct statements of first principles ever penned. Though originally condemned by nine states in the late 1790s, the Resolutions' cogent reasoning won acceptance in the marketplace of ideas.[8]

The resolutions represent Jefferson's greatest contribution to a constitution which may well have been the offspring of "an assembly of demi-gods,"[9] but to which he had been able to take no part since he was minister to France at the time. In a sense, as we will see in the discussion on libertarian federalism, Jefferson felt that federalism was so important that it could at times override individual rights. For Jefferson, a centralized republic—one and indivisible—was always and necessarily tyrannical, even when if it formally recognized the natural rights of men. Over time, he would replace the "simple" natural rights doctrine of the origins with a genuinely federal construction of the body politic, because he came to recognize that "the true barriers of our liberty...are our State governments."[10]

Political tyranny increasingly came to be defined, in Jefferson's thought, as the consolidation of power in a single center. Individual rights certainly remained at the center of his political thought, but the strategic design to safeguard such rights would come to include the strengthening of the power of the states at the expense of the federal government.

It should also be kept in mind that this doctrinal dispute engaged American scholars and politicians for at least the first seventy years of the life of the union and, indeed, well beyond. In the end, it was not resolved by one theory overcoming the other on the strength of interpretation, scholarly consensus, or popular favor. What decided the issue was merely the force of arms. Yet the historian of political thought can hardly resign himself to the notion that the exchange of ideas and debate, however heated, is trounced by the logic of the fait accompli, conceivably cloaked in questionable theories on centralization as the specific form of American modernization. In fact, it is difficult to share the optimism of William J. Watkins, Jr., who believes that "though written over two centuries ago, the Resolves' [sic] insights into the American experiment with self-government remain instructive as we continue to debate the proper roles of the state and national governments."[11] As far as the role of the states in the American union is concerned, this was settled by the Civil War; they are administrative jurisdictions, mere provinces of a vast empire.

In order to elucidate the flow of events, it is necessary to dwell briefly on the historical context within which the Jeffersonian doctrine was elaborated, as well as the grueling political struggle that formed the backdrop to this novel interpretation of the nature of the American union.

Jefferson seized the first available opportunity offered by the Federalists overstepping the boundary of fair debate in order to seriously address the entire problem of constitutional interpretation, of the relations between the federal government and the states, and limitations on federal power. The limitations derived from the fact that the United States had been set up as a republic founded both on states' rights and individual rights (a natural rights "republic of republics"). The occasion was provided by the enactment of two legislative provisions that, at the very least, constituted "a gross violation of personal and civil liberties."[1] In summer 1798, the Alien and Sedition laws were passed when Jefferson was vice president, and they occasioned the final break between Jefferson himself and the Federalist Party. By the end of the 1790s, political strife and partisan anger had reached fever pitch. As Jefferson wrote to a correspondent, "The passions are too high at present, to be cooled in our day.... Men who have been intimate all their lives, cross the street to avoid meeting, and turn their heads another way, lest they should be obliged to touch their hats."[2]

In fact, during the preceding years the Federalists had found themselves grappling with the first serious opposition in American history, which had been organized by the Jeffersonian-Madisonian party and had been active since at least summer 1795. It was around that time that protest against the Jay's Treaty (ratified by the Senate on 24 June 1795) had erupted in a series of meetings and public demonstrations. Subsequently, the protest movement did not die away but was absorbed within the general antagonism toward the federal government fomented by the Democratic-Republican Party.[3] When observed from the broader perspective of the American political tradition, the notion of organized dissent as a factor of "progress," or in any case as a tolerable part of the life of a polity, was taking its first steps. The Federalists did certainly share the notion that political rifts were always pernicious; in the opinion of two important historians, they "never recognized the value of party opposition, and from their quarterdeck point of view the Republicans were little better than mutineers."[4] Similarly, other historians have taken a dim view of the behavior of the party in power at that particular historical juncture: "The Sedition Act was an implied acknowledgment by the Federalists that force and coercion rather than reason and argument were to be the ultimate arbiters of political controversy in the United States."[5]

As to the illiberal character of the above-mentioned laws, on this matter there can be little doubt. The law on aliens was composed of three legislative measures. The first concerned the period of residence required for naturalization, which was increased from five to fourteen years. In addition, it imposed compulsory registration on all aliens present in the country.[6] The second granted the president of the United States the power to order the expulsion from American soil, or the internment without trial, of any alien citizen. The third allowed the president to deport any alien in time of war or threat of war. Any alien refusing to comply promptly with the presidential decree would have to face the harsh disciplinary measures imposed by the law: three years in prison.

The foreigners present on American soil came mainly from France, Ireland, and Germany. While at first glance the law could be read as a device aimed at the French, given the enormous apprehension raised in America, as in Europe, by the French Revolution pouring out of its natural borders, the truth is that all immigrants were looked upon with the same attitude of mistrust. The Irish revolt, crushed by England in that very same year 1798, had triggered the first great Irish exodus toward America. Many of the Irish, in addition to being Catholic—which, in the American republic of the origins, was hardly a boon—were politically opposed to English dominion over Ireland, a cause that the Federalists abhorred and the Democratic-Republicans supported.

The Federalists' aversion to aliens was, naturally, of a political nature, for the latter were drawn en masse toward Thomas Jefferson's Democratic-Republican Party. Although generally "not in search of a Republic, but of bread,"[7] the number of English, Scottish, and Irish immigrants who arrived in America during the 1790s was significant, and among their ranks were more than a few political firebrands. As one historian has put it, at least seventy-four of these had already been militants back in their home country, before emigrating to the United States. Half of these were Irish, three-fifths of the remainder were English, and the rest were Scottish.[8] Thus, the Alien Laws were also intended to depict Jefferson's party, the first genuine organized opposition in the country, as a den of spies in the pay of Paris.

If the law on aliens, although extremely severe, basically remained a paper tiger, the case of the other law passed that same summer was quite a different matter. The law on sedition, an act for the punishment of certain crimes against the United States, stated that it was an offense, punishable with a fine of 5,000 dollars and five years in jail, to act in such a manner as to prevent the full implementation of a United States law. Further, it was an offense to intimidate anyone who sought to obtain a federal office or, more generally, to participate in any sort of seditious assembly. Furthermore, anyone found to be the author or publisher of scandalous or defamatory material that offended the president or Congress could be punished by a fine of 2,000 dollars and imprisonment for two years.[9] As has been pointed out by Frederick Allis, "The key words in the act were vague…'defaming' the government of the United States and 'bringing it into contempt or disrepute' had been a favorite sport of Americans ever since the birth of the republic."[10] But the basic result was that the First Amendment, the one establishing the right of every citizen to absolute and incoercible freedom of manifesting his or her own thought, was no longer in force, superseded by a mere act of Congress.[11] Thomas Paine noted a few years later, "The plan of the leaders of the faction was to overthrow the liberties of the New World[12]…that no investigation be made into its conduct [the Administration] intrenched itself within a magic circle of terror and called it a SEDITION LAW…. The pretended Sedition Law shut up the sources of investigation [into the Administration's conduct]…. The object, therefore…was the overthrow of the representative system of government."[13]

The Alien Laws remained virtually inoperative as it was hardly ever enforced, while the Sedition Law became the basic issue in a number of lawsuits against journalists and politicians, although the number of those actually convicted is difficult to determine. It is worth noting that one of the purposes of this law was to be the full restoration of the old common law action against seditious libel, which was widely invoked in the several convictions, despite the fact that it was held to have been superseded by the First Amendment.[14]

Thomas Cooper, a naturalized English scientist and a friend of Joseph Priestley, was one of the most illustrious victims of Judge Samuel Chase, a zealous Federalist and one of the signatories of the Declaration of Independence, who showed great determination in the enforcement of the

Sedition Law. When Cooper subsequently related the account of his trial, in which he brilliantly argued his own case (albeit with a very unsuccessful outcome, since he was sentenced to six months in prison and a 400-dollar fine), he warned: "The Citizens of this Country may learn some useful lessons from this trial; and principally, that if they mean to consult their own peace and quiet, they will hold their tongues, and restrain their pens, on the subject of politics."[15]

The long list of dissenters who ended up on trial for their disapproval of federal power also includes a number of other remarkable figures. Take, for instance, the case of the Irish-born Matthew Lyon, who fought in the Revolution and who was imprisoned for having merely sent a letter to the *Vermont Journal* in which he criticized the president. Elected to office while still in prison, he became one of the popular heroes of the resistance to Federalist persecution. Or consider William Duane, copublisher with Benjamin Franklin Bache[16] of the *Aurora*, the most important Jeffersonian mouthpiece, who landed in jail in 1799 on charges pertaining to the Alien Act, although he had been born in America to Irish parents. Immediately released, he was then rearrested on the basis of the provisions of the Sedition Act. Only the fortunate circumstance of Jefferson's election saved him from further prosecution. James Thomson Callender—the scandal-mongering journalist who would later embarrass the president by exposing his alleged affair with Sally Hemings—was imprisoned for nine months and fined the sum of 900 dollars.

These laws clearly overstepped the bounds of executive power, since no article of the Constitution vested the federal government with the power of regulating the status of aliens, much less with that of restricting the freedom of expression. The arguments advanced by the supporters of these laws in the attempt to show the full constitutionality of the provisions against sedition were based essentially on the general welfare clause (Article 1, Section 8, Clause 1) as well as on the necessary and proper clause (same article and section, Clause 18). It was within the general powers of Congress, so the argument ran, to provide for the "general welfare" by adopting the "necessary and proper" measures.[17]

As far as the Alien Laws were concerned, the most frequently voiced objection was that aliens had no constitutional right, since the Constitution granted rights only to citizens of the United States. Yet the full constitutionality of these laws must have appeared doubtful, even to the

Federalist themselves, for while in the Senate the ballot was favorable eighteen to six (by the irony of fate, the vote was held on 4 July 1798), it scraped through by a vote of just forty-four to forty-two in the House of Representatives, this despite the overwhelming Federalist majority in the House.

French Scare and Witch Hunt

The background to the illiberal measures was the so-called French scare, which spread like wildfire through America during the 1790s, fueled by the fear that the French Revolution would reach beyond its borders. While such a fear was more than justified in Europe, where the threatening nature of the exploits of young Napoleon were increasingly apparent, it was implausible for America to consider itself exposed to any real risk of invasion. Even John Adams privately acknowledged that this fear was totally unfounded and that the French threat was nonexistent: "At present there is no more prospect of seeing a French army here than there is in heaven."[18]

Shortly before the election of John Adams, the *Directoire* had authorized French naval ships to stop American merchantmen and confiscate any English goods they had aboard. The new president attempted to restore friendly relations with France and appointed a commission composed of three men to be sent to Paris: Charles C. Pickney, John Marshall, and Elbridge Gerry. However, the diplomatic mission turned out to be a miserable failure as the Americans, who received a lukewarm and informal welcome from the entourage of Foreign Minister Charles Maurice de Talleyrand, refused to pay either Talleyrand's aides or the French government the huge sums requested to begin negotiations. Back at home, there was great indignation when news of these demands became known, and scorn for the corrupt French government reached a peak with the publication of the transcripts of the dealings with three French agents (the latter being disguised with the letters XYZ, hence the name of this historical episode: the "XYZ Affair").

The nationalist indignation that was sweeping the country offered the Federalist Party the opening it needed for a further expansion of government. As John Ferling remarks:

> In this atmosphere the Federalists pushed through their program. By July Congress had created the Department of the Navy,

authorized the construction or refitting of thirty-seven warships, armed merchant vessels, and upgraded coastal fortifications. It was all to be paid for with revenues raised through new taxes on land, houses, and slaves.... Congress also took steps that Adams had not asked for. It more than tripled the existing army—to ten thousand men—and created a provisional army of another ten thousand as well, embargoed all trade with France, and abrogated the Franco-American treaties that the joyous public had welcomed twenty years before.[19]

To finance these warlike measures, Congress authorized a new federal tax on land, houses, and slaves. The XYZ Affair led to an undeclared naval war with France and to a veritable witch hunt back at home in America to ferret out secret French agents, who, of course were associated with the Jeffersonian party. "Homes and offices of Republican editors were attacked;...Republicans were condemned as infidels by Federalist preachers, who urged their congregations to hate the word 'revolution.'"[20] The climate had reached such feverish pitch that "good ladies expected to be murdered in their beds, or meet a fate worse than death, at the hands of the godless Frenchmen and wild Irishmen."[21] Harrison Gray Otis, from Massachusetts, voiced a common prejudice when he stated that "if some means are not adopted to prevent the indiscriminate admission of wild Irishmen & others to the right of suffrage, there will soon be an end to liberty & property."[22] Fear and hatred toward anything that looked or sounded French or "foreign" soon embraced whoever entertained a friendly attitude toward France or the French Revolution, to the point that "Jefferson became the chief target of the Federalist fusillade."[23]

Yet by then, at that stage of his life, Jefferson showed a rather jaundiced view of France and its revolution. In March 1799, after expressing a scathing judgment of French policy, Jefferson summarized in the following words the way his passions stood:

> The Anglomen and monocrats had *so artfully confounded the cause of France with that of freedom*, that both went down in the same scale. I sincerely join you in abjuring all political connection with every foreign power; and tho' I cordially wish well to the progress of liberty in all nations, and would forever give it the

weight of our countenance, yet they are not to be touched without contamination from their other bad principles. Commerce with all nations, alliance with none, should be our motto.[24]

Years later, reminiscing about the anti-French climate, Jefferson did not hesitate to dub the Jacobins assassins and openly spoke of the horrors of the Terror, thus correcting some aspects of the stance he had adopted in the early 1790s when he had warmly welcomed the French republican experiment. "The horrors of the French revolution, then raging, aided them [the Federalists] mainly.... Their Attorney General had the impudence to say to a Republican member, that deportation must be resorted to, of which, said he, 'you republicans have set the example'; thus daring to identify us with the murderous Jacobins of France."[25]

Naturally, the Federalists cared very little as to Jefferson's true opinions about the revolutionary events in France; by now, Republicans and Jacobins were considered one and the same.[26] As one historian has maintained,

This tendency to identify the Republicans with the French set the stage for congressional action not only against the external foe, but what the Federalist chose to call the "internal foe."... Under the guise of patriotic purpose and internal security, the Federalists enacted a program designed to cripple, if not destroy, the Jeffersonian party.... The authoritarian alien and sedition system was the logical culmination of Federalist political philosophy.[27]

Jefferson immediately stated that these laws should be considered "as merely an experiment on the American mind, to see how far it will bear an avowed violation of the Constitution. If this goes down, we shall immediately see attempted another act of Congress, declaring that the President shall continue in office during life, reserving to another occasion the transfer of the succession to his heirs, and the establishment of the Senate for life."[28] Jefferson did not overtly take sides during the debate in the Senate when he was vice president (it cannot be ruled out that, as a consummate politician, he secretly gloated over what he considered to be the political suicide of his adversaries), and he took great care to organize the opposition behind the scenes. For his rivals would have had no qualms about impeaching even the second-highest office in the country.

Yet Jefferson put an optimistic face on things, privately reassuring John Taylor, "A little patience, and we shall see the reign of witches pass over, their spells dissolve, and the people, recovering their true sight, restore their government to it's true principles."[29] However, his opposition to the measures could not have been more clear. In 1804, a few years after the end of the battle, Jefferson wrote to Abigail Smith Adams, the wife of John Adams and a fervent Federalist, "I considered and now consider that law to be a nullity as absolute and as palpable as if Congress had ordered us to fall down and worship a golden image."[30]

The election of 1800 was in many ways a watershed event, as recognized by scholars of all persuasions. Bruce Ackerman, for instance, sees the election of 1800 and the deadlock it provoked as "the rise of the plebiscitarian presidency."[31] Joyce Appleby notes that Jefferson's election to the presidency in 1800 "enabled...[him] to embark in a campaign to expunge the colonial residues that cluttered American's path...to a democracy that was social as well as political.... Jefferson's success in promoting democracy and freedom produced a blend of egalitarianism and individualism that has characterized American culture ever since."[32] But whatever the outcome, the core of the election was the battle between the Jeffersonians and the Federalists, and the center of that struggle was a radically different view on what happened in Philadelphia more than a decade earlier.

The Kentucky and Virginia Resolutions

In the Kentucky Resolutions, Jefferson for the first time clearly expounded the political and juridical foundations of the states' rights school of thought, which soon become the mainstream position in the American constitutional thought, retaining its primacy right up until the Civil War.[33] Taken up again after Jefferson and formulated in greater detail by John Caldwell Calhoun[34] (vice president, senator from South Carolina, and one of the major nineteenth-century American political theorists), this doctrine and its underlying assumptions became the true bone of contention between the states of the North and the South.

But what was the source of the school of states' rights? In the previous chapter, we saw that its earliest foundations could perhaps be traced back to that first Continental Congress, at the dawn of the Revolution. But the true coming of age of that first notion of relations between the states and the federacy must be placed a little later in time. Anti-federalist feelings were extremely strong in Virginia, where the constitutional plan was passed by a vote of eighty-nine members against as many as seventy-nine at the 1788 Convention. At the moment of ratification, the Virginia convention added a rider that was intended to provide a clearer statement of the meaning of this traumatic act of subscribing to the new constitution. The true birth of the doctrine of states' rights should be seen as residing essentially in this statement.[35]

> We, the delegates of the people of Virginia [do] declare and make known, that the powers granted under the Constitution, being derived from the people of the United States, may be resumed by them, whensoever the same shall be perverted to their injury or oppression, and that every power not granted thereby remains with them, and at their will; that, therefore, no right, of any denomination, can be cancelled, abridged, restrained, or modified, by the Congress, by the Senate or House of Representatives, acting in any capacity, by the President, or any department or officer of the United States, except in those instances in which power is given by the Constitution for those purposes; and that, among other essential rights, the liberty of conscience, and of the press, cannot be cancelled, abridged, restrained, or modified, by any authority of the United States.[36]

It is interesting to note that freedom of speech, as well as the notion later embodied in the Tenth Amendment and the nature of the Constitution as a compact voluntarily entered into, are indissolubly linked in this clear-cut pronouncement on exactly what the delegates of Virginia intended to ratify. The constitutional instrument was to be understood in this sense and the representatives of the people of Virginia approved no other constitution than that underlying in this specific interpretation. Ten years later, Virginia and Kentucky found themselves leading a battle that stemmed from the issue of freedom of speech and ultimately involved the entire interpretation of the Constitution.

The resolutions of Virginia and Kentucky, drafted, respectively, by Madison—who, after being a close associate of Hamilton in 1787–1788, changed his political stance, becoming a fervent supporter of states' rights to the point where his interpreters must distinguish between a "Hamiltonian" and a "Jeffersonian" Madison—and Jefferson, were the political response to the laws enacted by the Federalists. The battle took shape throughout the last two years of the eighteenth century and culminated in the election of Jefferson to the presidency. In effect, "The Kentucky and Virginia resolutions were the opening guns of the campaign of 1800."[37] This is not to say that the election of Jefferson was a sort of referendum on the constitutional doctrine expounded by the resolutions. Remarkably, however, the notion that the victory of the Jeffersonian party in the election of 1800 was to be considered a popular endorsement of the Kentucky and Virginia resolutions was suggested by a subcommittee of the Ohio state assembly in 1821.[38]

Undoubtedly, the view of the union advanced by Jefferson was controversial and suspect in the eyes of many state assemblies. A reading of contemporary writings, though, makes clear that most Americans were keenly aware of the problematic constitutional standing of the laws passed by the Federalists. At that time, a theoretical subordination of the states to federal legislation deemed unconstitutional—or merely unfair—could hardly be contemplated.[39]

The Jeffersonian resolutions were delivered to Wilson Cary Nicholas, who acted as Jefferson's substitute in the House of Representatives, with the understanding that the North Carolina assembly would discuss and approve them. Jefferson had chosen the North Carolina assembly because it was there that his party was going from strength to strength. John Breckinridge from Kentucky happened to be on a visit to Virginia, and Nicholas proposed, instead, that he should present them in his own state. This decision turned out to be extremely effective. The outcome was enormously successful. On 10 November 1798, the House of Representatives of Kentucky approved the nine resolutions with only one vote against the first, two against the second, third, fourth, fifth, sixth, seventh, and eighth, and three against the ninth.[40] However, Kentucky, which had been admitted to the union only a few years earlier, turned out to be a rather controversial choice as far as the political impact was concerned. Breckinridge proved to be a useful ally—and above all extremely discreet, since secrecy about the authorship of the resolutions was essential for the success of the plan—and despite the fact that the version of the Jeffersonian document he presented to his own state was watered down on several crucial points. Breckinridge added an appeal to the other states to unite and repeal the Alien and Sedition laws, which greatly weakened the Jeffersonian view of state's rights, since it originally envisaged that every single state was entitled to declare null and void in its own territory any federal law exceeding the delegated powers, without the need that other states join in such a declaration. Moreover, the Kentuckian deleted entirely the passage on nullification.[41]

The controversy presents two aspects which, although historically linked, can be kept distinct from a logical point of view. The first relates to the struggle to preserve the rights and civil liberties enjoyed by Americans, so brazenly jeopardized by the actions of the Federalists.[42] The second pertains to the political/juridical debate on the nature of the American union. In any case, the two perspectives are so inextricably connected that they need to be addressed simultaneously. Although this was the first great attempt to endow the federal compact with sense and meaning, the fact that the whole affair was sparked by a controversy on individual rights is by no means unimportant.

Today, mainstream political and constitutional thought holds that federal citizenship is unthinkable without common and uniform juridical protection of individual freedoms. That is to say, contemporary scholars almost unanimously agree that individual rights enjoy a greater protection under federal than state power and that, in any case, there should be no disparity of treatment among the various states on this sensitive issue. Indeed, in the eyes of many contemporary scholars, the essence of a federation resides specifically in the equality of its citizens before the law, and this cannot but be guaranteed at the federal level.

Thomas Jefferson declared exactly the opposite: It was not the federacy but the states—the buffers against the Federalists' attempt to lump the American population into a single polity—that were the true safeguard of the freedom of the citizens. As has been rightly emphasized by Charles Wiltse, one of the consequences of the battle was the shift in American political discourse from the paradigm of natural rights to that of states' rights. "It was the *Alien and Sedition Acts* that led to the first gloss upon the Constitution, made the states rather than the courts the defenders of individual liberty, and completed the transformation of the natural rights dogma into the far more powerful and effective doctrine of state rights."[43]

The Kentucky Resolutions are, first and foremost, an acknowledgment of the irreplaceable role played by the states in safeguarding the constitutional balance against the risk of consolidation of federal power. Hamilton immediately grasped the potential implicit in the theory embodied in the resolutions and complained of "the tendency of the doctrines advanced by Virginia and Kentucke [sic] to destroy the Constitution of the U[nited] States."[44] Hamilton went as far as advocating recourse to a mobilization of the militia: "In the mean time the measures for raising the Military force should proceed with activity.... When a clever force has been collected let them be drawn toward Virginia for which there is an obvious pretext—& then let measures be taken to act upon the laws & put Virginia to the Test of resistance."[45] A recent scholar voices a common opinion when he agrees with the idea of Hamilton in considering the Jeffersonian doctrine a veritable coup d'etat. "What Jefferson had proposed [in the Kentucky Resolutions] was nothing less than the overthrow of the constitutional settlement of 1787–88, for nullification would have emasculated the national government and restored the states to the predominant position they had occupied under the Articles of Confederation."[46]

It should be remembered, though, that in the *Federalist* (no. 26 and 28), the New Yorker himself had made mention in clear and unequivocal terms of the means available to the states when the federal government overstepped its powers so that the liberties enjoyed by citizens could be protected.[47] While needing elaboration in greater depth, and undeniably hard to reconcile with the spirit of centralization that pervades the entire body of Hamiltonian thought, these reflections may appear as a forerunner of Jeffersonian doctrine.

It is now appropriate to quote the core of the arguments set forth in the resolutions, as contained in the first resolved in the manner in which it was drawn up by Jefferson:

> The several States composing the U.S. of America are not united on the principle of unlimited submission to their general government; but that by a compact under the style and title of a Constitution for the United States, and of amendments thereto, they

constituted a general government for special purposes—delegated to that government certain definite powers, reserving, each State to itself, the residuary mass of right to their own self-government; and that whenever the general government assumes undelegated powers, its acts are unauthoritative, void and of no force: that to this compact each State acceded as a State, and is an integral party, its co-States forming, as to itself, the other party: that the government created by this compact was not made the exclusive or final judge of the extent of the powers delegated to itself; since that would have made its discretion, and not the Constitution, the measure of its powers; but that, as in all other cases of compact among powers having no common judge, each party has an equal right to judge for itself, as well of infractions as of the mode and measure of redress.[48]

Jefferson asserted that the states, inasmuch as they were sovereign parties entering into the constitutional compact, had created the federal government simply as their agent, subordinate to their own power, and designed to carry out limited and well-defined functions. As a result, the federal government had no right to expand its own sphere of authority without the agreement of the contracting parties.

In Jefferson's original formulation, each individual state, when dealing with controversies that concerned the Constitution, had the right to establish two things: 1) whether the pact had been breached and 2) the measures required to restore the order that had been disrupted. Jefferson argued in favor of the existence of a "natural right" of each state to declare the illegitimacy of an act of Congress deemed to be contrary to the constitutional contract. Furthermore, in the draft submitted to the Kentucky assembly, he had used the term *nullification* to refer specifically to that particular right.[49]

This term would prove to be of crucial importance in American history. The nullification crisis of the early 1830s, which saw the state of South Carolina pitted alone and defiantly against the government of the United States and President Andrew Jackson, is generally considered to be one of the landmark stages on the path toward the great crisis that eventually culminated in the Civil War.

That Jefferson was the author of the document had always been strongly suspected, but when in 1832 the original version of the resolutions was found among his papers, complete with the word "nullification" in his unmistakable handwriting, the nullifiers scored a decisive point in their favor and began to regard the Virginia and Kentucky resolutions as part of the constitution of the country. The authorship of Jefferson was revealed by the *Richmond Enquirer* on 16 March 1832. The debate of the right of a state to nullify on its own territory a federal law was of such moment that the paper engaged in a veritable philological exercise, comparing the document approved by the Virginian assembly with the Jeffersonian original. The writer, although declaring himself an opponent of the right of nullification, felt the obligation to redress the mistaken position of the paper, which had published several attacks to the views of Calhoun, in which the fundamental difference between them and the ideas advanced by Jefferson was posited.[50]

At any rate, the most crucial passage was contained in the eighth Kentucky resolution, the one which addresses the issue of how to set things right in the case of a constitutional infringement.

> In cases of an abuse of the delegated powers, the members of the General Government, being chosen by the people, a change by the People would be the Constitutional Remedy; but, where powers are assumed which have not been delegated, a nullification of the act is the rightful remedy: that every State has a natural right in cases not within the compact (*casus non foederis*,) to nullify of their own authority all assumptions of power by others.[51]

Essentially, then, in the case of "ordinary abuses," those occurring within the scope of the powers that the Constitution firmly vests into the federal government, the remedy would lie in the free succession of political majorities and minorities (in a nutshell, democracy), without the states acting in their own right. Whereas, when the federal government reached for powers that had not been delegated, the state would become the champion of its own citizens and the guarantor of the original constitutional compact. This function, whereby the state protects its own citizens against the encroachments of the federal government—effectively shielding them from unconstitutional laws—would later come to be called a power of interposition, a term preferred by Madison, as we will see.[52]

The resolutions passed by the Kentucky assembly, as mentioned above, did not feature some of the most significant sections that were actually contained in the copy Jefferson had given to John Breckinridge, the trusted aide who presented the document to the legislature. In particular, the eighth resolved omitted the above-mentioned passage on nullification. One cannot but agree with Ethelbert Warfield, one of the first historians to have addressed the entire issue, when he offers the following comments on the main characters of the affair: "Mr. Madison has expressed the most guarded sentiments. Mr. Breckinridge…still holds a somewhat imperfectly defined middle ground, and Mr. Jefferson represents the most advanced type of States' rights found in any of the accepted formulas of 1798 and 1799."[53]

The Reactions of the Other States

The resolutions drafted by the two Virginians ended with an appeal to the *co-states*, urging them to orchestrate common actions in order to banish the horrors brought about by the 1798 acts from the legal system. What were the reactions of the other states to the political and constitutional doctrine enshrined in the resolutions? And, more generally, how was the "Kentucky doctrine" received in the America of that time?

One clear division to emerge was that of its "sectional" character. While south of the Potomac the states simply did not respond to the two Virginians' exhortations, all the northern states protested vociferously, through their legislatures, asserting first and foremost the full constitutionality of the Alien and Sedition Acts. But the difference was of a political nature. In the Southern states, Jefferson's party was gaining strength, while the whole of the North was firmly in the hands of the Federalists. In the North, the states debated and passed documents stating their formal disapproval of the resolutions, while in the South the strength of the Republicans was sufficient to forestall any action of this kind, but not enough to pass motions of approval of the Kentucky and Virginia doctrines.

The tone of the states' responses varied widely, but the lead theme seems to have been that the states were not empowered to judge federal laws, for which there already existed an arbiter: the Supreme Court. Only Vermont actually questioned the premise that the union originated in a contract entered into by the parties, and this is a clear indication that the notion of the union advanced by Jefferson and Madison was not a truly contentious issue.[54]

Let us delve into just a few examples. The Delaware assembly flatly asserted that it considered "the resolutions from the state of Virginia, as a very unjustifiable interference with the general government and constituted authorities of the United States, and of dangerous tendency."[55] Rhode Island grounded its opposition on a case of constitutional construction: "The judicial power shall extend to all cases arising under the laws of the United States [the Constitution] vests in the federal courts exclusively, and in the Supreme Court of the United States ultimately, the authority of deciding on the constitutionality of any act or law of the Congress of the United States."[56] A similar approach was adopted by the Massachusetts legislature: "The people in that solemn compact, which is declared to be the supreme law of the land, have not constituted the state legislatures the judges of the acts or measures of the Federal Government, but have confided to them the power of proposing such amendments of the Constitution, as shall appear to them necessary."[57] In addition, it was argued that the Alien and Sedition Acts were constitutional and that the First Amendment was not violated because, and this appears to be a very odd reading of the first amendment, "The genuine liberty of speech and the press, is the liberty to utter and publish the truth."[58] The senate of the state of New York declared "their incompetency, as a branch of the legislature of this state, to supervise the acts of the general government."[59]

The importance of the resolutions stemmed above all from the assumption that the Constitution was a compact in which the states were the contracting parties. John Miller contends that Jefferson and Madison for the first time in history put forward "the theory...that the Federal government was created by a compact between the states: 'we, the people' acceded only as states.... Thus, the states became not only the legitimate judges of the Constitution but the executors of their decisions with regard to the constitutionality of Federal laws."[60] This crucial point was refuted directly only by Vermont, whose assembly ventured a brief foray into an interpretation which—perhaps also for the first time in American history—took up a position of direct hostility to the contractual and state-based model of the genesis of the Constitution: "The people of the United States formed the federal constitution, and not the states, or their Legislatures. And although each state is authorized to propose amendments, yet there is a wide difference between proposing amendments to the constitution, and assuming, or inviting, a power to dictate and control the General Government."[61]

The extremely brief propositions voted by the assemblies of Kentucky ("to this compact each State acceded as a State, and is an integral part, its co-States forming, as to itself, the other party") and Vermont ("the people of the United States formed the federal Constitution, and not the States, or their Legislatures") embody the whole of the controversy that would rack the union during its first decades of life. The subsequent doctrinal reflections of John C. Calhoun and Daniel Webster in the 1830s embellished the arguments with erudite and sophisticated analyses, adding historical, logical, and philosophical rigor to a controversy born in this simple opposition. And even though in 1798 slavery had nothing to do with the issue at hand, it is interesting to note that the notion of the Constitution being a compact, founded on the states and entered into voluntarily, was championed by the South, while the centralizing and "consolidating" credo—summarized in the quite bizarre notion that the American people were to be considered as a whole—was expounded by a Northern state.

Nevertheless, it would be misleading to believe that the notion of states' rights as the proper foundation of the union was embraced only by the South. The idea of an association formed by a pact voluntarily entered into enjoyed considerable support in the North as well, and it effectively represented the most widespread view of the union right up until the mid-nineteenth century. To give just one example, in a pamphlet on states' rights, a politician from a Northern state asserted the following.

> Questions which involve the reserved rights—the moral exist-ence—the sovereignty of the States, individually, must be settled—not by the General Government, but by the States collectively—the States—the parties—the only parties to the compact which established, and still, in the main, so nobly sustains the Union—the States themselves—the source of political power, and not the General Government—a mere creation of this power, for limited purposes.[62]

Similarly, a few years later, the opposition of many a Northern Federalist to the Louisiana Purchase was expressed in unabashedly states' rights terms.

High Federalists from New England…did not question the authority to acquire territory, defending it as an inherent power,…but they insisted that it could not be incorporated in the Union; since the Union was a compact among the states, to absorb the territory would be to alter the nature of the compact…. [Timothy] Pickering argued that the incorporation of the Louisiana Territory could not be accomplished even by a constitutional amendment: every state would have to approve.[63]

On the other hand, neither should the significance of the responses by the other states vis-à-vis the resolutions be overestimated. Voting in the several legislatures proceeded on strict party lines, with the Federalists favorable to the Alien and Sedition Laws and the Democratic-Republicans siding with Virginia and Kentucky. All the assemblies that responded to the challenge, as mentioned earlier, were in the hands of the Federalists.

The Union as an Experiment

The correspondence between Jefferson and John Taylor is particularly illuminating in order to grasp the focus of concern in the Republican Party during those crucial months. The two thinkers were perfectly attuned with each other's views. So much so, in fact, that John Taylor had written to Jefferson a few months before the drafting of the Kentucky Resolutions declaring that "the right of the State governments to expound the constitution, might possibly be made the basis of a movement towards its amendment."[64] In a letter written from Philadelphia in June 1798 that was addressed to Taylor (who was suggesting that Virginia and North Carolina should leave the union without delay, lest they suffer further under the yoke of Massachusetts and Connecticut), Jefferson dwelt on the question of political parties and of the relative importance of party divisions.

First and foremost, the latter could not, per se, constitute a sufficient cause to leave the union. "It is true that we are completely under the saddle of Massachusetts & Connecticut, and that they ride us very hard, cruelly insulting our feelings as well as exhausting our strength and substance…. But our present situation is not a natural one." In his view, a difference in political opinions and the predominance of a party, even if territorially localized, could not lead to secession, for otherwise, "no federal government can ever exist." Furthermore, the possibility of a chain reaction triggering a cascade of secessions should not be overlooked, and this would put a very powerful card in the hands of political factions. "What a game, too, will the one party have in their hands by eternally threatening the other that unless they do so & so, they will join their Northern neighbors...who can say what would be the evils of a scission, and when & where they would end?" In any case, though, since dissent is a feature of all human associations and must be tolerated, it behooves us to "keep our New England associates...than to see our bickerings transferred to others."[65]

Up to that moment—note that this letter was written before the passing of the Alien and Sedition Laws—the vice president was keen to pour oil on troubled waters, and he seemed sincerely concerned with upholding the solid bonds that formed the union. One year later, the situation had radically changed. In a letter to Madison dated August 1799, Jefferson proposed that Virginia and Kentucky should proceed side by side and in a decisive manner. Having taken note of the responses from the other states, he was now convinced that it was necessary to "answer the reasoning of such of the states that have ventured in the field of reason...they have given us all the advantage we could wish." Further, it was necessary to strongly reiterate the principles laid down a few months earlier, and to "express in affectionate & conciliatory language our warm attachment to the union with our sister-states" but at the same time to make it clear that "[we are] determined, were we to be disappointed in this, to sever ourselves from that union we so much value, rather than give up the rights of self government which we have reserved, and in which alone we see liberty, safety & happiness."[66] It was only the cautious Madison, as Jefferson recalled in a letter to Wilson C. Nicholas written just a few months later, who succeeded in persuading him to remove this sentence from the proposed resolution.[67]

Rarely do we find a clearer expression of the view that a preference for freedom and limited government can imply the relative decrease of the significance of the union. Jefferson was in no way an unconditional unionist. From that moment on, this was to become one of the classic Jeffersonian themes: Freedom and self-government cannot be subordinated to the union. It is hard to disagree with Koch and Ammon when they state that "by his willingness to consider the grave possibility of separation from the union, Jefferson showed that he placed no absolute value upon 'union.'

Compared to the *extreme* evil of ruthless violation of liberty, a destruction of the compact which bound the states together was the *lesser* evil."[68]

Jefferson's feelings toward the union were far from isolated in the America of that time. As Dumas Malone points out, "At the time, to be sure, there was nothing particularly startling in the idea that the Union was dissoluble.... Quite clearly, the author of the Declaration of Independence no more valued union for its own sake than he did government. He judged it, as he did every other manmade institution, by the ends it served."[69]

For Jefferson, as for many political thinkers of the period prior to the Civil War, the union was an experiment in liberty and in no way constituted an end in its own right. During his presidency, Jefferson wrote to Joseph Priestley that it was ultimately of little relevance to the happiness of Americans whether the union was preserved or abandoned in favor of Atlantic and Mississippi confederacies. In Jefferson's words, if an upheaval of this kind occurred, the people "of the western confederacy will be as much our children & descendants as those of the eastern, and I feel myself as much identified with that country, in future time, as with this."[70] It was the right of self-government, and not necessarily the union, that was the guarantee of the safety and happiness of citizens.

While many scholars recognize that Jefferson's way of thinking hardly differed from the general consensus of political opinion among his contemporaries, Peter Onuf is unwilling to take this plain statement at face value and calls it an example of "Jefferson's paradoxical thinking."[71] But the paradox is created by the distinguished professor when he affirms, rightly, that "Jefferson could be sanguine about the prospects of disunion because it would not bring into existence new nations that would be 'hostile' to each other" and that "in any event the American nation would survive and prosper."[72] Now the reader is really puzzled, because if one admits that Jefferson believed the nation could survive the union (which seems to be the logical implication of Onuf's argument), then it is difficult to reconcile this with the fact that Jefferson was as stanch a unionist as Onuf portrays him.

At its outset, the union arose essentially as a result of the urgent situation caused by the Revolution, and it won its laurels on the battlefield. The fear of geographic fissures led some, especially during the debate on the ratification of the Constitution, to depict the union as being in itself the bearer of prosperity and security. The governor of Virginia, Edmund Randolph, asserted that "our very quiet depends upon the duration of the

Union."[73] But these feelings were offset by many dissenting voices who were wary of these emotionally charged notions lest they jeopardize the future of the union. Richard Henry Lee, a leader of the Anti-Federalists, recognized that "our greater strength, safety, and happiness, depends on our union; but I am as clear that this union had infinitely better be on principles that give security to the just rights and liberties of mankind, than on such principles as permit rulers to destroy them."[74] The union performed the function of guaranteeing security, but at the same time it raised an ominous threat to freedom—the "consolidation" of powers in a single center. Therefore, a balance had to be struck between these opposite tendencies.

The New York *Examiner* of 9 October 1814 raised the following query: "Is it certain that the union and liberty are inseparable? Is it certain that they are compatible?"[75] At the time of the debate on the Missouri Compromise, William Pinkney, senator from Maryland, was compelled to recall, "The Union is a *means*, not an *end*. By requiring greater sacrifices of domestic power, the end is sacrificed to the means. Suppose the surrender of all, or nearly all, the domestic powers of legislation were required; the means would there have swallowed up the end."[76] The line of reasoning is somewhat tortuous, but the gist is that the goal of freedom coincides fully with the power of the states. The states represented the freedom of Americans, while the union, on the contrary, represented the limitations placed on freedom, and potentially its destruction.

The view that the union was simply an experiment naturally entailed the idea that it could be modified and even dissolved without excessive turmoil. In effect, throughout the generation of the Revolution—as well as in the following generation—there was a widespread tendency to entertain a rather cavalier attitude toward the future of the union.

During the 1820s, Thomas Jefferson's predictions with regard to this future and, above all, about the possibility of maintaining a constitutional, limited, government in America grew increasingly pessimistic. A letter written a few months before his death shows him favoring secession and even armed resistance, but only as a matter of principle, for the time had not yet arrived. "Not yet, nor until the evil...shall be upon us, that of living under a government of discretion."[77]

Jefferson had confessed to a friend just a few days before that he was extremely concerned about the consolidation of federal power. "I see, as you do, and with the deepest affliction, the rapid strides with which the federal branch of our government is advancing towards the usurpation of all the rights reserved to the States, and the consolidation in itself of all powers, foreign and domestic."[78] Moreover, he went on, in what may appear to be a disavowal of his trust in reason and democratic rules:

What is our resource for the preservation of the constitution? Reason and argument? You might as well reason and argue with the marble columns.... The representatives chosen by ourselves? They are joined in the combination, some from incorrect views of government, some from corrupt ones, sufficient voting together to out-number the sound parts; and with majorities only of one, two, or three, bold enough to go forward in defiance.[79]

On the question as to whether it would be proper to take up arms in order to separate from the union, Jefferson gave a negative answer, yet without categorically ruling out the recourse to arms:

That must be the last resource, not to be thought of until much longer and greater sufferings. If every infraction of a compact of so many parties is to be resisted at once, as a dissolution of it, none can ever be formed which would last one year. We must have patience and longer endurance then with our brethren while under delusion;...and separate from our companions only when the sole alternatives left, are the dissolution of our Union with them, or submission to a government without limitation of powers. Between these two evils, when we must make a choice, there can be no hesitation.[80]

This fairly pragmatic attitude toward the union and the total refusal to resort to coercion in order to preserve it can be perceived very clearly in a letter the president wrote at the time of the Louisiana Purchase. Jefferson certainly could hardly fail to notice the enormous territorial increase and the problems this created, yet he was not willing to treat the union as if it were a totem. The Federalists, he argued, "see in this acquisition the formation of a new confederacy, embracing all the waters of the Mississippi, on both sides of it, and a separation of it's Eastern waters from us." He harbored serious doubts about this prospect, but still declared,

> [I]f it should become the great interest of those nations to separate from this, if their happiness should depend on it so strongly as to induce them to go through that convulsion, why should the Atlantic States dread it?... We think we see their happiness in their union, & we wish it. Events may prove it otherwise; and if they see their interest in separation, why should we take side with our Atlantic rather than our Mississippi descendants? It is the elder and the younger son differing. God bless them both, & keep them in union, if it be for their good, but separate them, if it be better.[81]

Basically, the real alien notion seems to be the mystical doctrine of the union as supreme end, as the absolute good to be defended at all costs, as sketched by Daniel Webster and then afterwards, in a completely novel form, by Abraham Lincoln.

For these reasons, then, a reading of Jefferson's attitude toward the union as that expounded by Peter Onuf[82] seems to be as interesting as questionable. Onuf's book begins with the most astonishing claim: "Thomas Jefferson cherished an imperial vision for the new American nation.... This rising empire would be sustained by affectionate union, a community of interests, and dedication to the principles of self-government."[83] Onuf immediately strikes a reassuring note, reminding us that "for provincial Britons "empire" did not evoke, as it now does, centralized, despotic, and arbitrary rule," and that the empire Jefferson yearned for "was...republican in several senses, most conspicuously in its rejection of the aristocratic and monarchical old regime and its corrupt state apparatus."[84]

But a series of rather surprising characterizations of this purported Jeffersonian unionism follow. "In our minds Jefferson's federalism is closely associated with a union-destroying devotion to states' rights, local privilege, and the defense of slavery [amounting to the] reactionary and regressive tendencies of Jeffersonian Republicanism.... The union, the new republican empire of liberty that Jefferson saw spreading across the continent, was to him the whole point of the American Revolution."[85]

When was it that Jefferson gave a hint that the union, and not self-government and/or the rights of man, was the object of the Revolution?

But to Onuf everything in Jefferson's mind was subordinated to the union, as "Jefferson's great political project [was] liberation from tyranny in order to achieve union."[86] Mind, union, not liberty. Indeed, for Jefferson, it was the very notion of union that was subordinated to each and every primary political ends.

Peter Onuf is not the only one to believe that Jefferson's first inaugural is "a paean to the immortal nation."[87] In fact, a student of political rhetoric, Stephen Howard Browne, has devoted a short book to Thomas Jefferson's first inaugural, *Jefferson's Call for Nationhood*.[88] In Browne's opinion, Jefferson's vision was not only that of a nation, but of "a people…the living embodiment of his imperial ideal." Not only that, Jefferson was actually a globalist, reaching out for a united world: "American nationhood was supposed to be the first great step to the republican millennium, when the self-governing peoples across the world would join in peaceful, prosperous, harmonious union." In short, "Jefferson's great invention [is] American nationhood."[89]

While there might have been some exaggerations in depicting Jefferson as the natural father of the Confederate States of America, as it was common many years ago, this recent construction of the third president as a resolute unionist, empire lover, nationalist, and potentially "one-worlder,"—will he become a UN icon in the next few years?—frankly amounts to fairy tale, the story of a new America that needs to redraft its super-icon according to the spirit of the times (and who could deny that we live in a Zeitgeist that commands esteem for the union, love for the empire, and admiration for the nation with the prospect of a uniting world of "free" republics?). All this seems closer to a Jeffersonian nightmare than to the actual political dreams of the sage of Monticello.

Historically, it was Daniel Webster who played a paramount role in keeping alive and spreading the idea of the union and its transcendent value. A scholar recently depicts in a very effective manner Webster's influence.

> Of [nationalist] leaders, none was more important than Webster when it came to establishing a priority of values for developing nationhood. His talent was to use the founders, particularly Washington, to advance the Federalist agenda, often in the guise of making a ceremonial speech. Because of him, *the Union* became

the God-term that Lincoln was to use to justify the North's prosecution of the Civil War. The Union was Webster's heaven on earth; the Constitution was his Ten Commandments.[90]

In his rejoinder to the Calhounian resolutions on states' rights, submitted to the Senate in 1833, Webster stated that "the Union is not a temporary partnership of states. It is the association of the people, under a constitution of government, uniting their power, joining together their highest interests, cementing their present enjoyments, and blending, in one indivisible mass, all their hopes for the future."[91]

James Bryce, in his classic work *The American Commonwealth* (1888), was very harsh on this line of reasoning, as he referred to the claim of the perpetuity of the union as being tantamount to "a mass of subtle and, so to speak, scholastic metaphysics regarding the nature of government."[92] Yet the idea of the existence of a single American people and its union—if not genuinely metaphysical, then at least metahistorical—was gradually gaining ground, although it remained a marginal position at least up to the Civil War.

Lincoln went far beyond the views of Webster. The notion that a sort of moral catastrophe would ensue from the dissolution of the union, which was the constant refrain of Lincolnian statements, must have struck a profound chord in many European (and more than a few American) hearts during that era of surging nationalism. But it was much too fragile a construction to warrant going to war. Not surprisingly, the man from Springfield resorted to other expedients that sent more immediate shockwaves through American political circles. In particular, he crafted the myth whereby unionist majorities in the South were cast as being overpowered by a few rebellious troublemakers, so that their Northern compatriots were duty-bound to "liberate" the South. In actual fact, if one looks at the elections held at all levels and at the results through which the states that were later to form the Confederacy dissolved the union, from December 1860 to the following May, then there can be little doubt as to the extreme popularity of this decision in public opinion. In some states, the resolution to reverse the ratification of the U.S. Constitution was voted by the states' assemblies. The first of such debates was held in South Carolina on 20 December 1860, and the resolution was adopted unanimously by the assembly. In the other states, secession was very popular. In Texas, which ratified the decision by a popular ballot, secession was approved by 75 percent of the voters; similar percentages were recorded in Tennessee, while Virginians proved to be even more enthusiastic.[93]

But when the crisis reached a peak, on 4 July 1861, Lincoln conveyed a message to Congress, which had by now been called upon to prepare for war. In his message, Lincoln denied the states any standing whatsoever, and, with more than a degree of misrepresentation of historical truth, he warned that outside of the union they would have no reason to exist:

> The States have their status in the Union, and they have no other legal status. If they break from us, they can only do so against law and by revolution. The Union, and not themselves separately, procured their independence and their liberty. By conquest or purchase the Union gave each of them whatever of independence and liberty it has. The Union is older than any of the States, and, in fact, it created them as States.[94]

This parricide of Lincoln (which would shortly thereafter also see the involvement of his armies—with a far greater force of persuasion), carried out in the name of the union against the states, contributed to ushering in a new view into American politics, namely an organicist view of almost continental scope. This had been looming on the horizon for decades but had never heretofore been expressed with such lucid clarity. A letter dating from 1864 outlined the justification for recourse to court-martialing as a means of putting civilians on trial, clearly one of the most blatant among the many infringements of the Constitution committed by the president: "Was it possible to lose the nation, and yet preserve the constitution? By general law life and limb must be protected; yet often a limb must be amputated to save a life; but a life is never wisely given to save a limb. I felt that measures, otherwise unconstitutional, might become lawful, by becoming indispensable to the preservation of the constitution through the preservation of the nation."[95]

The fact that it was none other than this man, claiming as he did to hold Jefferson in higher estimation than any other thinker, who actually imported the categories of the nation-state into America is one of the cruelest ironies of American history. It serves to show how far the

Jeffersonian political legacy was already on the verge of being hijacked by his natural adversaries long before the New Deal.

States' Rights and Federal Supremacy

The resolutions include a very clear enunciation of a classical postulate of liberal constitutionalism. "Confidence is everywhere the parent of despotism—free government is founded in jealousy, and not in confidence.... In questions of power, then, let no more be heard of confidence in man, but bind him down from mischief by the chains of the Constitution."[96] According to David Mayer, this embodies "the most succinct expression of...Jefferson's constitutionalism."[97] As can be seen, although the author of the Declaration was known for his boundless trust in man's unlimited potential to improve himself through education and the use of reason, when it was a matter of political power, and thus of the authority some men exert over others of their kind, then he was not at all inclined to embrace a meaningless and generic "anthropological optimism."

But are the resolutions to be understood in the light of constitutionalism or more extensively as a great battle for the civil rights of Americans? Koch and Ammon argue that "however interesting these famous Resolutions may be for the constitutional doctrine they contain, they were intended *primarily* as a defense, practical and spirited, of civil liberties.... The Resolutions were measures of 'solemn protest' meant to limit the scope of the illiberal laws and to guard against their serving in the future as precedent for Congressional legislation."[98] The conclusion reached by the authors may seem correct as far as the entire battle is concerned, in the light of Madison's "moderating" function. Yet it strikes me as rather debatable if applied to Jefferson.

For Jefferson had been musing on such issues for almost a decade, or at least since the beginning of his clash with Hamilton. Moreover, Jefferson was hardly the type who would wield a constitutional sledgehammer to squash the gnat of a political diatribe. In fact, the construction of the Constitution put forward in the resolutions is to be seen as the attempt to build up an impregnable bulwark against the doctrine of implicit powers formulated by Alexander Hamilton. Such a defense centered on the Tenth Amendment to the Constitution as the keystone of the whole American federal system; notably, the amendment is cited twice and at full length in the resolutions.

Far from being a political expedient,[99] the whole of the battle waged in those years corresponded to Jefferson's deepest convictions. Such a conclusion is borne out by a little known episode. Jefferson was set to dwell on his constitutional theory in considerable depth during his inaugural message. However, Albert Gallatin and Madison persuaded him to desist, convinced as they were that by setting out what had now come to be called the "Kentucky doctrine," he would arouse the opposition of the Federalists, and the whole matter would be understood as spoiling for a fight. In fact, the first inaugural address delivered by President Jefferson was instead very conciliatory in tone. The part excised by the draft reads, "Each department is truly independent of the others and has an equal right to decide for itself what is the meaning of the Constitution...especially when it is to act ultimately and without appeal."[100]

Surely, the arguments Jefferson put forward on the nature of the union contain a "core of common sense." Stripped to the bone, the essence of the concept delineated in the resolutions goes as follows: The States are the ultimate judges of the constitutionality of any federal legislative measure. This undeniably involves a rigorously contractual and voluntary basis for the union. But let us analyze other possible interpretations. First, the one that ultimately became predominant during the twentieth century, but which could already be glimpsed in the answers given by the states controlled by the Federalists: The Supreme Court (that is, a branch of the federal government) is the arbiter in conflicts between the states and the federal government itself. In this respect, Jefferson's objection appears not altogether unreasonable. It is the very structure of the Constitution itself that is undermined, since the extent of the powers of a part of the federal system is being adjudicated by the part itself and not by the Constitution. More generally, it is difficult to deny that if the states had been required to comply with any federal law whatsoever, whether in accordance with the Constitution or in flagrant disregard of the latter, then the system of guarantees known as "federalism" would become a mere *flatus vocis*.

One point that needs to be emphasized is that the United States constitutional tradition knows no principle comparable to that of the *Bundestreue*, worked out by the German Constitutional Court as organic development of the pseudofederal concept, which prevailed from the age of Bismarck onwards. This principle of federal "fidelity" requires all the subjects of the legal system to behave according to the spirit of the union and has, like many others deriving from continental European juridical doctrine, no place within American political and constitutional thought, at least in Jeffersonian times.

The first myth to be debunked in order to grasp the reasons supporting an unbiased assessment of Jeffersonian thought on the nature of the union is the statement, so dear to twentieth-century jurists, that the Constitution contains some sort of "federal supremacy" clause.

The Tenth Amendment is a foreclosing rule within the American legal system. It summarizes the partitioning of spheres of authority between the federal government and state governments. However, many scholars of public law hold this to be in sharp contradiction with Article 6 of the Constitution, which they understand to establish a federal supremacy clause.[101] The Tenth Amendment and Article 6 should jointly constitute one of the "conflict resolution rules" to be observed when determining the validity of laws, but they are, in the view of many jurists, contradictory provisions.[102] As has been pointed out by a number of scholars, the string of assumptions marshaled by legal theorists in their quest to assert the supremacy of federal legislation is rather vast and, at least from an historical perspective, debatable on each one of its points. "The supremacy clause is binding inasmuch as the interpreters of the Constitution agree on the fact that sovereignty derives from the people, that one generation can place binding constraints on a subsequent generation and that the 1787 Philadelphia convention and the ensuing ratification process were effectively an expression of the national will to set up a lasting form of government."[103]

In any case, the articles would not resolve the problem of the antinomies within the United States legal system. For we are faced here with an exclusive alternative. Either the federal supremacy clause applies, in which case any state law contrary to the federal law "disappears," or the point of view is inverted and a court can judge whether the federal law oversteps the powers that have been delegated to it, in which case it falls into abeyance.

It was John C. Calhoun who moved an objection to this castle of cards. It is an objection which, to my mind, is decisive and worth considering here because it seems to be fully in line with the Jeffersonian analysis. "The clause [within Article 6] is declaratory;...it vests no new power whatever in the government, or in any of its departments;" in effect, the article does not establish anything at all, much less a supremacy of the federal order, which "results from the nature of the relation between the federal government, and those of the several states, and their respective constitutions and laws." For when a common constitution and government are set up "the authority of these, *within the limits of the delegated powers*, must, of necessity, be supreme.... Without this, there would be neither a common constitution and government, nor even a confederacy." The entire construction would be nonexistent: "But this supremacy is not an absolute supremacy.... It does not extend beyond the delegated powers— all others being reserved to the States and the people of the States. Beyond these the constitution is as destitute of authority, and as powerless as a blank piece of paper; and the measures of the government mere acts of assumption."[104]

James Madison: The Contrite States' Righter

It is interesting to emphasize that at the time of this debate hardly anyone noticed a feature which today appears perfectly clear to everyone: Namely, the greater radicalism of the constitutional doctrine put forward by the Kentucky assembly as opposed to that of Virginia. Or, to put it another way, the more conciliatory tone adopted by Madison in comparison to Jefferson. According to Koch and Ammon,

> The disagreement between Jefferson and Madison...is evident in every line of the Virginia Resolutions. Madison accepted the theory that the Union was based upon a compact among the states, but he did not think, as did Jefferson, that under the Constitution the state was justified in declaring federal laws 'null, void, and no effect.' Nor did he believe that the state was the ultimate judge of both the violation and the mode of redress.[105]

It should be noted, though, that even in the Virginia Resolutions, which were presented to the assembly by John Taylor, the word "unconstitutional" was followed by a phrase referring to federal laws that overstepped their delegated powers. That phrase was "and not law, but utterly null, void, and of no force or effect." During the debate, Taylor himself proposed striking out this latter version, which was deemed to be too strong. His offer of retraction was probably prompted by Madison, the great moderator (often the great puzzler, from a doctrinal point of view) of heated clashes.[106]

While nullification implied the concept of federal legislation being null and void, with effects limited to the state that opted to annul the provision, the notion of state interposition advanced by Madison aimed to be an appeal to the other states to expunge an unconstitutional provision from their legal system. It was a "warning" to call the federal government to a halt, made public in order to induce those who were originally party to the constitutional compact to join in the "protest."

The fundamental difference between Madison's thoughts and Jefferson's concerns the extent of states' rights envisaged in the two documents. Madison conceived the issue as the right of the states to declare—that is to say, to make it publicly known to all and sundry—that any laws of the United States found to overstep their delegated powers should be regarded as unconstitutional. Jefferson believed instead that the states, inasmuch as they were party to the original constitutional compact, had created the federal government simply as an agent, subordinated to their own will, designed to perform limited and well-defined functions. Consequently, the federal government could not increase or expand its own authority purely upon its own initiative.

Madison, unlike Jefferson, never mentioned the right of the state to oppose federal laws, in the sense of revoking them within the state's own territory, but merely that of declaring their unconstitutionality. This fundamental distinction stems from the fact that Madison did not conceive of the government as a mere agent of the federation of sovereign states. Rather, he entertained the notion of a government fully authorized to conduct the general political affairs of the country, even above and conceivably against the will of the states. According to Jefferson, on the other hand, it was only through the power to nullify any laws overstepping the agent's sphere of authority that the states could maintain supremacy over their agent, the federal government. The central point obviously revolves around the entitlement—collective, according to Madison, and vested into the individual states in Jefferson's approach—of the right to expunge an unconstitutional federal law.

The problem is familiar for Madison's scholars.[107] In order to make sense of his serpentine path, it is often presumed that he was under the political spell of his two more consistent and gifted mentors: Hamilton and

Jefferson. It is a well-known fact that in his first political alliance with the New Yorker, he sought to bring about as strong and as centralized a federal government as possible, while later he worked with Jefferson in order to oppose that same plan. While it could be argued that the "Father of the Constitution" was reacting to the different situations of 1788 and 1798, so that "though his thinking about federalism was variable, the variations reflected the relative strengths of the federal and state governments at different times,"[108] his ultimate political coherence has been questioned by many scholars.

Clyde Wilson put it bluntly and persuasively: "There were in the early Republic only two honest positions to take. One was to side with Hamilton, Marshall, and Webster in the pursuit of a vigorous centralized government. The other choice was to follow Jefferson, John Taylor, and Calhoun in defending the agrarian republic."[109] The third way that Madison was always trying to follow, although at times in tune with the Constitutional compromise itself, was not theoretically so alluring, at least considering the modest success it had in early America.

In 1835, challenged by John Calhoun and his supporters, who had revived the Madisonian–Jeffersonian doctrine, James Madison resolved to go public with his firm condemnation of the nullifiers and Calhounites. Faced with the endless and explicit references by Calhoun to the writings of Madison himself and Jefferson, and having to deal with the public opinion of the South, which by now regarded the two resolutions as part of the Constitution, Madison (by that time the most important Founding Father alive) was compelled to once more take a position on this issue. He declared that there was no connection whatsoever between South Carolina's doctrine of nullification and the resolutions. And he did so in a meticulously detailed study designed to set apart the Calhounian doctrine of nullification from its historical precedents. In the *Notes on Nullification*, Madison managed to make an almost hopeless tangle of the whole issue of the right of nullification. If scholars portray for the most part a Madison swinging between a "Hamiltonian" and a "Jeffersonian" perspective, the views expressed in the *Notes on Nullification* are perhaps the most significant work of the "authentic" Madison, the "Madisonian Madison."[110]

Madison started with the quite dubious assertion that the resolutions of 1798 had never been intended by their authors as a prescription for action. Rather, he stated, their most important aim was to induce the other states to acknowledge and affirm the principle. Thus, the right of a state to declare a law unconstitutional was not to be understood as "nullification" and was not a way to expunge the legal system of the state of the unconstitutional measure but was, instead, purely a declaratory act. The Virginia legislature in 1798 had as an "immediate object to produce a conviction everywhere, that the Constitution had been violated."[111] But the crux of the matter did not escape the Virginian politician George K. Taylor, a staunch opponent of the document in 1798. During the debate on the resolutions, he asserted that the population was actually being invited to regard such laws as nonexistent and thus to disregard them completely.[112]

Madison further distinguished his position from the Calhounites' (and involuntarily from Jefferson's stance as well) by arguing that while Calhoun's approach granted the right of nullification or interposition to any given individual state, the power of interposition should actually be awarded only to the states collectively.[113] Madison believed that any action resulting from a declaration of unconstitutionality should be undertaken by the states collectively and not individually. Jefferson, in contrast, had explicitly stated the right of any single state to declare the unlawfulness of an act of Congress, if such an act proved to be contrary to the constitutional pact.

From a purely logical perspective, the Madisonian notion of a collective right of interposition of the states, discussed at length in the 1830s, rests on rather shaky foundations. The states collectively—or better, a majority of three-quarters—are endowed with the power to do as they please with the Constitution, on the basis of amending power, which is absolute as it knows no boundaries. It follows that claiming that the power of nullification or interposition is awarded to the states collectively simply equates to the statement that such a power does not exist at all.

A crucial point for Madison is the distinction between the right to revolution ("the natural and universal right of resisting intolerable oppression")[114] and a state's constitutional right to nullify a law while remaining in the union. It was to the latter sort of "legal revolution" that he objected firmly. Madison tried to use the authority of Thomas Jefferson, whose draft of the Kentucky Resolution had been published just a few years earlier, to show that his old friend was indeed arguing in favor of the "appeal to heaven" and not of a constitutional right.

In this Document [Jefferson's draft of the Kentucky Resolutions] the remedial right of nullification is expressly called a *natural* right, and consequently not a right derived from the Constitution, but from abuses or usurpations.... The right of nullification meant by Mr. Jefferson is the natural right, which all admit to be a remedy against insupportable oppression.... [He] would...revolt at the doctrine of South Carolina, that a single state could constitutionally resist a law of the Union while remaining within it.[115]

James Madison was entirely off the mark in reading between the lines of his old friend. What Jefferson meant by "natural right" is indeed very easy to assess. He entertained the idea that natural was the proper right to be applied to any situation in which no positive or municipal law could be appropriate. As the states stand vis-à-vis each other as individuals in the state of nature (having no common judge), reason and the law of nature are the only categories that can help the observer discern right from wrong. Nullification is, to be sure, the natural right of a state, as he declared clearly, but such a right derived entirely from the nature of the American union as it had been historically constructed and not from the general properties of political associations, as Madison strongly asserted.

Basically, then, the arguments Madison put forward fail to clarify whether the doctrine of interposition/nullification means that the states are, in the last analysis, supreme judges of constitutional violations, or whether it was merely a question of the right to denounce the unconstitutionality of a federal act. Later, Madison defended the reasonableness and moderation of his 1798 position, but he was in contradiction with his own views. Those resolutions, which he claimed were simply documents for a limited political battle designed to obtain the nullification of the Alien and Sedition Laws, had now become the crux of Calhoun's nullification doctrine. And however much he endeavored to demonstrate the mistaken nature of the Carolinian's position, his arguments still remained largely unconvincing.

Yet it is to Madison that we owe a conceptual clarification that would turn out to be of enormous importance in the subsequent evolution of the states' rights school. Both of the resolutions spoke of the states as parties to the constitutional contract. A repartee by an anonymous writer who signed himself as "a citizen of Westmoreland County," but who was probably Henry Lee, mistakenly read the expression "state" as "governmental authorities" and objected that the state governments were none other than the agents of the people of the several states, who were the real parties to the federal Constitution:

> To this Constitution the state governments are not parties in any greater degree than the general government itself. They are in some respect the agents for carrying it into execution, and so are the Legislature and the Executive of the Union; but they are not parties to the instrument, they did not form, or adopt it, nor did they create or regulate its powers. They were incapable of either. The people, and the people only, were competent to these important objects.[116]

In his *Report on the Resolutions*, drawn up in 1799 on behalf of the Virginia assembly in order to assess the responses of the states to the resolutions, Madison appears to have specifically had Lee's criticisms in mind. He thus offers a clear explanation of exactly what should be understood by the term "state." In effect, Madison pointed out, the term state had often been used in a rather vague sense. "It sometimes means the separate sections of territory occupied by the political societies within each; sometimes the particular governments, established by those societies; sometimes those societies as organized into those particular governments; and, lastly, it means the people composing those political societies, in their highest sovereign capacity."[117]

The preference for the latter meaning of "state" would become one of the cardinal points of the doctrine of states' rights. It would also be seen as the synthesis achieved between the doctrine of sovereignty of the people and that of the sovereignty of the states of the American union.

Alexander Addison, drafting a Federalist critique of this Madisonian belief, sought to prove through a series of rather unconvincing disquisitions that Madison's statements would make sense only if the state assemblies had been party to the constitutional contract, whereas it had actually been the conventions of the various states that ratified the Constitution.[118] But on closer inspection Addison's pamphlet does little more than testify to the fact that the notion of the Constitution as a contract and a compact was a widely held view. It shows that no one, not even in the opposing fold, was prepared to call upon the metaphysical entity "people of the United States" to counter what would go down in American history as the Principles of Ninety-Eight.

Libertarian Federalism and Common Law

The Jeffersonian vision is that of a libertarian federalism. If emphasis is placed on the noun, one finds therein the idea of a government entrusted with a limited number of functions, and of a federal power strictly regulated by a constitutional pact, and only able to expand its powers with the consent of the contracting parties (the states). In this view, the rights of local self-government limit and circumscribe an agent, the federal government, whose referent is not a single people, but the peoples of the several states. If, on the other hand, emphasis is placed on the adjective "libertarian," we find that natural rights are the supreme political end for which governments have been legitimately constituted among men. By the same token, federalism should be prima facie nothing other than the form of government most suited to achieving a vital political end of paramount importance; that is, the freedom of individuals to enjoy their own natural rights.

Yet this is not the case. The self-government of the states and their supremacy over the federal government have a peculiar and highly distinctive status in Jeffersonian thought, so much so that federalism can in no way be relegated to the role of a simple means for achievement of an end, albeit the supreme political end of individual freedom. The federal division of powers is not one of the possible devices to obtain the goal of liberty; rather, it is an end in itself.

The two-year period 1798–1799 was a time during which an underlying political consensus grew up around the great questions of the age on the Jeffersonian side under the onslaught of the centralist tendencies embodied by the Federalist Party.[119] If the public debt and the Bank of the United States had been the consensus-building factors of the early 1790s, by the end of the decade the most deeply felt problem was the consolidation of power, the recognition that within the American system the potential despot was the government in Washington and not the governments of the states. All moves leading to an increase in federal powers beyond the limits enshrined in law should be firmly opposed. States' rights became the last bulwark of Jeffersonian republicanism.

One of the notions most detrimental to states' rights, and a view that pervaded the entire Federalist faction, was that there existed an American common law. Of course, the boundaries of this general federal legal system were rather vague, but the claim was made that the Revolution had, in some sense, spared the English legal tradition, or alternatively, if this had indeed been broken, then the Articles of Confederation and eventually the Constitution itself had effectively reinstated at the federal level the principles of common law. The response to this claim blended the two central aspects of Jefferson's political thought, the same that have been addressed throughout this work. First, in Jefferson's view the introduction of common law was a rejection of the revolutionary break. It was tantamount to a return to a remote past and to a huge step backwards as far as the essence of the American experiment was concerned. It was reason and not English precedent that was intended to be the foundation of a rightful government among men. Second, the introduction of the English legal tradition into the living body of American laws would lead to an indiscriminate increase in the powers of Congress, of the president, and, above all, of the federal judiciary.

Jefferson's ideas on a common law of the United States can be properly appreciated only in the light of his general theory of federalism. In the third Kentucky resolution, he declared that the First Amendment had brought any issue regarding freedom of religion, defamation, freedom of the press and of speech outside the cognizance of the federal courts. This was partly by virtue of the combined provisions of the First and Tenth amendments, whereby the powers not delegated to the union were reserved to the states or the people, so that only the states were empowered to legislate on such issues. Thus, in Jefferson's view, the Bill of Rights was to be taken literally: *Congress shall make no laws* means that the restriction applies specifically to the Congress of the United States, not to the individual states. Otherwise stated, the federal courts could only deal with cases falling within the province of federal jurisdiction, as specifically delegated by the Constitution or prohibited by its amendments.

Jefferson rejected the existence of a federal common law. There were as many common law systems as there were states, and these systems were enclosed within their own boundaries, but there existed no American common law. Let us now dwell in greater detail on the arguments put forward in the third resolution, which is likewise of extreme importance yet frequently underestimated by scholars.

No power over the freedom of religion, freedom of speech, or freedom of the press being delegated to the United States by the Constitution, nor prohibited by it to the States, all lawful powers respecting the same did of right remain, and were reserved to the States or the people.... In addition...another and more special provision has been made by one of the amendments to the Constitution, which expressly declares, that "Congress shall make no law respecting an establishment of religion, or prohibiting the free exercise thereof, or abridging the freedom of speech or of the press" thereby guarding in the same sentence, and under the same words, the freedom of religion, of speech, and of the press: insomuch, that whatever violated either, throws down the sanctuary which covers the others, and that libels, falsehood, and defamation, equally with heresy and false religion, are withheld from the cognizance of federal tribunals.[120]

Jefferson clearly intended the Bill of Rights to act as a limit to federal, but not state, powers.[121] This was by no means a sudden flight of fancy, a phrase dropped almost casually into an official document. On the contrary, it was a crucial point that can be fully apprehended only in relation to Jefferson's federalist principles. In order to delve into this question in further depth, it is necessary to look at the correspondence dating from this period and from later days as well. The specific point is clarified in an unequivocal manner in a letter from 1804 addressed to Adams's wife: "The power...is fully possessed by the several state legislatures. It was reserved to them and denied to the general government, by the constitution according to our construction of it. While we deny that Congress have a right to controul [sic] the freedom of the press, we have ever asserted the right of the states, and their exclusive right to do so."[122]

As early as 1799, Jefferson had focused on this issue in extremely general terms in a letter to his friend Edmund Randolph. "Of all the doctrines which have ever been broached by the federal government, the novel one, of the common law being in force & cognizable as an existing law in their courts, is to me the most formidable."[123] All the other

The Political Theory of Thomas Jefferson   201

infringements "have been solitary, unconsequential, timid things, in comparison with the audacious, barefaced and sweeping pretension to a system of law for the U.S., without the adoption of their legislature, and so infinitively beyond their power to adopt. If this assumption be yielded to, the state courts may be shut up."[124]

The United States, he added, are a nation *"for special purposes only."*[125] And since the association was strictly limited by the Constitution, the espousal of a common law by the federal power would have wrought upheaval in the system of government "because it would have embraced objects on which this association had no right to form or declare a will."[126] Jefferson concluded with a recommendation and a note in a saddened tone: "I think it will be of great importance...to portray at full length the consequences of this new doctrine, that the common law is the law of the U.S., & that their courts have, of course, jurisdiction coextensive with that law, that is to say, general over all cases & persons. But, great heavens! Who could have conceived in 1789 that within ten years we should have to combat such windmills."[127]

The task assigned with these words was entrusted to Madison. The most extensive and convincing confutation of the claim that common law had been introduced into the American federal legal system is to be found in the 1799 *Report.* Madison's manner of proceeding is unexceptionable. Starting out from the colonial status of the country, he traced the effects of the Revolution that "converted the colonies into independent states," then went on to analyze the changes brought about by the Articles of Confederation, and finally ended with a reflection on "the Constitution of 1788, which is the oracle that must decide the important question."[128]

During the colonial period, common law "was the separate law of each colony within its respective limits" and had most certainly not been conceived as "a law pervading and operating through the whole, as one society."[129] Could the Revolution have led to a change of perspective as far as common law was concerned? Clearly not, since the very essence of the Revolution was that Great Britain had no right to establish laws designed to be valid for the other parts of the empire. "Such being the ground of our Revolution, no support nor colour can be drawn from it, for the doctrine that the common law is binding on these states as one society. The doctrine, on the contrary, is evidently repugnant to the fundamental principle of the Revolution."[130]

During the time of the Confederation, any logical inference on the possible operation of common law in the whole of the United States was ruled out by Article 2, which declared, "That each state retains its sovereignty, freedom, and independence, and every power, jurisdiction, and right, which is not by this confederation expressly delegated to the United States, in Congress assembled."[131]

With regard to the Constitution, Madison did not deny that some parts of common law might be held to form part of the American legal system by virtue of an explicit mention in the Constitution. But the real problem was the stable entry of an ambiguous English-American common law into the republican legal order. Those who support this position, Madison argued, base their arguments on the provision of Article 3, Section 2: "The judicial power shall extend to all cases *in law and equity*, arising *under this Constitution*, the laws of the United States, and treaties made or which shall be made under their authority." Yet constitutional language by no means allows such an extensive construction, and if it did, the whole of criminal law would in any case remain excluded. Madison also focused attention on a long series of technical/juridical obstacles that foil any such enterprise, namely the determination of the "quantity" and "type" of common law to be introduced in America.[132]

The point that most seriously worried both Jefferson and Madison was that if common law became part of the American federal legal system, Congress would ipso facto, by recourse to legal measures, have the possibility of revising and integrating the principles of common law, as in the case of the English system, which is a notorious blend of customary law and law enacted by the Parliament. If this were to occur, any constitutional limitation to the action of federal power would be swept away in an instant. For if "the authority of Congress is co-extensive with the objects of common law [it] would, therefore, be no longer under the limitations marked out in the Constitution. They would be authorized to legislate in all cases whatsoever."[133] If, on the other hand, common law were to be introduced as a limitation on federal legislative activity, then it would be the judiciary that would have "a discretion little short of a legislative power."[134] Taken together, this would mean that, once common law became established within the American system, nothing would ever be the same again. Change would affect not only the features of the federal government but also the relation between the latter and state governments. In conclusion, common law would become a body of law that could "sap the foundation of the Constitution as a system of limited and specified powers."[135]

Madison reiterated his aversion "to the doctrine that the 'Common Law' as such is a part of the law of the U.S. in their federo-national capacity" in a letter to Duponceau in August 1824.[136] In doing so, he restated the revolutionary generation's belief in the doctrine of natural rights. "If the Common Law has been called our birthright, it has been done with little regard to any precise meaning.... As men our birthright was from a much higher source than the common or any other human law.... And as far as it might belong to us as British subjects it must with its correlative obligations have expired when we ceased to be such."[137]

In *United States v. Hudson and Goodwin* (1812),[138] Jefferson and his party scored an important victory. The issue was whether the circuit courts of the United States could exercise a common law jurisdiction in criminal cases. The court denied: "The legislative authority of the Union must first make an act a crime, affix a punishment to it, and declare the court that shall have jurisdiction of the offence."[139]

The abolition of common law crimes in 1812 represented a moment when the implications of the Constitution's structure ultimately caught up with experience. It crystallized the recognition—suggested in 1798—that the Constitution and the common law could not coexist and that the American system of government had broken off from its English antecedents more sharply than anyone had appreciated.

Peter DuPonceau, author of a work on jurisdiction in the early republic, expressed this opinion:

> The revolution has produced a different state of things in this country. Our political institutions no longer depend on uncertain traditions, but on the more solid foundation of express written compacts.... The common law...is to be considered in the United States in no other light than that of a system of jurisprudence,...[and] no longer the *source* of power or jurisdiction.... But old habits of thinking are not easily laid aside; we might have gone on for many years longer confounding the English with the American common law, if cases had not been brought before the federal Courts, so serious in their nature, and apparently fraught with such dangerous

consequences, that hesitation was produced, and the public attention was at last drawn to this important subject.[140]

In spite of the Jeffersonian consensus that was building up around these issues, the nationalists were not inactive. In 1816, Joseph Story stated that "it can hardly be doubted, that the constitution and laws of the United States are predicated upon the existence of the common law." The common law served as an essential ingredient in the "construction and interpretation of federal powers."[141] "In my judgment, nothing is more clear than that the…exercise of the vested jurisdiction of the courts of the United States must…be governed exclusively by the common law." Story went on to elaborate the types of crimes subsumed under the common law: "All offences against the sovereignty, the public rights, the public justice, the public peace, the public trade and the public police of the United States, are crimes and offences against the United States."[142] Story's seemingly modest desire to provide the fragile United States government power to protect itself against criminals contained illimitable implications. Just as the Jeffersonians had predicted, Story was ready to vest the national government with an indefeasible sovereignty, using federal common law as a Trojan horse.[143]

Behind the whole dispute on federal common law lies another, which is of even greater significance. Freedom of speech, in Jefferson's view, was one of the preeminent natural rights of the individual, as has been underscored a number of times in this book. Yet he was prepared, theoretically at least, to imagine that the states could occasionally violate it. But never would the federal government be allowed to encroach upon it. Between libertarianism, which implied that any infringement of a sacred and inviolable law is totally disallowed, and federalism, founded on the full self-government of the states and on rigid, precisely defined fields of federal intervention, Jefferson seems to have been almost more inclined to jettison the former in order to go the whole way in pursuing the latter.

At the end of the day, Jefferson was a classical liberal who believed in the people as the best safeguard of freedom and natural rights. What prevented him from assuming the existence of a vast political community denominated United States, or, simply America, devoted to the protection of the natural rights of individuals and complying with majority rule? Why does the *angst* about the consolidation of powers in the hands of the federal government recur over and over again in his writings? Why is it that the states, and not the federal government, are the "the true barriers of our liberty"? Plainly, in Jefferson's eyes federalism was not merely the manner in which the American republic had historically become structured, but something immeasurably more important; that is, the very essence of the American experiment in self-government.

Jefferson used the terms monarchic and Anglophiles (actually, *Anglomen*, one of the many phrases he introduced into the English language, together with *monocrats*, a word used to indicate exponents of the Federalist Party) to refer to his political opponents. It mattered little that the latter perhaps had no intention of importing a monarch into America. What he sought to stress was the nature of the English model they were trying to impose. The essence of that model, as he saw it, lay in the "parliamentary sovereignty" typical of the English system as it had been produced by the Glorious Revolution. For "parliamentary sovereignty" had permanently supplanted the concept of "popular sovereignty," even though popular sovereignty had been enshrined in a doctrinal formulation worked out by his champions of the Whig tradition. Jefferson was convinced that parliamentary sovereignty was just as dangerous a notion as the concept of monarchy, and was, in fact, in many ways indistinguishable from it.

Thomas Jefferson had grasped something that eluded many of his contemporaries, namely that the parliament was the true heir of the sovereign, and, in particular, Congress represented the true heir of the English crown. The struggle of political Enlightenment risked being reproduced indefinitely if the new sovereign (the legislature) were not bound by a well-defined scope and insurmountable limits. Only in this context could one fully appreciate the significance of his statements on the nonexistence of an American common law and those on the Bill of Rights as a limit applying only to federal power; that is, on the predominance of the states vis-à-vis their agent.

What Jefferson feared was the rise of something we might today describe as "legal globalism." It should never be forgotten that if the author of the Declaration is, in a sense, the first *Homo Americanus*—the one who was the first to use the term "Americanism"—he was also very clear on what he meant by "my country." Whenever he used this expression, he always meant Virginia. This is not a case of localism or particularism, coming as it does from one of the greatest exponents of Enlightenment cosmopolitanism. Furthermore, in American political history, the negative connotation of the term "localism" has not gained much ground. The dominating political culture in America, above and beyond the situations shaped in the different historical periods and their resulting general political trends, has always interpreted the relation between localism and freedom as being of the utmost importance.

Jefferson, with his opposition to universal frameworks and to legal cosmopolitanism, seems to be in tune with the somewhat popular mood even nowadays in his own country. In Europe, on the contrary, a view prevails similar to the one expounded by Jürgen Habermas, in which the age of economic globalization makes necessary a "global governance of the economy," possibly entailing uniform taxation, worldwide social services, a global health system, and the like. The process of global democratic integration is supposed to unfold by means of the extension all over the world of justiciable and uniform "social rights."[144] The prospect of a "world government," along the lines of the Kantian tradition that was long one of the warhorses of "progressive" culture, seems to have run its course in America, and even one of the major political philosophers, a cult figure of the noncommunist left, the late John Rawls, denied that the *Weltrepublik* (world republic) holds any attraction. However, the Harvard philosopher debatably credited Kant himself with the idea that the global political society holds little appeal: "I follow Kant's lead in *Perpetual Peace*...in thinking that a world government—by which I mean a unified political regime with the legal powers normally exercised by central governments—would either be a global despotism or else rule over a fragile empire torn by frequent civil strife."[145]

The Ward-Republic

In the years following his withdrawal from active political life, Jefferson worked on a rather fascinating idea, that of the ward-republic, in which the federal relation took on a special ethical connotation. It was an idea that perhaps aimed to represent the bonding of popular sovereignty and natural rights. Federalism was no longer merely the manner in which the American republic had taken shape, nor a commendable model for the division of powers on a territorial basis, nor even was it a pattern that could supersede certain simple models of republican representation. It became, instead, a relation of an ethical nature between the one and the many, between the individual and society, a guideline to be applied to any political community in all places.[146]

Jefferson's most important statement on the ward-republic is found in a well-known letter to Joseph C. Cabell, dated 2 February 1816. But it is of interest to place it in its correct setting in order to note how the vision of a "republic of republics," in which power progressively decreased toward the top (where the officials are furthest away from the people), is in harmony with his ideal of limited government, even in the field where Jefferson was apparently willing to grant greater powers to the government—as opposed to the ward—namely education.

Discussion on this matter started out from some considerations on a bill concerning primary education. Jefferson was informed that his system did not seem to be received very favorably and that a statewide system seemed likely to be more advantageous. To which Jefferson commented, "If it is believed that these elementary schools will be better managed by the governor and Council, the commissioners of the literary fund, or any other general authority of the government, than by the parents within each ward; it is a belief against all experience."[147] To convey his thought even more clearly, he added, sarcastically, "Try the principle one step further, and amend the bill so as to commit to the governor and Council the management of all our farms, our mills, and merchants' stores. No, my friend, the way to have good and safe government, is not to trust it all to one, but to divide it among the many, distributing to every one exactly the functions he is competent to."[148]

Those responsible for the education of their children are their parents and not the government. Men must be educated precisely in order to be able to provide themselves with a shield against the government. For the government has to be made "good and safe," tamed like a wild beast. In this passage, one perceives the gulf that separated Jefferson's conception from the view that sees "tyranny" (exploitation, prevarication, dominion, and so forth) as the natural product of social interaction and political power as a possible solution. I have been unable to find a single passage in which Jefferson's outspoken opposition to privilege, abuse of power, and the benefits enjoyed by the rentier class was not directly linked to that of the public policies that had brought about such adversities. Indeed, one has the feeling that for Jefferson the possibility of systematic coercion simply cannot exist outside of the political arena. Government and freedom are diametrically opposed, and the advancement of the one entails a diminishment of the other. The struggle, as he asserted in 1788, was clearly moving toward the paired terms government tyranny: "The natural progress of things is for liberty to yield and government to gain ground."[149]

Thus, in the light of these and other considerations, the most unfounded interpretations of the Jeffersonian thought appear to be those current in the age of the New Deal, when the attempt was made of enlist the author of the Declaration among the ranks of the champions of government interventionism.

But for Jefferson, the concept of the ward-republic was not a simple division of political powers. It starts from the individual and reaches the summit of the federation, allowing the arms of government increasingly fewer powers of coercion. This is clarified in greater depth immediately afterwards:

> Let the national government be entrusted with the defence of the nation, and its foreign and federal relations; the State governments with the civil rights, laws, police, and administration of what concerns the State generally; the counties with the local concerns of the counties, and each ward direct the interests within itself. It is by dividing and subdividing these republics from the great national one down through all its subordinations, until it ends in the administration of every man's farm by himself; by placing under every one what his own eye may superintend, that all will be done for the best.[150]

But why is it necessary to divide and subdivide all the powers over man? As Jefferson saw it, this necessity derived from the very nature of power, from its tendency to spill over beyond its boundaries and become oppressive. Why was this, he wondered. "What has destroyed liberty and the rights of man in every government which has ever existed under the sun?"[151] The answer is plain and simple: "The generalizing and concentrating all cares and powers into one body, no matter whether of the autocrats of Russia or France, or of the aristocrats of a Venetian senate."[152] The secret to set men free is thus no longer to be identified as residing in mere respect for natural rights, since the government tends naturally to impinge on such rights, but rather in the diffusion and division of power.

> I do believe that if the Almighty has not decreed that man shall never be free (and it is a blasphemy to believe it,) that the secret will be found to be in the making himself the depository of the powers respecting himself, so far as he is competent to them, and delegating only what is beyond his competence by a synthetical process, to higher and higher orders of functionaries, so as to trust fewer and fewer powers in proportion as the trustees become more and more oligarchical.[153]

This reflection came at a time when Jefferson's political journey had come to an end and he had witnessed the entire course of the American experiment, from the separation of the colonies to the foundation of the republic of natural rights, to the Federalist "Thermidor," right up to his own attempt to bring the government back within the strict limits established by the Constitution. From the height of an experience that has no parallels among the Founding Fathers, he was able to observe that one single enemy stood out as a threat against the toils to achieve freedom, an enemy summarized in the concentration of powers at a higher level. It is worth noting that Jefferson never believed that the separation of federal powers was a meaningful guarantee against the consolidation of government; the most reliable bulwark was the states' governments.

This Jeffersonian conception is the reverse image of that of Immanuel Kant. For the German thinker, an ethical approach required existing states to grant increasingly wide-ranging powers to a superstructure, the world Republic designed to guarantee peace.[154] The American held that exactly the opposite was true: It is the free individual owner who is the pivotal element of the system, the freeholder who delegates increasingly smaller powers the further one moves away from him, from that which is most visibly before his vigilant and suspicious eyes. It is his careful attitude and his direct participation, and not the concept of shifting sovereignty further and further upwards, that forms the moral guarantee of the system. Consequently, the fewer powers are delegated, the less these powers are diverted away from the individual's sight, and the greater will be the result in terms of freedom. Obviously, though, the comparison between the two political visions is intended here purely as a thought-provoking suggestion. The two men ignored each other (or rather, Jefferson was not acquainted with Kant's writings), and the circumstance of partaking of such a vast category as that of political Enlightenment could not necessarily cause a meeting of minds in Königsberg and Monticello.

The Nature of the Union According to Jefferson

The strong assumption on which the entire Jeffersonian construct of states' rights is grounded is the analogy between relations among men and relations among the states within the federal compact. This notion immediately recalls the (very theoretical) concept put forward by Immanuel Kant in his *Perpetual Peace* (1795), but it is also sharply distinct from the Kantian view.[155] The German philosopher's vision was favorable to a pact among the world's nations with the aim of entering into a commitment to certain rules and establishing an overarching sovereignty in order to overcome the disruptions caused by state sovereignty. In Kant, the whole edifice is built upon a contractual base. Nations wage war against one another because they are in a "state of nature"—that state of international anarchy which for innumerable scholars of subsequent periods has become a sort of refrain— and the transition to political society, which has worked so nicely among men within individual countries, must be extended to the nations themselves. Furthermore, according to the author of *Perpetual Peace*, this change is a moral imperative (as had been man's move beyond the state of nature), and morals can thus be seen as a growing and general commitment to a cosmopolitan law.

For Jefferson, such a scheme could not be valid. First, because as a true Lockean, he believed the prepolitical state to be perfectly moral—and already well governed by the law of nature. Likewise, he held "municipal" laws to be acceptable only insofar as they were a reflex of natural law. But, above all, he believed that there exists no common judge among the parties to the constitutional compact. Among the states, the transition to political society simply has not taken place. Since the parties cannot appeal to a judge, they are therefore sovereign in establishing the just remedy for a violation of the pact. The ratification of the Constitution notwithstanding, the states find themselves facing one another while still fully endowed with all their natural rights, exactly like individuals in the "state of nature."

The crucial question of the common judge in the American compact remains somewhat controversial. As early as the end of the eighteenth century, the Supreme Court tended to assume the function of arbiter of conflicts between the states and the federal government, even though this was not necessitated by any specific provision of the Constitution. Section 25 of the 1789 Judiciary Act, approved shortly after the new constitution had come into force, allowed the Supreme Court to decide on the appeals concerning sentences issued by the courts pertaining to matters regulated by the Constitution, or to laws approved by Congress, or to treaties of the United States. One crucial conflict between Jefferson's federal theory and what had, by then, become the approach adopted by the American federal system in that period specifically concerned the powers of the Supreme Court.

While, as we have seen, Rhode Island, Massachusetts, New York, New Hampshire, and Vermont firmly argued that the highest federal office of the judiciary was also the final arbiter of the constitutionality of federal laws, Jefferson and Madison strongly denied this claim, reiterating a crucial point of their resolutions. Madison clarified the question in a fairly persuasive manner in his 1799 *Report*: "However true, therefore, it may be, that the judicial department, is, in all questions submitted to it by the forms of the Constitution, to decide in the last resort, this resort must necessarily be deemed the last in relation to the authorities of the other departments of the government; not in relation to the rights of the parties to the constitutional compact, from which the judicial as well as the other departments hold their delegated trusts."[156]

When the problem of whether a federal legislative measure did or did not comply with the Constitution was left to the operation of the clever system of checks and balances, then the ultimate judge could in no way be the Supreme Court, which was a creation of the pact itself, inasmuch as it was a department of the federal government. Rather, the ultimate judge was the individual state, as an original party to the constitutional compact.

But, naturally, according to the most widely held opinion (both today and at the time of Jefferson), a judge of last resort is needed, one who provides a definitive resolution and establishes justice in controversies between the states and the federation once and for all, and who provides the final word on any question. Jefferson's answer concerning the final arbiter is unexceptionable and coherent with the whole of his political thought, as well as with Article 5 of the Constitution. In 1823, he wrote to Judge William Johnson on the occasion of a discussion on the case *Cohens v. The State of Virginia* in which Chief Justice Marshall had maintained that there necessarily had to be an ultimate arbiter: "The ultimate arbiter is the people of the Union, assembled by their deputies in convention, at the call of Congress, or of two-thirds of the States.[157] Let them decide to which they mean to give an authority claimed by two of their organs. And it has been the peculiar wisdom and felicity of our constitution, to have provided this peaceable appeal, where that of other nations is at once to force."[158]

Thus, it is the people who have the final word. Not a metaphysical and constitutionally nonexistent American people, assembled in a single mass, but rather the peoples of the various states represented in purpose-convened conventions with the aim of amending, abolishing, or modifying the government of the union. Exactly as prescribed by Article 5 of the Constitution.

In a letter to the Virginian judge Spencer Roane, important because it dwells on the limits of the powers of the Supreme Court, Jefferson strongly denied that the Court should have any power of interpreting the Constitution of the United States. This was true, he maintained, not just in relation to controversies among states, or between the latter and the federal government, but also among the arms of the federal government itself.[159] For there could be no common judge among the parties of the constitutional compact, neither the Supreme Court, nor, much less, the federal government itself, since the latter was not the arbiter of the pact but was instead its object. In fact, though, the perceived "need for a mechanism to settle disputes between the states and national government" seems to be settled in favor of the Supreme Court. However, as William Watkins notes, "While the Supreme Court as final arbiter does provide certainty, we must ask ourselves whether such a state of affairs can be squared with the people's position as ultimate sovereigns."[160]

Once again, John Locke provided Jefferson with a clarification of when men are to be deemed to live in a state of nature, and when not: "Those who are united into one body, and have a common established law and judicature to appeal to, with authority to decide controversies between them and punish offenders, are in civil society one with another; but those who have no such common appeal...are still in the state of Nature, each being where there is no other, judge for himself."[161]

As mentioned earlier, in a different historical and doctrinal context, John Calhoun took up the Jeffersonian theory again, but, in releasing it from the conceptual framework of natural law, he upheld it purely on the grounds of the sovereignty of the individual federated state. For Jefferson, on the other hand, the "natural law model" of Lockean inspiration was sufficient, once it had been transposed by pure analogy from individuals to the states, to allow him to assert the characteristics of the American union. Thus, he never resorted to a theory of "sovereignty" (a term that does not even appear in the Resolutions) in order to claim that the states are "free and independent." It is the nature of their bond with each other that makes them such and not their character as original political communities.

This must be a starting point to appreciate the unity and internal coherence of Jeffersonian thought on federalism. It is nonetheless a complex approach, contrasting with a large part of the body of thought elaborated by subsequent theory, and, most crucially, at variance with the distinction between federation and confederation of states, a distinction as disputable as it was successful.[162]

To reconstruct Jefferson's thought on federalism, it is necessary to set aside the mental attire lazily donned in the form of the juridical theory of federalism that was formulated during the nineteenth and twentieth centuries. Attention must be directed in quite another direction, following the conceptual path of almost half a century of political reflections, leading from the rights of man to the rights of the states, from the Declaration of Independence to the Kentucky Resolutions, right up to the notion of the ward-republic as a solution to the problem of freedom by means of "fractional representation."

Conclusions

And...the State was nowhere to be seen.[1]

The figure of Thomas Jefferson looms large over at least three revolutionary developments of the wider American historical setting of his age. Such developments led to unparalleled changes in the political and doctrinal circumstances of the young American republic, and they were to provide the backdrop to many a heated debate at least until the Civil War. The first of these developments is the theory of natural law of the origins, the second is the fervent support for the powers of the states as rivals of—and a constraint on—federal government, and the third is the discovery of the politics of opposition as a tool to promote inquiry and change.

Jefferson's view of natural law, of reason as the one and only guide to building a just society, took shape in the colonial period and was an integral part of his thought for the rest of his days. As I have tried to show, Jefferson had an unconditionally Lockean approach to natural law, based on the positive notion of the state of nature and on the assumption that government is established to safeguard the preexistent rights of individuals that men possess inasmuch as they are human beings. Such rights, Jefferson believed, do not have a contractual nature, for it is government that is the object of the contract, not the rights themselves.

Jefferson also represents the fulfillment of the tradition that spans from Coke through the Levellers and John Locke, right up to Trenchard and Gordon. A sort of *terminus ad quem*, which the theory of self and limited government cannot overstep. In that period, individual freedom and democracy seemed compatible, and it was perhaps Jefferson who most strongly believed in this possibility. I have also tried to demonstrate that the Jeffersonian concept of democracy and popular control actually has very little to do with present-day practices of democratic countries or with contemporary speculations. The notion of using democracy against "capitalism" was totally inconceivable in his days, and he certainly was *not* the early champion of these practices.

Rather, with Jefferson it was the entire Whig tradition that reverted to its prior tradition, rejecting the shift from the sovereignty of the people to that of parliament, which had caused the English revolutionary progress of 1688 to "lose its way." Jefferson's theoretical achievement during the years in retreat at Monticello—that of the ward-republic—aimed at making every citizen the master of his own house precisely through a sort of concentric representation, in which the most important powers remained firmly entrenched in the hands of the individual.

Thus, Jefferson's entire system springs from the desire to find mechanisms that can place society above government and can make political power separate from and under the control of society itself. At the heart of his thinking, there is always the freeholder, the free individual who manages his own life, liberty, and property, fully aware of the fact that freedom is not free.

The other two facets of his theory are the result of the political battles he waged in the republic of the 1790s. The theory of the contractual nature of the union, the strict construction of the Constitution, and states' rights were the particular innovations to which Jefferson gave voice and a first theoretical framework. They subsequently became an integral part of the Jeffersonian credo and forged a political ruling class, first in the opposition and later in power within the first decades of the nineteenth century.

Jefferson's lifelong struggle may be thought of as a grand attempt to do away with competition for power. The government was to be limited precisely in order to achieve this end, so that no one should delude himself into believing it could be exploited for personal interests. Government should not be a coercive power over society, ready to grant favors to some behind the backs of others. Jefferson's view of government and its aims is so restricted as to make the third president one of the champions of classical liberalism, as indeed most scholars freely admit.

In the course of this work, I have concentrated on "liberal" (in the modern, American meaning of the term, namely of a left-leaning bent) readings of the thought of Thomas Jefferson, with the deliberate aim to refute them. I would very much regret if a casual reader came away with the impression of these positions being commonly accepted and the opposite school of thought being a scant minority. This book, in contrast with some recent academic output, belongs to the mainstream scholarly undertakings of Jeffersonian studies in the recent past, which is the continuation of past works on this subject. Under this respect, it is instead the view of democratic radicalism as the characterizing feature of

Jeffersonian thought that is to be seen as a historiographical detour, whose enduring after effects must necessarily be challenged by any scholar.

Jefferson's faith in the people and popular majorities, which he carefully nurtured, is perhaps one of his greatest delusions. His belief that the people, by exercising their power to make majority-based decisions, were the best defenders of their natural rights has, to say the very least, been cut down to size by the course of history.

The optimism Jefferson showed in his answer to John Adams, who was despairing about the future of self-government in Europe, where reactionary regimes seemed to have wiped out the vestige of any revolutionary improvement, appears to be groundless: "The Generation which commences a revolution can rarely compleat [*sic*] it.... A first attempt to recover the right of self-government may fail; so may a 2d. a 3d., etc., but as a younger and more instructed race comes on, the sentiment becomes more and more intuitive, and a 4th or a 5th or some subsequent one of the ever renewed attempts will ultimately succeed."[2]

The republican government that Jefferson believed to be "the only form of government which is not eternally at open or secret war with the rights of mankind,"[3] has given such proof of itself—from Jefferson's death right up to the present day—as to lead one to deem his statement and his confidence to have been vastly overblown. It is difficult to still share his confidence after witnessing many instances of totalitarian governments (soft and hard) born from or sanctioned by relatively free elections.

In short, the changes Jefferson fought against, from the diminished role of the states to the centralization of political and economic life, were perfectly compatible with the expansion of democracy, in the sense of expansion of the franchise and the growing role assumed by majority decisions at all levels. However, it is perhaps also on account of this specific Jeffersonian heritage, namely the dream—a dream that history seems to condemn as contradictory—of achieving a minimal government based on the widest possible popular participation that America still appears to many observers among the ranks of "liberal democracies," the most democratic, and also the least illiberal country. The propensity to use democracy against capitalism, which is perhaps the most evident characteristic of the century that has just come to a close, still encounters greater hurdles in America than in Europe. There is a range of factors that contribute to making the United States a radically democratic country, and yet a country that is not totally hostile to the free market. Among these many factors, I do not deem the least significant the fact that the most loved, most highly regarded, and best remembered Founding Father devoted his entire lifetime to creating a republic founded as much on "popular sovereignty" as on the respect of natural rights.

Jefferson had one of the best legal minds of his day and believed that constitutionalism was a revolutionary achievement of his times and his country. Even the contractual theory of the union was nothing other than a restatement of the theory of limited government in the American context. Limitations on government are always related to the extent of the power of coercion over individuals. Where simple human rights are not sufficient to curb government despotism—inasmuch as a consolidated republic is equivalent to a monarchy—then another device comes to the rescue: the Constitution and the territorial apportionment of powers provided by it. Thus, in Jefferson's political theory, the Constitution becomes the bulwark of states' rights and the states themselves are the only instrument left to citizens in order to safeguard their natural rights. The function of veritable barricades on behalf of their own citizens properly vested in the states' governments is the strongest check on the transgressions of the federal government beyond the limits established in the Constitution. The strict construction of the document was not, however, the preordained outcome of the struggles in the early 1790s. On the contrary, at the beginning, it was the Federalists themselves who appealed for a strict construction of the constitutional instrument.

Among the unintended consequences of the actions of the Jeffersonian party, one of the most important was without doubt the crystallization of the political debate on the Constitution. The canonization of the document and its makers was to occur after Jefferson's lifetime, but many of these tendencies had already come to the fore during the period of the struggle against the Federalists. At a certain point in the constitutional debate, Jefferson used what is now called "originalism"; that is, adherence to the original principles according to the interpretation that was held correct at the time of stipulation. He and his followers no longer based their political arguments on principles, on rational awareness of what was the "best government," but rather on a written document. Toward the end of his life, Jefferson summed up his battle for a strict construction of the Constitution as follows: The text should be understood "according to the plain and ordinary meaning of its language, to the common intendment of the time and those who framed it."[4] And, if it was genuinely necessary to make logical inferences, then the procedure should be to "carry ourselves back to the time when the constitution was adopted, recollect the spirit manifested in the debates, and instead of trying what meaning may be squeezed out of the text, or invented against it, conform to the probable one in which it was passed."[5]

In the struggle of the 1790s, it was easy for Jefferson and his followers to show that the Federalists held "their" very Constitution in utter disregard. But he knew perfectly well that the document was understood in different ways by different people, and he believed that it featured elements that could drive it in the direction of either a monarchical or a republican government.

The Jeffersonian insistence on a strict construction of the Constitution imposed a straitjacket on the American political debate and shackled it to the constitutional document. As a result, although the Constitution did feature a number of provisions for its change and amendment, its development was left to the evolutionary construction by the Supreme Court and was rarely submitted to the judgment of popular sovereignty. Moreover, the idea of a fixed Constitution ultimately militated against the notion of generational sovereignty, so often emphasized by Jefferson. Of this, he was well aware. Remarking that his generation and the Constitution itself were becoming an object of worship, he stated in 1816:

> Some men look at constitutions with sanctimonious reverence, and deem them like the arc of the covenant, too sacred to be touched. They ascribe to the men of the preceding age a wisdom more than human, and suppose what they did to be beyond amendment. I knew that age well; I belonged to it, and labored with it. It deserved well of its country. It was very like the present, but without the experience of the present; and forty years of experience in government is worth a century of book-reading;...laws and institutions must go hand in hand with the progress of the human mind.... We might as well require a man to wear still the coat which fitted him when a boy, as civilized society to remain ever under the regimen of their barbarous ancestors.[6]

This book does not deal with the drama of Jefferson in power, as it focuses on his political ideas. How he was worn down by the burden of daily political concerns during his two presidential mandates is not part of this inquiry; much less does attention center on his personality, the character issue. It would take another entire volume to show how the legacy of a government that became too powerful to be reined in acted like a dead weight over the entire body of his governmental activity (a sort of veritable mortmain of the recent past). For the Anti-Federalists, the alternative was clear: Empire *or* Liberty. And they had made it clear which way their preferences lay. Jefferson believed he had a solution to the dilemma: With the Louisiana Purchase of 1803, his aim was to create an Empire *for* Liberty.[7]

In the endeavor to restrain the federal government within the limits of the Constitution, Jefferson turned to what has historically been the gravedigger of limited government and the midwife of the omnipotent state: majoritarian democracy. In the end, after decades of hostilities, which today give the impression of having been rearguard battles, albeit only because they were conquered by the force of the arms, the supporters of limited government and states' rights were eventually defeated in an election, that of 1860, which marked the end of the American experiment in self-government, at least in its original form. This event opened a new chapter in American history in which the federal government was destined to be the almost unchallenged protagonist.

From a doctrinal point of view, the playing field was now completely different. The natural law tradition that had dominated the early Republic had given way to a construction based on the dogma of sovereignty, though in an enormously looser understanding than the same-named variety worked out by the European jurists. The clash was now between those who championed the sovereignty of the individual states and those who championed the sovereignty of the federation. The term "sovereignty," which never appeared in Jefferson's Kentucky Resolutions, put in a timid appearance in the 1814 Hartford Convention,[8] subsequently bursting obsessively onto the scene on the occasion of the 1832 South Carolina nullification ordinance controversy. In that context, the constitutional theory upheld by Madison in the *Federalist*—that of a sovereignty divided between states and federation—became no longer operative. As is well known, the advocates of federal sovereignty emerged victorious, with their understanding of the expression "we, the people of the United States" as "we, the American people." It was conveniently forgotten that the first draft of the Constitution bore the names of all the states, and that the change into "We, the People" was recommended by the Committee on Style lest the enumeration of all the states by name caused embarrassment in those which may later not ratify the Constitution itself (in the event, none). In fact a "people of the Union" is never mentioned in the document and, from the institutional point of view, simply does not exist.

It is not easy to share the optimism of Michael Zuckert when he says that "Jefferson's...commitments...remain for the most part our commitments."[9] But clearly such a statement must be read in light of the irrepressible drive (that even the best scholars experience) of rendering the most eminent Founding Father our contemporary. What could be called the "institutional hypnosis"—the bizarre delusion that since the Constitution is basically the same, then this country must bear some similarities to the early republic—tends to cast the shadow of Jefferson over a time that does not belong to him in any way, namely our own. Although the questions surrounding "Jefferson today" have been avoided throughout this book, and with good reasons, the political heritage dilemma might be worth considering. The "whose icon" problem is indeed as difficult to solve as it is simple to answer. Thomas Jefferson would be the perfect icon—as well as the only legitimate one—of a conservative movement, if there were one in this country that was truly ready to be conservative in a Jeffersonian manner; that is, conservative of the American classical liberal tradition.

The decline of the natural law tradition during the nineteenth century was not an exclusively American phenomenon, but in the American context it involved specific problems and complexities, if for no other reason than the founders had taken the theory of natural law very seriously.[10] Its demise opened the floodgates to notions of government that were limited only on paper. Similarly, for the specific form assumed by American constitutional liberalism of the origins, namely federalism, as interpreted by Jefferson and his followers, its very success proved to be its undoing. Having lost its moorings in the theory of natural rights, it then became increasingly transformed into an instrument of ideological conflict between the two sections of the country, which were by now tantamount to veritable distinct nations.

In the end it was the presidency of Lincoln—the statesman who said, "The principles of Jefferson are the definitions and axioms of free society"[11]—that decided the destiny of the American experiment in limited and self-government. One of the major consequences of the metaconstitutional theory of the union as an end in and of itself, equating its dissolution with a "moral catastrophe," as embraced by Abraham Lincoln, was that of making American political thought more receptive to European theories, particularly the theory of sovereignty.[12] During what many historians call the Second Founding of the United States,[13] America proceeded toward a "normalization" of sorts, growing ever more similar to Europe. This process of convergence was to gather momentum during the last century, and it will probably go on unabated for generations.

Jefferson's America may perhaps be born again at any moment. Indeed, as the "shining city upon a hill" in political rhetoric, it has never died. But with regard to historical reality, it vanished forever at Gettysburg.

Notes

Chapter 1

[1] Thomas Jefferson, *Notes on the State of Virginia*, ed. William Peden (Chapel Hill: University of North Carolina Press, 1955) 147.

[2] The first edition of this volume, printed in a limited number of copies reserved for Jefferson's friends, was entitled Notes on the State of Virginia; written in the year 1781, somewhat corrected and enlarged in the winter of 1782, for the use of a foreigner of distinction...Paris, 1784–1785. The French translation is Morellet's Observations sur la Virginie (Paris: Barrois, 1786). The many errors and misrepresentations in this translation persuaded Jefferson to publish his work in England, with the title Notes on the State of Virginia (London: Stockdale, 1787) and later in America (Philadelphia: Prichard and Hall, 1788). On this point, see Dorothy Medlin, "Thomas Jefferson, André Morellet, and the French Version of Notes on the State of Virginia," William and Mary Quarterly 3rd series, 1/35 (January 1978): 85–99. Medlin argues that it was, in fact, a good standard translation for the times, and that Jefferson exaggerated disapproval of the French translation chiefly because he was not satisfied with his own work. The latest critical edition is edited by Frank Shuffelton (New York: Penguin Books, 1999).

[3] Jefferson to James Madison, 18 November 1788, *The Papers of Thomas Jefferson*, ed. Julian Boyd et al. (Princeton NJ: Princeton University Press, 1950) 14:188 (henceforth cited as *Papers*). Jefferson added: "The three authors have been named to me.... And was satisfied there was nothing in it by one of those hands, and not a great deal by a second. It does the highest honor to the third," Ibid. While it is true that John Jay ("one of those hands") wrote very few of the *Federalist*'s essay, Alexander Hamilton (the "second" hand referred to in the above quote) authored the vast majority of them. It thus appears that Jefferson was misinformed.

[4] James Parton, *Life of Thomas Jefferson, Third American President* (Boston: J. R. Osgood, 1874) iii.

[5] Merrill D. Peterson, *The Jefferson Image in the American Mind* (New York: Oxford University Press, 1960) vii.

[6] *New York Times Magazine*, 23 August 1992, quoted in Joyce O. Appleby, "Introduction: Jefferson and His Complex Legacy" in *Jeffersonian Legacies*, ed. Peter S. Onuf (Charlottesville: University Press of Virginia, 1993) 1.

[7] Fernand Braudel, *A History of Civilizations*, trans. and ed. R. Mayne (New York: Penguin Books, 1993) 458. It is noteworthy that the translator of this work did not bother to correct such a blatant error. The Gallic disregard for this particular point in American history has been displayed by the former French president Valery Giscard d'Estaing, who, presenting the draft Constitutional Treaty of the European Union, compared himself to Thomas Jefferson, "author of the American Constitution."

[8] Joseph Ellis, American Sphinx: The Character of Thomas Jefferson (New York: Vintage Books, 1998).

[9] Peterson, The Jefferson Image, 9.

[10] Akbar S. Ahmed, "Jefferson and Jinnah: Humanist Ideals and the Mythology of Nation-Building" in *The Future of Liberal Democracy: Thomas Jefferson and the Contemporary World*, ed. R. K. Ramazani and Robert Fatton, Jr., (New York: Palgrave, 2004) 88.

[11] Garrett W. Sheldon, *Jefferson & Atatürk: Political Philosophies* (New York: Peter Lang, 2000) ix.

[12] Ibid., xi.

[13] Yasushi Akashi, "Thomas Jefferson, Rights, and the Contemporary World" in *The Future of Liberal Democracy*, 153.

[14] Appleby, "Introduction: Jefferson and His Complex Legacy," 1.

[15] Although most people haven't seen those bills in a long time (they went out of print in the early 1980s and before that were used mostly at racetracks), it is interesting that those banknotes had the Jefferson effigy.

[16] Garrett W. Sheldon, *What Would Jefferson Say?* (New York: Berkeley, 1998).

[17] Charles M. Wiltse, *The Jeffersonian Tradition in American Democracy* (Chapel Hill: University of North Carolina Press, 1935) and James T. Adams, *The Living Jefferson* (New York: Scribner, 1935).

[18] Adams, The Living Jefferson, 14.

[19] Samuel B. Pettengill, *Jefferson, the Forgotten Man* (New York: America's Future, 1938).

[20] Ibid., 1–2.

[21] Ibid., ix.

[22] Merrill D. Peterson, "Afterword" in *Jeffersonian Legacies*, ed. Onuf, 462.

[23] George F. Hoar, "Introduction" in *The Writings of Thomas Jefferson*, ed. Andrew A. Lipscomb and Albert E. Bergh (Washington DC: Thomas Jefferson Memorial Association, 1904–1907), 1: 6–7 (henceforth cited as *Writings*).

[24] Leonard W. Levy, *Jefferson and Civil Liberties: The Darker Side* (Cambridge MA: Harvard University Press, 1963).

[25] John C. Miller, The Wolf by the Ears. Thomas Jefferson and Slavery (New York: Macmillan, 1977).

[26] Fawn M. Brodie, *Thomas Jefferson: An Intimate History* (New York: Norton, 1974).

[27] The charge of concubinage with the young slave was first levelled against the president by a disgruntled former ally, James Thomson Callender, in 1802 in the pages of the *Richmond Recorder* (1 September 1802). Cf. Michael Durey, *"With the Hammer of Truth": James Thomson Callender and America's Early National Heroes* (Charlottesville: University Press of Virginia, 1990) 158.

[28] Cf. Annette Gordon-Reed, *Thomas Jefferson and Sally Hemings: An American Controversy* (Charlottesville: University Press of Virginia, 1997).

[29] Peterson, The Jefferson Image, 187.

[30] This now seems a legitimate topic for the most serious historians; cf. *Sally Hemings and Thomas Jefferson: History, Memory and Civic Culture*, ed. Jan E. Lewis and Peter S. Onuf (Charlottesville: University Press of Virginia, 1999).

[31] On the basis of DNA tests, the author concluded,"The simplest and most probable explanation for our molecular findings are that Thomas Jefferson...was the father of Eston Hemings Jefferson." Eugene A. Foster, "Jefferson Fathered Slave's Last Child," *Nature* (5 November 1998) 27.

[32] Winthrop Jordan, *White over Black* (Chapel Hill: University of North Carolina Press, 1968). Jordan came to this decisive trail of evidence by the painstaking and accurate research on Jefferson's life carried out by Dumas Malone, one of the staunchest deniers of the whole affair.

[33] Daniel Jordan, President of Thomas Jefferson Memorial Foundation, "Statement on the TJMF Research Committee Report on Thomas Jefferson and Sally Hemings" (Thomas Jefferson Memorial Foundation, Inc., 2000) 1.

[34] A book that refutes the Jefferson-Hemings affair is *The Jefferson-Hemings Myth: An American Travesty*, ed. Eyler R. Coates (Charlottesville: Jefferson Editions, 2001).

[35] Vernon Parrington, Main Currents in American Political Thought: An Interpretation of American Literature from the Beginnings to 1920: The Colonial Mind (New York: Harcourt Brace, 1927) 1:345–65. For other influential sketches of the Jeffersonian thought, see Richard Hofstadter's The American Political Tradition and the Men Who Made It (New York: Vintage Books, 1974) 22–56 and Daniel J. Boorstin's The Genius of American Politics (Chicago-London: University of Chicago Press, 1953) 84–94. Hofstadter tried to restore Jefferson to his proper place,

namely among the Founding Fathers, in tune with the most widespread ideas of his times, particularly on the matters of life, liberty, and property, the natural rights for whose protection a government can legitimately be established among men.

[36] Abraham Lincoln to H. L. Pierce et al., 6 April 1859, *The Collected Works of Abraham Lincoln*, ed. R. P. Basler (New Brunswick NJ: Rutgers University Press, 1953) 2:374–76. The letter is also reprinted in *The Writings of Thomas Jefferson*, 1:15.

[37] I am referring in particular to two Italian books on Jefferson: Malcolm Sylvers, *Il pensiero politico e sociale di Thomas Jefferson* (Manduria Italy: Lacaita, 1993) and Federico Mioni, *Thomas Jefferson e la scommessa dell'autogoverno: virtù, popolo e "ward system"* (Reggio Emilia Italy: Diabasis, 1995). Among the American works offering a view of Jeffersonian thought ranging from the communitarian to the proto-socialist, see Staughton Lynd, *Intellectual Origins of American Radicalism* (New York: Random House, 1968) 67–88; Garry Wills, *Inventing America: Jefferson's Declaration of Independence* (New York: Doubleday, 1978); and Richard K. Matthews, *The Radical Politics of Thomas Jefferson. A Revisionist View* (Lawrence: University Press of Kansas, 1984).

[38] Cf. Howard L. Parsons, *Self, Global Issues, and Ethics* (Amsterdam Netherlands: Grüner, 1980) 49–66.

[39] Cf. Ronald T. Takaki, Iron Cages: Race and Culture in Nineteenth-Century America (New York: Knopf, 1979) 36–65.

[40] A. M. Karimskii, "The Problem of Human Rights in the 'Declaration of Independence' and Current Ideological Conflicts in the United States," *Soviet Studies in Philosophy* 16/1 (Winter 1977–1978) 35–51.

[41] Jim Blissett, Agrarian Socialism in America. Marx, Jefferson, and Jesus in the Oklahoma Countryside 1904–1920 (Norman: University of Oklahoma Press, 1999) 66.

[42] Ibid., 183. The author, however, does not provide specific examples of the socialists' utilization of Thomas Jefferson as one of their patron saints.

[43] Parrington, *Main Currents in American Thought*, 347–62, and Stuart G. Brown, *Thomas Jefferson* (New York: Washington Square Press, 1966) 220–23.

[44] Lawrence K. Kaplan, *Jefferson and France: An Essay on Politics and Political Ideas* (New Haven CT: Yale University Press, 1967) 36.

[45] Cf. Conor C. O'Brien, *The Long Affair: Thomas Jefferson and the French Revolution, 1785–1800* (Chicago: University of Chicago Press, 1996).

[46] Cf. ibid., 144.

[47] Cf. ibid., 12.

[48] Paul M. Spurlin, *Rousseau in America 1760–1809* (Tuscaloosa: University of Alabama Press, 1969) 65.

[49] More generally, "Every indication points to the fact that Americans did not consider Rousseau's treatise of paramount importance." Ibid., 66.

[50] Jefferson to Antoine Louis Claude Destutt de Tracy, 26 January 1811, *Writings*, 13:20. This suggests that B. B. Kendrick was right when he said in 1941 that Jefferson was a "Girondist" (a term from the French political spectrum). See B. B. Kendrick, "The Colonial Status of the South," *Journal of Southern History* 8 (February 1942) 3–22.

[51] William Leggett, *The* (New York) *Plaindealer*, 15 April 1837, in *Democratick* [sic] *Editorials: Essays in Jacksonian Political Economy*, ed. L. H. White (Indianapolis: Liberty Press, 1984) 54–55.

[52] Charles A. Culberson, "Jefferson and the Constitution," *Writings*, 9:10.

[53] Ernest M. Halliday, *Understanding Thomas Jefferson* (New York: HarperCollins, 2002) 140.

[54] Thomas Jefferson, "Report of the Commissioners for the University of Virginia," 4 August 1818, in *Early History of the University of Virginia, as contained in the letters of Thomas Jefferson and Joseph C. Cabell* (Richmond VA: J. W. Randolph, 1856) 501.

[55] Thomas Jefferson, "Response to the Citizens of Albemarle," 12 February 1790, *Papers*, 16:179.

[56] J. W. Cooke, "Jefferson on Liberty," *Journal of the History of Ideas* 34/4 (October–December 1973): 575.

[57] Ibid.

[58] Michael Zuckert, "Response" in *Thomas Jefferson and the Politics of Nature*, ed. Thomas S. Engeman (Notre Dame IN: University of Notre Dame Press, 2000) 197.

[59] Cf. Patrick Riley, The General Will Before Rousseau: The Transformation of the Divine into the Civic (Princeton NJ: Princeton University Press, 1986).

[60] Gordon S. Wood, "The Trials and Tribulations of Thomas Jefferson" in *Jeffersonian Legacies*, ed. Onuf, 400.

[61] Jefferson to John Adams, 12 September 1821, *The Adams-Jefferson Letters. The Complete Correspondence Between Thomas Jefferson and Abigail and John Adams*, ed. Lester J. Cappon (Chapel Hill: University of North Carolina Press, 1988) 575 (henceforth cited as *The Adams-Jefferson Letters*).

[62] Jefferson to Joseph Priestley, 21 March 1801, *Writings*, 10:229.

Chapter 2

¹ Junius Americanus (Arthur Lee), *Boston Evening Post*, 4 May 1772, quoted in Steven M. Dworetz, *The Unvarnished Doctrine. Locke, Liberalism and the American Revolution* (Durham NC: Duke University Press, 1990).

² Cf. *Annals of the Congress of the United States*, 1st Cong., 1st sess., 22 May 1789 (Washington DC: Government Printing Office, 1834–1856) 418–22. This episode is also narrated in Walter Berns, "Religion and the Founding Principle" in *The Moral Foundations of the American Republic*, ed. R. H. Horowitz (Charlottesville: University Press of Virginia, 1986) 215–16. Thomas Jefferson recalled this vote in 1819, stressing the purely political nature of the decision: "In the cases of two persons..., the federal court had determined that one of them (Duane) was not a citizen; the House of Representatives nevertheless determined that the other (Smith, of South Carolina) was a citizen, and admitted him to his seat in their body. Duane was a republican, and Smith a federalist, and these decisions were made during the federal ascendancy." Jefferson to S. Roane, 6 September 1819, *The Writings of Thomas Jefferson*, ed. Andrew A. Lipscomb and Albert E. Bergh (Washington DC: Thomas Jefferson Memorial Association, 1904–1907) 15:215 (henceforth cited as *Writings*).

³ In the April and May 1800 issues of the *Historisches Journal*, published in Berlin, Gentz wrote two parts of a long essay on the American and the French Revolutions. It was immediately translated and published as Friedrich von Gentz, *The Origin and Principles of the American Revolution Compared with the Origin and Principles of the French Revolution* (Philadelphia: Asbury Dickins, 1800) and reprinted as *The French and American Revolutions Compared* with an introduction by Russell Kirk (Chicago: Regnery, 1955).

⁴ Von Gentz, Revolutions Compared, 47.

⁵ Ibid., 56.

⁶ Edmund Burke, "Speech in Support of Resolutions for Conciliation with the American Colonies," 22 March 1775, in *On the American Revolution*, ed. Elliot R. Barkan (Gloucester MA: Peter Smith, 1972) 82.

⁷ John Reid, "The Irrelevance of the Declaration" in *Law in the American Revolution and the Revolution in the Law: A Collection of Review Essays on American Legal History*, ed. Hendrick Hartog (New York: New York University Press, 1981) 47.

⁸ Ibid., 87–88.

⁹ John Reid, Constitutional History of the American Revolution: The Authority of Rights (Madison: University of Wisconsin Press, 1986) 90.

¹⁰ Robert E. Brown, *Reinterpretation of the Formation of the Constitution* (Boston: Boston University Press, 1963) 21.

¹¹ Russel Kirk, *The Conservative Mind. From Burke to Eliot* (Chicago: Gateway, 1986) 72. This was first published as *The Conservative Mind, from Burke to Santayana* (Chicago: Regnery, 1953).

¹² Cf. Otto Vossler, Die Amerikanischen Revolutionsideale in Ihren Verhältnis zu den Europäischen: Untersuch an Thomas Jefferson; English edition: Jefferson and the American Revolutionary Ideal, with an introduction by Bernard Wishy, trans. Catherine Philippon and Bernard Wishy (Washington DC: University Press of America, 1980). Cf. also Robert R. Palmer, "A Neglected Work: Otto Vossler on Jefferson and the Revolutionary Era," William and Mary Quarterly 3rd series, 12/3 (July 1955): 462–71.

¹³ John Davis, "A Preface Dedicatory," Le Primer Report des Cases et Matters en Ley, quoted in Charles H. McIlwain, The Growth of Political Thought in the West. From the Greeks to the End of the Middle Ages (New York: Macmillan, 1953) 365.

¹⁴ James Otis, "The Rights of the British Colonies Asserted and Proved," *Pamphlets of the American Revolution (1750–1765)*, ed. Bernard Bailyn (Cambridge MA: Harvard University Press, 1965) 444.

¹⁵ Quoted in Edward S. Corwin, *The "Higher Law" Background of American Constitutional Law* (Ithaca NY: Cornell University Press, 1955) 24.

¹⁶ Thomas Jefferson, *Notes on the State of Virginia*, ed. William Peden (Chapel Hill: University of North Carolina Press, 1955) 65.

¹⁷ Cf. Jefferson, "Draft Instructions to the Virginia Delegates in the Continental Congress" (MS text of *Summary View, &c.*), *The Papers of Thomas Jefferson*, ed. Julian Boyd et al. (Princeton NJ: Princeton University Press, 1950) 1:121–37 (henceforth cited as *Papers*).

¹⁸ Cf. H. Trevor Colbourn, The Lamp of Experience: Whig History and the Intellectual Origins of the American Revolution (Chapel Hill: University of North Carolina Press, 1965).

¹⁹ Alessandro Passerin D'Entrèves, *La dottrina del diritto naturale* (Milano Italy: Edizioni di Comunità, 1980) 65.

²⁰ Berns, "Religion and the Founding Principle," 217.

²¹ Yehoshua Arieli, *Individualism and Naturalism in American Ideology* (Cambridge MA: Harvard University Press, 1964) 25–26.

²² Edward J. Erler, "The Great Fence to Liberty: The Right to Property in the American Founding" in *Liberty, Property, and the Foundations of the American*

Constitution, ed. Ellen Frankel Paul and Howard Dickman (Albany: State University of New York Press, 1989) 47.

[23] Carl L. Becker, The Declaration of Independence, a Study in the History of Political Ideas (New York: Harcourt Brace, 1922).

[24] Ibid., 79.

[25] Louis Hartz, The Liberal Tradition in America: An Interpretation of American Political Thought since the Revolution (New York: Harcourt Brace, 1955) 140.

[26] For two articles that put into focus what was going on in American historiography, cf. Robert E. Shalhope, "Toward a Republican Synthesis: The Emergence of an Understanding of Republicanism in American Historiography," *William and Mary Quarterly* 3rd series, 29/3 (January 1972): 49–80, and idem, "Republicanism and Early American Historiography," *William and Mary Quarterly* 3rd series, 39/2 (April 1982): 334–56.

[27] Jefferson to John Trumball, 18 January 1789, *Papers*, 14:561.

[28] Jefferson to Benjamin Rush, 16 January 1811, *Writings*, 13:4.

[29] Jefferson to Thomas Mann Randolph, 30 May 1790, *Papers*, 16:449.

[30] Cf. in particular, Garry Wills, *Inventing America: Jefferson's Declaration of Independence* (New York: Doubleday, 1978). This book has been criticized with well-deserved severity; cf. Ronald Hamowy, "Jefferson and the Scottish Enlightenment: A Critique of Garry Wills's Inventing America," *William and Mary Quarterly* 3rd series, 36/4 (October 1979): 503–23, and Kenneth S. Lynn, "Falsifying Jefferson," *Commentary* 66/4 (October 1978): 66–71.

[31] Cf. Wills, *Inventing America*, and Richard K. Matthews, *The Radical Politics of Thomas Jefferson. A Revisionist View* (Lawrence: University Press of Kansas, 1984).

[32] Cf. Caroline Robbins, The Eighteenth-Century Commonwealthman. Studies in the Transmission, Development, and Circumstances of English Liberal Thought from the Restoration of Charles II Until the War of the Thirteen Colonies (Cambridge MA: Harvard University Press, 1959).

[33] Among the severest critiques—to the point of being a virtual obituary for the entire school—is Daniel T. Rodgers, "Republicanism: The Career of a Concept," *Journal of American History* 79/1 (June 1992): 11–38; cf. also Shalhope, "Republicanism and Early American Historiography."

[34] It is the title of a lecture held by Pocock in 1980 and later published as J. G. A. Pocock, "The Myth of John Locke and the Obsession with Liberalism" in *John Locke*, ed. J. G. A. Pocock and Richard Ashcraft (Los Angeles: William Andrews Clark Memorial Library, University of California, 1980). The major works of the

school, as far as the founding of America is concerned, are Bernard Bailyn's *The Ideological Origins of the American Revolution* (Cambridge MA: Harvard University Press, 1967); Gordon S. Wood's *The Creation of the American Republic, 1776–1787* (Chapel Hill: University of North Carolina Press, 1969); J. G. A. Pocock's *The Machiavellian Moment. Florentine Political Thought and the Atlantic Republican Tradition* (Princeton NJ: Princeton University Press, 1975); and Lance Banning's *The Jeffersonian Persuasion, Evolution of a Party Ideology* (Ithaca NY: Cornell University Press, 1978).

[35] Wood, The Creation of the American Republic, 60–61.

[36] Cf. Rodgers, "Republicanism," 18.

[37] Ibid., 16. On the same page, the author terms this Pocockian lineage "exhilarating."

[38] Cf. John M. Murrin, "The Great Inversion, or Court versus Country: A Comparison of the Revolution Settlements in England (1688–1721) and America (1776–1816)" in *Three British Revolutions: 1641, 1688, 1776*, ed. J. G. A. Pocock (Princeton NJ: Princeton University Press, 1980) 368–453.

[39] Cf. Pocock, The Machiavellian Moment and Banning, Jeffersonian Persuasion.

[40] J. G. A. Pocock, "Virtue and Commerce in the Eighteenth Century," *Journal of Interdisciplinary History* 3/1, (Summer 1972): 124.

[41] Such a language can also be understood in a different way. Various works challenge the view that virtue was a uniquely republican notion: John Diggins, *The Lost Soul of American Politics: Virtue, Self-Interest, and the Foundations of Liberalism* (New York: Basic Books, 1984) and James T. Kloppenberg, "The Virtues of Liberalism: Christianity, Republicanism, and Ethics in Early American Political Discourse," *Journal of American History* 74 (June 1987): 11–16. These publications argue very persuasively that the colonists shared a belief in a protestant and distinctively Lockean concept of virtue. Analyzing colonial political language, Jack Green concludes that "the significance of the concept of civic virtue in early America may have been considerably inflated" (Green, "The Concept of Virtue ·in Late Colonial British America" in *Virtue, Corruption, Self-Interest. Political Values in the Eighteenth Century*, ed. Richard K. Matthews [Cranbury NJ: Associated University Press, 1994] 48).

[42] In 1965, Pocock, while reviewing Caroline Robbins's, *The Eighteenth-Century Commonwealthman*, one of the first republican endeavors, stated, "It is clear that the textbook account of Augustan political thought as Locke *et praeterea nihil* [and nothing more] badly needs revision" (J. G. A. Pocock, "Machiavelli, Harrington, and English Political Ideologies in the Eighteenth Century," *William*

and *Mary Quarterly* 3rd series, 22/3 [October 1965]: 551). In the following decades, however, he decided to go against this notion of "Locke *et praeterea nihil*," and his research program became so bold that in order to go along with his stunning scholarship, one has to forget almost everything learned from other authors, especially those trapped in the Lockean myth. No doubt he "has been the most insistent in repudiating Locke's influence on the entire century," Isaac Kramnick, *Republicanism and Bourgeois Radicalism. Political Ideology in Late Eighteenth-Century England and America* (Ithaca NY: Cornell University Press, 1990) 167. Cf. also John H. Hexter, "Republic, Virtue, Liberty, and the Political Universe of J. G. A. Pocock" in *On Historians: Reappraisals of Some of the Makers of Modern History* (Cambridge MA: Harvard University Press, 1979) 293–303. Pocock's influence has been rather impressive: Jürgen Habermas's reflections on "Verfassungpatriotismus" (constitutional patriotism), for instance, are largely a philosophical elaboration on republican and Pocockian themes; cf. Jürgen Habermas, *Faktiziät und Geltung* (Frankfurt Germany: Suhrkamp, 1992) and *Die Einbeziehung des Anderen* (Frankfurt Germany: Suhrkamp, 1996). English versions: Jürgen Habermas, *Between Facts and Norms. Contributions to a Discourse Theory of Law and Democracy*, trans. William Rehg (Cambridge MA: MIT Press, 1996) and idem, *The Inclusion of the Other. Studies in Political Theory*, ed. Ciaran Cronin and Pablo De Greif (Cambridge MA, MIT Press, 1998). Habermas does not seem to be fully aware of the fact that Pocock's research program has been effectively challenged and many of his followers have settled for a much more modest paradigm.

[43] Dworetz, The Unvarnished Doctrine, 12.

[44] Joyce O. Appleby, *Liberalism and Republicanism in the Historical Imagination* (Cambridge MA: Harvard University Press, 1992) 133.

[45] Cf. Philip Pettit, *Republicanism. A Theory of Freedom and Government* (Oxford: Clarendon Press, 1997) and Quentin Skinner, *Liberty Before Liberalism* (Cambridge: Cambridge University Press, 1998) 80–86.

[46] Isaac Kramnick, "Republican Revisionism Revisited," *American Historical Review* 87 (June 1982): 630.

[47] Wood, *The Creation of the American Republic*, 59. We also are left with a little puzzle here: How is it that American culture is nowadays individualist, while at the founding it was not?

[48] J. G. A. Pocock, Virtue, Commerce, History, Essays on Political Thought and History, Chiefly in the Eighteenth Century (Cambridge: Cambridge University Press, 1985) 40–41.

[49] Pettit, *Republicanism*, 271.

[50] Wood, The Creation of the American Republic, 53.

[51] Gordon S. Wood, The Radicalism of the American Revolution. How a Revolution Transformed a Monarchical Society into a Democratic One Unlike Any That Had Ever Existed (New York: Knopf, 1992) 178.

[52] Pocock, Virtue, Commerce, History, 48.

[53] Joyce O. Appleby, Capitalism and a New Social Order: The Republican Vision of the 1790s (New York: New York University Press, 1984) 18.

[54] Wood, The Creation of the American Republic, 68.

[55] Pocock, The Machiavellian Moment, 499.

[56] William Galston, *Liberal Purposes: Goods, Virtues, and Diversity in the Liberal State* (Cambridge: Cambridge University Press, 1991) 225.

[57] Jefferson to Francis W. Gilmer, 7 June 1816, *Writings*, 15:24.

[58] Cf. Michael Zuckert, Natural Rights and the New Republicanism (Princeton NJ: Princeton University Press, 1994) and Zuckert, The Natural Rights Republic, Studies in the Foundation of the American Political Tradition (Notre Dame IN: University of Notre Dame Press, 1996).

[59] Zuckert, Natural Rights and the New Republicanism, 165.

[60] Richard H. Fallon, Jr., "What is Republicanism and Is It Worth Reviving?" *Harvard Law Review* 102/7 (May 1989): 1698–99.

[61] In order to appreciate the ideology of Pocock, very much in line with the old Labour Party that is as fiercely anti-free market as anti-Marxist, cf. the prefaces to the various editions of his methodological studies: J. G. A. Pocock, *Politics, Language and Time. Essays on Political Thought and History* (New York: Atheneum, 1971) and particularly the new preface of the revised edition of 1989 (Chicago: University of Chicago Press, 1989). Kramnick, one of Pocock's favorite polemical targets, notes with some truth, "Pocock sees liberalism as a mere popular front for Marxism" (Kramnick, *Republicanism and Bourgeois Radicalism*, 37). Joyce Appleby is probably right in her harsh judgment of Pocock: "One sometimes gets the impression that Pocock entered the world of civic humanism as a scholar and remained to become a partisan" (Appleby, *Liberalism and Republicanism*, 133).

[62] Michael J. Sandel, *Democracy's Discontent, America in Search of a Public Philosophy* (Cambridge MA: Harvard University Press, 1996) 123–67.

[63] Michael J. Sandel, review of John Diggins's *The Lost Soul of American Politics* in *The New Republic* (10 June 1985): 39. Of course, one can expect something so candid only from a public intellectual.

[64] Michael J. Sandel, "Morality and the Liberal Idea," *The New Republic* (7 May 1984): 17. For a Communitarian and republican complete blending, cf. Adrian Oldfield, *Citizenship and Community: Civic Republicanism and the Modern World* (London: Routledge, 1990).

[65] Alasdair MacIntyre, *After Virtue: A Study in Moral Theory* (London: Duckworth, 1981) 69.

[66] Michael Walzer, "The Communitarian Critique of Liberalism," *Political Theory* 18/1 (February 1990): 19.

[67] Ibid., 20.

[68] Ibid., 204.

[69] Cf. Cass Sunstein, "Beyond the Republican Revival," *Yale Law Journal* 98/8 (1988): 1539–90.

[70] Cass Sunstein, "Naked Preferences," *Columbia Law Review* 84/7 (1984): 1731.

[71] Jean-Jacques Rousseau, *The Social Contract and Discourses*, trans. G. D. H. Cole (London: J. M. Dent, 1946) 68.

[72] Pocock, The Machiavellian Moment, 504.

[73] Maurizio Viroli, *Jean-Jacques Rousseau and the 'Well-Ordered Society'* (Cambridge: Cambridge University Press, 1989) 11.

[74] Ibid., 6. In the same page, we learn that "Rousseau…sees the State as a guarantor of property rights."

[75] Richard Dagger, *Civic Virtues: Rights, Citizenship, and Republican Liberalism* (New York: Oxford University Press, 1997) 92.

[76] Ibid., 97.

[77] For a critical assessment of Sandel's Rousseau, cf. Jonathan Marks, "Jean-Jacques Rousseau, Michael J. Sandel and the Politics of Transparency," *Polity* 33/4 (June 2001): 619–43.

[78] Sandel, Democracy's Discontent, 319.

[79] Ibid., 347.

[80] Asher Horowitz and Richard K. Matthews, "'Narcissism of the Minor Differences': What Is at Issue and What Is at Stake in the Civic Humanism Question," *Polity* 30/1 (Autumn 1997): 7–9.

[81] Cf. Dagger, *Civic Virtues*.

[82] Lance Banning, "The Republican Interpretation: Retrospect and Prospect" in *The Republican Synthesis Revisited, Essays in Honor of George Athan Billias*, ed. M. M. Klein, R. D. Brown, and J. B. Hench (Worcester MA: American Antiquarian Society, 1992) 93–94.

[83] Zuckert, The Natural Rights Republic, 208–209.

[84] Lance Banning, "Jeffersonian Ideology Revisited: Liberal and Classical Ideas in the New American Republic," *William and Mary Quarterly* 3rd series, 43/1 (January 1986): 11n.

[85] "The American Revolution was therefore an American Secession and not a British Revolution," J. G. A. Pocock, "Political Thought in the English-Speaking Atlantic, 1760–1790. Part 1: The Imperial Crisis" in *The Varieties of British Political Thought 1500–1800*, ed. J. G. A. Pocock (Cambridge: Cambridge University Press, 1993) 280. This clearly is a fundamental change of perspective for the editor and inspirer of *Three British Revolutions*.

[86] Zuckert, The Natural Rights Republic, 209.

[87] Wood, The Radicalism of the American Revolution, 7.

[88] On this point, cf. Joyce Appleby's criticism of Wood: Joyce O. Appleby, "The Radical Recreation of the American Republic" in *William and Mary Quarterly* 3rd series, 51/4 (1994): 679–83.

[89] Wood, The Radicalism of the American Revolution, 369.

[90] Cf. Zuckert, Natural Rights and the New Republicanism; Zuckert, The Natural Rights Republic; Dworetz, The Unvarnished Doctrine; Richard C. Sinopoli, The Foundations of American Citizenship: Liberalism, the Constitution, and Civic Virtue (New York: Oxford University Press, 1992).

[91] Paul A. Rahe, Republics Ancient and Modern: Classical Republicanism and the American Revolution (Chapel Hill: University of North Carolina Press, 1992) 570.

[92] Jerome Huyler, *Locke in America. The Moral Philosophy of the Founding Era* (Lawrence: University Press of Kansas, 1995) 39.

[93] Cf. Diggins, The Lost Soul of American Politics, 364–65.

[94] Cf. Jennifer Nedelsky, Private Property and the Limits of American Constitutionalism. The Madisonian Framework and Its Legacy (Chicago: University of Chicago Press, 1990).

[95] Cf. Pocock, *Virtue, Commerce, History*, 44–48.

[96] Jefferson to James Madison, 9 June 1793, *Papers*, 26:240.

[97] Hannah Arendt, *On Revolution* (New York: Viking, 1963) 125–26.

[98] Ibid., 115.

[99] Ibid., 258–59 (italics added).

[100] Pocock, The Machiavellian Moment, 529–33.

[101] Cf. Pocock, *Virtue, Commerce, History*, 77–84.

[102] Pocock, "Political Thought in the English-Speaking Atlantic, 1760–1790," 281.

[103] Ibid., 282.

[104] In fact, Pauline Maier is correct when she suggests that the Declaration must be thought of as a whole American endeavor. However, dissenting "from any suggestion that Jefferson alone was responsible for the Declaration of

Independence...or that the full story of the Declaration can be told apart from that of the Independence it declared and the process that led to it" (Pauline Maier, *American Scripture. Making the Declaration of Independence* [New York: A.J. Knopf, 1997] xvii) should not be carried to the extremes. Thomas Jefferson was not the principal or the most important drafter of the Declaration, as it is fashionable to hint nowadays, he authored it. Joint writing had not been invented in those times, and arguably it is not still perfected in ours. He was the author, the committee made comments, Congress reshaped it, but it was a rather less "collective enterprise" than the independence the document was declaring. The "harmonizing sentiments" needed a harmonizer and Thomas Jefferson became the instrument. Until new evidence is found on this subject, there isn't any need to amend the account passed on by the revolutionary generation. (In addition, would Jefferson lay on his deathbed by appropriating a document whose paternity he could not claim because it was the work of a committee?)

[105] Cf. Lance Banning, The Quarrel with Federalism: A Study in the Origins and Character of Republican Thought, Ph.D. diss. (St. Louis MO: Washington University, 1971).

[106] Lance Banning, "Republican Ideology and the Triumph of the Constitution, 1789 to 1793," *William and Mary Quarterly* 3rd series, 31/2 (April 1974): 178–79.

[107] Cf. Banning, Jeffersonian Persuasion.

[108] Bailyn, Ideological Origins.

[109] Cf., among others, James H. Hutson, "Country, Court, and Constitution: Antifederalism and the Historians," *William and Mary Quarterly* 3rd series, 38/3 (July 1981): 337–68.

[110] Forrest McDonald, *The Presidency of Thomas Jefferson* (Lawrence: Kansas University Press, 1976) 19–22.

[111] Jefferson to W. S. Smith, 13 November 1787, *Papers*, 12:356.

[112] In this respect, Peter S. Onuf might be correct in stating that "spending on education constituted the grand and significant exception to Jefferson's minimal state, for this was precisely the kind of public investment that would foster the welfare of the rising generation without wasting its future prospects." Onuf, *Jefferson's Empire*, 119. See also Jennings L. Wagoner, Jr., *Jefferson and Education* (Monticello VA: Thomas Jefferson Foundation, 2004).

[113] Joyce O. Appleby, "What Is Still American in the Political Philosophy of Thomas Jefferson," *William and Mary Quarterly* 3rd series, 39/2 (April 1982): 293.

Chapter 3

[1] Frédéric Bastiat, "Property and Law" in *Selected Essays on Political Economy*, trans. Seymour Cain, ed. George B. de Huszar (Irvington-on-Hudson NY: Foundation for Economic Education, 1964) 97.

[2] Cf. Peter S. Onuf, "The Scholars' Jefferson," *William and Mary Quarterly* 3rd series, 50 (October 1993): 671–99.

[3] Jefferson, "Original Rough Draught of the Declaration of Independence," *The Papers of Thomas Jefferson*, ed. Julian Boyd et al. (Princeton NJ: Princeton University Press, 1950) 1:423–24 (henceforth cited as *Papers*). The quotation is from the first version drafted by Jefferson.

[4] This change was once attributed to Benjamin Franklin then generally deemed as inserted by Jefferson himself. Cf. Boyd, "Editorial Note," Papers, 1:427. More recently, the view that the author of the change could actually have been Franklin is gaining favor. Cf. for the pro-Franklin view, Walter Isaacson, *Benjamin Franklin: An American Life* (New York: Simon & Schuster, 2003).

[5] Michael Zuckert ("Self-Evident Truth and the Declaration of Independence," *Review of Politics* 49/2 [Summer 1987]: 319–39) contends that "self-evident" is to be related to the initial "we hold," thus weakening the axiomatic basis of natural rights and stressing its political significance.

[6] The pursuit of happiness captured the scholars' attention in past generations, but it is now the "self-evident" truths that draw most of the intellectual consideration. Cf. Allen Jayne, *Jefferson's Declaration of Independence: Origins, Philosophy, and Theology* (Lexington: University Press of Kentucky, 1998) 109–38 and Hans L. Heicholz, *Harmonizing Sentiments: The Declaration of Independence and the Jeffersonian Idea of Self-Government* (New York: Peter Lang, 2000).

[7] Cf. Morton White, *The Philosophy of the American Revolution* (New York: Oxford University Press, 1978) 9–96.

[8] Cf. the discussion of Locke's concept of self-evidence in White, *The Philosophy of the American Revolution*, 15–20, 23–36.

[9] Jefferson to James Madison, 6 September 1789, *Papers*, 15:392.

[10] Jefferson to Thomas Earle, 24 September 1823, *The Writings of Thomas Jefferson*, ed. Andrew A. Lipscomb and Albert E. Bergh (Washington DC: Thomas Jefferson Memorial Association, 1904–1907) 15:470 (henceforth cited as *Writings*; italics added).

[11] Joyce O. Appleby, "Thomas Jefferson and the Psychology of Democracy" in *The Revolution of 1800. Democracy, Race, and the New Republic*, ed. James

Horn, Jan Ellen Lewis, and Peter S. Onuf (Charlottesville: University of Virginia Press, 2002) 161.

[12] Jefferson to John Cartwright, 5 June 1824, *Writings*, 16:44.

[13] Cf. Richard B. Bernstein, "Thomas Jefferson's Letter to Roger D. Weightman" in *Roots of the Republic: American Founding Documents Interpreted*, ed. Stephen L. Schechter (Madison WI: Madison House, 1990) 444.

[14] Jefferson to Roger Weightman, 24 June 1826, *The Writings of Thomas Jefferson*, ed. Paul L. Ford (New York: Putnam, 1892–1898) 10:391–92 (henceforth cited as *Writings* [Ford]).

[15] See, for instance, Ronald Hamowy, "Jefferson and the Scottish Enlightenment: A Critique of Garry Wills's *Inventing America*," *William and Mary Quarterly* 3rd series, 36/4 (October 1979): 507–508.

[16] John Locke, "An Essay Concerning the True Original, Extent, and End of Civil-Government," *Two Treatises on Government* (London: Awnsham and Churchill, 1698) 2/19 "Of the Dissolution of Government," §225, 341 (henceforth cited as *Two Treatises*).

[17] Jefferson, "Original Rough Draught of the Declaration of Independence," *Papers*, 1:424.

[18] Locke, *Two Treatises*, 344–45.

[19] Hamowy, "Jefferson and the Scottish Enlightenment," 519.

[20] "Whenever any Form of Government becomes destructive of these ends, it is the Right of the People to alter or to abolish it." Jefferson, "Original Rough Draught of the Declaration of Independence," 424.

[21] Jefferson to James Madison, 30 January 1787, *Papers*, 11:92–93.

[22] Jefferson to Edward Carrington, 16 January 1787, *Papers*, 11:49.

[23] Robert K. Faulkner, "Jefferson and the Enlightened Science of Liberty" in *Reason and Republicanism. Thomas Jefferson's Legacy of Liberty*, ed. Gary L. McDowell and Sharon L. Noble (Lanham MD: Rowman & Littlefield, 1997) 33.

[24] Jefferson to Edward Carrington, 27 May 1788, *Papers*, 13:208.

[25] Joseph J. Ellis, *American Sphinx: The Character of Thomas Jefferson* (New York: Vintage Books, 1998) 69.

[26] Cf. James R. Stoner, Jr., Common Law and Liberal Theory: Coke, Hobbes, and the Origins of American Constitutionalism (Lawrence: University Press of Kansas, 1992) 137.

[27] In a letter to Madison, Jefferson noted, "Richard Henry Lee charged it as copied from Locke's treatise on government." Jefferson to James Madison, 30 August 1823, *Writings*, 15:462. Lee was one of the few people to receive a copy of the

original rough draft, and he believed that Congress had worsened the document. Cf. Dumas Malone, *Jefferson the Virginian* (Boston: Little, Brown, 1948) 230.

[28] Jefferson to Henry Lee, Jr., 8 May 1825, *Writings*, 16:118.

[29] Jefferson to Benjamin Rush, 16 January 1811, *Writings* [Ford], 9:296.

[30] Richard K. Matthews, *The Radical Politics of Thomas Jefferson. A Revisionist View* (Lawrence: University Press of Kansas, 1984) 135.

[31] Jefferson, "From the Minutes of the Board of Visitors," University of Virginia, 3 October 1825, *Writings*, 29:461.

[32] Cf. Willmore Kendall, *John Locke and the Doctrine of Majority Rule* (Urbana: University of Illinois Press, 1965).

[33] Garry Wills, *Inventing America: Jefferson's Declaration of Independence* (New York: Doubleday, 1978). As illustrated in chapter 2, this work has been attacked with well-deserved severity. Cf. Ronald Hamowy, "Jefferson and the Scottish Enlightenment" and Kenneth S. Lynn, "Falsifying Jefferson," 66–71.

[34] Garrett W. Sheldon, The Political Philosophy of Thomas Jefferson (Baltimore: Johns Hopkins University Press, 1991); Michael Zuckert, The Natural Rights Republic: Studies in the Foundation of the American Political Tradition (Notre Dame IN: University of Notre Dame Press, 1996) 209.

[35] Forrest McDonald, *Novus Ordo Seclorum: The Intellectual Origins of the Constitution* (Lawrence: University Press of Kansas, 1985) 1.

[36] Vernon L. Parrington, Main Currents in American Political Thought: An Interpretation of American Literature from the Beginnings to 1920: The Beginnings of Critical Realism in America, 1860–1920 (New York: Harcourt Brace, 1930) 3:410–11.

[37] Abraham Lincoln to H. L. Pierce et al., 6 April 1859, *The Collected Works of Abraham Lincoln*, ed. R. P. Basler (New Brunswick NJ: Rutgers University Press, 1953) 2:374–76.

[38] Ibid.

[39] Charles E. Merriam, *History of American Political Theories* (New York: Macmillan, 1903).

[40] J. Allen Smith, *The Spirit of American Government* (New York: Macmillan, 1907).

[41] Charles A. Beard, An Economic Interpretation of the Constitution of the United States (New York: Macmillan, 1913) and Beard, Economic Origins of Jeffersonian Democracy (New York: Macmillan, 1915).

[42] Nedelsky, Private Property and the Limits of American Constitutionalism, 1.

[43] Edmund S. Morgan, "The American Revolution: Revisions in Need of Revising," *William and Mary Quarterly* 3rd series, 14/1 (January 1957): 11.

[44] Ibid., 12.

[45] Claudio J. Katz, "Thomas Jefferson's Liberal Anticapitalism," *American Journal of Political Science* 47/1 (January 2003): 1.

[46] Ibid., 2.

[47] Ibid., 8.

[48] Ibid., 13.

[49] Jefferson to Dr. Cooper, 10 September 1814, Thomas Jefferson, *Political Writings*, ed. Joyce Appleby and Terence Ball (Cambridge: Cambridge University Press, 1999) 137.

[50] Ibid.

[51] Ibid., 138.

[52] Ibid.

[53] Ibid., 139.

[54] Ibid.

[55] Ibid., 140.

[56] Cf. Matthews, *Radical Politics*, 19–29 and Edward Dumbauld, *Thomas Jefferson and the Law* (Norman: University of Oklahoma Press, 1978) 153.

[57] On this point, I am very much indebted to Michael Zuckert, "Thomas Jefferson on Nature and Natural Rights" in *The Framers and Fundamental Rights*, ed. Robert A. Licht (Washington DC: American Enterprise Institute, 1991) 166–69.

[58] Letter 62 (20 January 1721) in John Trenchard and Thomas Gordon, *Cato's Letters, or Essays on Liberty, Civil and Religious, and Other Important Subjects*, ed. Ronald Hamowy (Indianapolis: Liberty Press, 1994), 1:427.

[59] Jefferson to F. W. Gilmer, 27 June 1816, *Writings* [Ford], 10:32 (italics added).

[60] "I amused myself with reading seriously Plato's Republic.... I laid it down often to ask myself how it could have been that the world should have so long consented to give reputation to such nonsense as this?" Jefferson to John Adams, 5 July 1814, *The Adams-Jefferson Letters*, 432.

[61] Jefferson to Thomas Mann Randolph, 30 May 1790, *Papers*, 16:449.

[62] Parrington, Main Currents in American Thought, 1:350.

[63] Gisela Tauber, "Notes on the State of Virginia: Thomas Jefferson's Unintentional Self-Portrait," *Eighteenth Century Studies* 26/4 (Summer 1993): 645. It is a peculiarly preposterous idea, as well as unquestionably at odds with Lockean and Jeffersonian thought, that only property holders have property rights.

[64] Roots of the Republic, 154.

[65] Ibid., 196.

[66] "Pennsylvania Declaration of Rights, 1776" in *The Roots of the Bill of Rights*, ed. Bernard Schwartz (New York: Random House, 1971) 2:264.

[67] "New Hampshire Constitution, 1784" in *The Roots of the Bill of Rights*, 2:375.

[68] 129 Wis. 190, 108 N.W. (1906) 629 quoted in Stanley N. Katz, "Republicanism and the Law of Inheritance in the American Revolutionary Era," *Michigan Law Review* 66/1 (1977): 6.

[69] That it had been an aesthetic choice is affirmed by, among others, Adrienne Koch, *Power, Morals, and the Founding Fathers* (Ithaca NY: Cornell University Press, 1961) 28.

[70] Adrienne Koch, *The Philosophy of Thomas Jefferson* (New York: Columbia University Press, 1943) 175.

[71] Cecelia M. Kenyon, "Republicanism and Radicalism in the American Revolution: An Old-Fashioned Interpretation," *William and Mary Quarterly* 3rd series, 19/2 (April 1962): 172.

[72] William B. Scott, In Pursuit of Happiness: American Conceptions of Property from the Seventeenth to the Twentieth Century (Bloomington: Indiana University Press, 1977) 42.

[73] Jefferson, "Declaration of the Causes and Necessity for Taking up Arms," June–July 1775, *Papers*, 1:197 (italics added).

[74] Jefferson, "Declaration and Protest of the State of Virginia, 1825," *Writings*, 17:446 (italics added).

[75] Jefferson, "Reply to the Virginia Assembly, 1809," *Writings*, 16:33 (italics added).

[76] Jefferson to Admantios Coray, 31 October 1823, *Writings*, 15:489 (italics added).

[77] Jefferson, "Third Annual Message (17 October 1803)," *Writings*, 3:353 (italics added).

[78] Trenchard and Gordon, *Cato's Letters*, 4 February 1720, 1:110.

[79] Gilbert Chinard, *Thomas Jefferson: The Apostle of Americanism* (Boston: Little, Brown, 1929) 233. For a mention of this very same alleged anecdote, cf. Wills, *Inventing America*, 238.

[80] Jefferson, "Lafayette's Draft of a Declaration of Rights" (July 1789), *Papers*, 15:230.

[81] Julian Boyd, "Editorial Note," *Papers*, 15:233

[82] William Blackstone, *Commentaries on the Laws of England* (1765) (Chicago: University of Chicago Press, 1979) 1:134.

[83] Cf. *The Letters of Lafayette and Jefferson*, ed. Gilbert Chinard (Baltimore-Paris: Johns Hopkins Press and "Les Belles Lettres," 1929) 138.

[84] The letter is found in the Jefferson Papers at the Library of Congress and has been published in *The Complete Writings of Thomas Paine*, ed. Philip S. Foner (New York: Citadel Press, 1945) 2:1298–99.

[85] Cf. Chinard, *Thomas Jefferson*, 81. However, mistakes of this kind tend to multiply. Years later, one could come across articles that discussed Jefferson's view of property that based their major arguments on Paine's letter. Cf. Joyotpaul Chaudhuri, "Possession, Ownership, and Access: A Jeffersonian View of Property," *Political Inquiry* 1/1 (Fall 1973): 78–95.

[86] Gilbert Chinard, *Thomas Jefferson: The Apostle of Americanism*, rev. ed. (Ann Arbor: University of Michigan Press, 1957) 80.

[87] Cf. White, The Philosophy of the American Revolution, 195–228.

[88] The first scholar to draw attention to the Burlamaqui connection was Ray F. Harvey, *Jean Jacques Burlamaqui: A Liberal Tradition in American Constitutionalism* (Chapel Hill: University of North Carolina Press, 1937) 119–23.

[89] White, The Philosophy of the American Revolution, 214.

[90] Jean M. Yarbrough, "Jefferson and Property Rights" in *Liberty, Property, and the Foundations of the American Constitution*, ed. Ellen Frankel Paul and Howard Dickman (Albany: State University of New York Press, 1989) 69.

[91] Jean M. Yarbrough, *American Virtues: Thomas Jefferson on the Character of a Free People* (Lawrence: University Press of Kansas, 1998) 90.

[92] A. John Simmons, "Inalienable Rights and Locke's Treatises," *Philosophy and Public Affairs* 12/3 (Summer 1983): 175–204. The same essay has been reproduced with very significant alterations in A. John Simmons, *On the Edge of Anarchy: Locke, Consent, and the Limits of Society* (Princeton NJ: Princeton University Press, 1993) 101–46.

[93] Simmons, "Inalienable Rights," 180.

[94] Ibid.

[95] Jefferson to Handsome Lake, 3 November 1802, *Writings*, 16:395.

[96] Michael Zuckert, *Natural Rights and the New Republicanism* (Princeton NJ: Princeton University Press, 1994) 245.

[97] Zuckert, Natural Rights and the New Republicanism, 245–46.

[98] Jefferson, "From the Minutes of the Board of Visitors, University of Virginia, 1822–1825, Report to the President and Directors of the Literary Fund," 7 October 1822, *Writings*, 19:416.

[99] Ulpianus, *Digestæ*, 1.4.1.

[100] Cf. Jefferson to Isaac McPherson, 13 August 1813, *Writings*, 13:333–36; cf. David N. Mayer, *The Constitutional Thought of Thomas Jefferson* (Charlottesville: University Press of Virginia, 1994) 78.

[101] For the best case argued in the Jeffersonian and Rothbardian tradition, cf. N. Stephan Kinsella, "Against Intellectual Property," *Journal of Libertarian Studies* 15/2 (Spring 2001): 1–53.

[102] Murray N. Rothbard, *Man, Economy, and State* (Los Angeles: Nash, 1970) 652–60.

[103] Jefferson to Isaac McPherson, 13 August 1813, *Writings*, 13:335.

[104] Ibid.

[105] Jefferson to James Madison, 6 September 1789, *Papers*, 15:392–97. For well-reasoned comments on this letter, cf. Herbert Sloan, "The Earth Belongs in Usufruct to the Living" in *Jeffersonian Legacies*, ed. Peter S. Onuf (Charlottesville: University Press of Virginia, 1993) 281–315; Daniel J. Boorstin, *The Lost World of Thomas Jefferson* (Chicago: University of Chicago Press, 1948) 204–13; Adrienne Koch, *Jefferson and Madison: The Great Collaboration* (New York: Oxford University Press, 1964) 62–96; and Merrill D. Peterson, "Mr. Jefferson's 'Sovereignty of the Living Generation,'" *Virginia Quarterly Review* 52/3 (Summer 1976): 437–47.

[106] Jefferson to James Madison, 6 September 1789, *Papers*, 15:397.

[107] Locke, *Two Treatises*, 168–69.

[108] Jefferson to James Madison, 6 September 1789, *Papers*, 15:392.

[109] Ibid., 395.

[110] Boyd, "Editorial Note," *Papers*, 15:388.

[111] Noble E. Cunningham, Jr., *In Pursuit of Reason: The Life of Thomas Jefferson* (New York: Ballantine Books, 1988) 127.

[112] Jefferson to James Madison, 6 September 1789, *Papers*, 15:397.

[113] Ibid. Jefferson was soon to find out how wrong he was.

[114] Edmund Burke, "Speech on a Committee to Inquire into the State of the Representation on the Commons in Parliament, 1782," *The Portable Burke*, ed. Isaac Kramnik (London-New York: Penguin, 1999) 177.

[115] Ibid., 176–77.

[116] Ibid., 176.

[117] Ibid., 174.

[118] For a sample of unpersuasive pages on this Jeffersonian reflection, cf. Staughton Lynd, *Intellectual Origins of American Radicalism* (New York: Random House, 1968) 67–88; Matthews, *Radical Politics*, 19–29; and Wills, *Inventing America*, 132–48.

[119] Lynd, American Radicalism, 77.

[120] For a synthetic statement of this view, presented by this author in numerous works, cf. Crawford B. Macpherson, "The Social Bearings of Locke's Political Theory," *Western Political Quarterly* 7/1 (March 1954): 8.

[121] Henry George, *Progress and Poverty* (1877) (New York: Robert Schalkenbach Foundation, 1979) 347.

[122] On the Lockean proviso and its economic relevance, cf. Geoffrey Miller, "Economic Efficiency and the Lockean Proviso," *Harvard Journal of Law and Public Policy* 10/2 (1989): 401–10. Many economists of Austrian inclinations consider the Lockean proviso totally indefensible. Cf. Israel M. Kirzner, "Entrepreneurship, Entitlement, and Economic Justice" in *Reading Nozick: Essays on Anarchy, State, and Utopia*, ed. Jeffrey Paul (Totowa NJ: Rowman & Littlefield, 1981) 385–413; and Murray N. Rothbard, *The Ethics of Liberty* (New York: New York University Press, 1998) 244.

[123] Jefferson to James Madison, 28 October 1785, *Papers*, 8:682.

[124] Locke, *Two Treatises*, 185. This passage has given some legitimacy to the socialist interpretation of John Locke. Cf. Max Beer, *The History of British Socialism* (London: National Labour Press, 1921).

[125] Locke, *Two Treatises*, 185.

[126] Ibid.

[127] Ibid., 189–90.

[128] Ibid., 189.

[129] Compare and contrast paragraphs 27, 32, and 33 of *Two Treatises*.

[130] Cf. John L. Mackie, *Ethics: Inventing Right and Wrong* (Middlesex, England: Penguin, 1977) 176 and Jerome Tully, *A Discourse on Property: John Locke and his Adversaries* (Cambridge: Cambridge University Press, 1980) 163–70. According to these authors, Locke provided a specific window of opportunity for private property: from Creation to the invention of money. Were this not a fallacious interpretation, Jefferson could be considered both a consistent Lockean and a genuine enemy of private property.

[131] Locke, *Two Treatises*, 200.

[132] Ibid., 202 (italics added).

[133] Rothbard, The Ethics of Liberty, 244.

[134] Israel M. Kirzner, "Discovery, Private Property, and The Theory of Justice in Capitalist Society," *Journal des Économistes et des Études Humaines* 1/3 (October 1990): 221.

[135] Rothbard, The Ethics of Liberty, 49.

[136] Ibid.

[137] Robert Nozick, *Anarchy, State, and Utopia* (New York: Basic Books, 1974) 175–82.

[138] One should keep in mind that, according to the doctrines of Grotius, Vattel, and many others, *jus gentium* (international law) was, in fact, natural law. This was peculiarly so for Jefferson, who, in 1810, translated a Roman law passage "*Quod per Alluvionem agro tuo flumen adjecit*, jure gentium *tibi acquisitur*" in this manner: "What the river adds by Alluvion to your field becomes yours *by law of nature.*" Jefferson, *The Proceedings of the Government of the United States in Maintaining the Public Right to the Beach of the Mississippi, adjacent to New Orleans, against the Intrusion of Edward Livingston* (New York: Ezra Sargeant, 1812) 42 (italics added).

[139] Jefferson to James Madison, 6 September 1789, *Papers*, 15:396.

[140] Cf. James Madison to Jefferson, 4 February 1790, *Papers*, 16:147–50.

[141] Sloan, "The Earth Belongs in Usufruct to the Living," 303.

[142] Scott, In Pursuit of Happiness, 43.

[143] Jefferson to John Cartwright, 5 June 1824, *Writings*, 16:45.

[144] Jefferson, "Note on Destutt de Tracy's Political Economy" (6 April 1816), *Writings*, 14:466.

[145] Jefferson to John Wayles Eppes, 24 June 1813, *Writings*, 13:277.

[146] Jefferson to Pierre Samuel Dupont de Nemours, 24 April 1816, *Writings*, 14:490.

[147] Jefferson to Samuel Kercheval, 12 July 1816, *Writings* [Ford], 10:39.

[148] Jefferson, "Comments on Soulé's Histoire" (3 August 1786), *Papers*, 10:396.

[149] Zuckert, The Natural Rights Republic, 240.

[150] Jefferson, "Note on Destutt de Tracy's Political Economy" (6 April 1816), *Writings*, 14:466.

[151] Jefferson, "First Inaugural Address" (4 March 1801), *Writings* [Ford], 8:3.

[152] Jefferson, "Second Inaugural Address" (4 March 1805), *Writings* [Ford], 8:344.

[153] Thomas Jefferson, *Notes on the State of Virginia*, ed. William Peden (Chapel Hill: University of North Carolina Press, 1955) 159.

[154] John Locke, *A Letter Concerning Toleration* (1689) (Chicago: Liberal Arts Press Book, 1955) 31.

[155] J. David Hoeveler, Jr., "Conservatism" in *A Companion to American Thought*, ed. Richard Wightman Fox and James T. Koppenberg (Oxford: Blackwell, 1995) 143.

¹⁵⁶ Jefferson to James Madison, 6 September 1789, *Papers*, 15:394 (italics added).

Chapter 4

¹ Jefferson to J. Gassaway, 17 February 1809, *The Writings of Thomas Jefferson*, ed. Andrew A. Lipscomb and Albert E. Bergh, (Washington DC: Thomas Jefferson Memorial Association, 1904–1907) 16:337 (henceforth cited as *Writings*).

² John Locke, *An Essay Concerning Human Understanding* (1689) (London: Routledge, 1894) 2:chap. 21, §50, 186.

³ Walter Euchner, *Naturrecht und Politik bei John Locke* (Frankfurt, Germany: Europäische Verlag, 1969) 107.

⁴ Cf. Leo Strauss, *Natural Right and History* (Chicago: University of Chicago Press, 1953) 202–51.

⁵ John Locke, "Essays on the Law of Nature; Essay V: Can the Law of Nature Be Known from the General Consent of Men? No." in *Political Essays*, ed. Mark Goldie (Cambridge: Cambridge University Press, 1997) 114.

⁶ Locke, *Human Understanding*, 2:chap. 21, §51, 187.

⁷ For a brief investigation of the influence of Locke on Jeffersonian conceptions of religious liberty, cf. Kessler Sanford, "Locke's Influence on Jefferson's 'Bill for Establishing Religious Freedom'" in *Journal of Church and State* 25/2 (Spring 1983): 231–52.

⁸ John Locke, *The Reasonableness of Christianity. As Delivered in the Scriptures* (1695), ed. G. W. Ewing (Washington DC: Regnery, 1965) 182.

⁹ John Locke, "Thus I Think," c. 1686–1688(?), MS Locke, *Political Essays*, 296.

¹⁰ John Locke, "Understanding," 8 February 1679, *Political Essays*, 264 and 261–62.

¹¹ John Locke, "Morality," c. 1677–1678, MS Locke, *Political Essays*, 267–68.

¹² Ibid.

¹³ As far as I can ascertain, there are only three occurrences of the term "happiness" in the *Second Treatise*. The first is in an investigation of fatherly power: "In the beginning of things," the rule of the father ensured to his children "all the political happiness they sought for in society," thus explaining the patriarchal form of early governments (Locke, *Two Treatises*, §107, 2:246). The term happiness occurs again when it is stated that absolute monarchy does not ensure any degree of "happiness and security;" this is the most common Jeffersonian parallel (Ibid., §92, 234). Finally, there is the injunction for children to abstain "from anything that may

ever injure or affront, disturb or endanger the happiness or life of those from whom he received his" (Ibid., §66, 214).

[14] Jefferson to Cooper, 29 November 1802, *Writings*, 10:342.

[15] Locke, *Two Treatises*, §87, 2:229.

[16] A. John Simmons, *On the Edge of Anarchy. Locke, Consent and the Limits of Society* (Princeton NJ: Princeton University Press, 1993) 26.

[17] John Locke, *Essays on the Laws of Nature* (1666), ed. W. von Leyden (Oxford: Clarendon Press, 1954) 206.

[18] Cf. Locke, *Two Treatises*, §88, 2:230–31.

[19] Martin Seliger, *The Liberal Politics of John Locke* (London: Allen & Unwin, 1968) 166.

[20] Jefferson, "First Inaugural Address" (4 March 1801), *Writings*, 8:3.

[21] Locke, *Two Treatises*, §13, 2:174.

[22] Cf. John Dunn, *The Political Thought of John Locke* (Cambridge: Cambridge University Press, 1969) and Dunn, *Locke* (Oxford: Oxford University Press, 1984).

[23] John Dunn, "The Politics of Locke in England and America in the Eighteenth Century" in *John Locke: Problems and Perspectives. A Collection of New Essays*, ed. J. Yolton (Cambridge: Cambridge University Press, 1969) 79.

[24] Ibid., 80.

[25] The research of Donald Lutz, based on the number of recognizable quotations in the most important pamphlets of the revolutionary age, shows that the quotations of Locke are paramount exactly in these two decades, to be ousted by Montesquieu's during the framing of the Constitution. Cf. Donald S. Lutz, "The Relative Influence of European Writers on Late Eighteenth Century American Political Thought," *American Political Science Review* 78/1 (March 1984) 189–97.

[26] Cf. *Roots of the Republic*, 29–35. On the colonial history of Connecticut, cf. Robert J. Taylor, *Colonial Connecticut: A History* (Millwood NY: KTO Press, 1979).

[27] Cf. Edmund S. Morgan, Inventing the People. The Rise of Popular Sovereignty in England and America (New York: Norton, 1988).

[28] Lutz, Origins of American Constitutionalism, 10–11.

[29] J. Allen Smith, The Growth and Decadence of Constitutional Government (New York: Holt, 1930) 14.

[30] Locke, *Two Treatises*, 201.

[31] Cf. Wesley F. Craven, "The Early Settlements: A European Investment in Capital and Labor" in *The Growth of the American Economy*, ed. H. Williamson (New York: Prentice-Hall, 1951) 19–32.

[32] Still today, any discussion of property and justice must depart from the thinking of Locke; cf. John T. Sanders, "Justice and the Initial Acquisition of Property," *Harvard Journal of Law & Public Policy* 10/2 (1987): 367–99.

[33] Robert Dahl, "On Removing Certain Impediments to Democracy in the United States" in *The Moral Foundations of the American Republic*, ed. R. H. Horwitz (Charlottesville: University Press of Virginia, 1977) 247.

[34] Cf. Willmore Kendall, *John Locke and the Doctrine of Majority Rule* (Urbana: University of Illinois Press, 1965).

[35] Crawford B. Macpherson, "The Social Bearings of Locke's Political Theory," *The Western Political Quarterly* 7/1 (March 1954): 2.

[36] Hugo Grotius, *De jure belli ac pacis*, book 2, chap. 2, section 2.

[37] Samuel Pufendorf, *Of the Law of Nature and Nations, Eight Books* (1672) (Oxford: L. Lichfield, 1703), book 4, ch.4, *Of the Origin of Dominion or Property*, §5 321.

[38] Locke, *Two Treatises*, 316.

[39] Harold J. Laski, *The Rise of Liberalism* (New York: Harper, 1936) 127.

[40] William S. Carpenter, *The Development of American Political Thought* (Princeton NJ: Princeton University Press, 1930) 103.

[41] Ibid.

[42] Locke, *Two Treatises*, 238.

[43] Ibid., 238 (italics added).

[44] Ibid., 238–39 (italics added).

[45] Ibid., 240.

[46] Charles E. Vaughan, *Studies in the History of Political Philosophy Before and After Rousseau* (1925), ed. A. G. Little (New York: Franklin, 1972) 1:166.

[47] Locke, *Two Treatises*, 240.

[48] Ibid.

[49] Ibid., 275–76.

[50] Ibid., 238.

[51] Locke, A Letter concerning Toleration, 17 (italics added).

[52] Jefferson to W. C. Jarvis, 28 September 1820, *Writings*, 15:276.

[53] Jefferson to J. F. Watson, 17 May 1814, *Writings*, 14:136.

[54] Jefferson "Notes on a Conversation with George Washington" (7 February 1793), *The Papers of Thomas Jefferson*, ed. Julian Boyd et al. (Princeton NJ: Princeton University Press, 1950) 25:154 (italics added; henceforth cited as *Papers*).

[55] Thomas Jefferson, *Notes on the State of Virginia*, ed. William Peden (Chapel Hill: University of North Carolina Press, 1955) 118.

[56] Jefferson to A. Caray, 31 October 1823, *Writings*, 15:480.

[57] Jefferson, Notes on the State of Virginia, 118.

[58] Ibid.

[59] Ibid., 119.

[60] Ibid., 121.

[61] Ibid., 120.

[62] Jefferson to J. Taylor, 28 May 1816, *Writings*, 15:18.

[63] Such a view was most famously expounded by Edmund Burke, particularly in his 1774 election speech at Bristol, in which he stated that "Parliament is not a *congress* of ambassadors from different and hostile interests, which interest each must maintain, as an agent and advocate, against other agents and advocates; but Parliament is a *deliberative* assembly of *one* nation, with *one* interest, that of the whole." Burke went on reminding his prospective constituents that "you choose a member, indeed; but when you have chosen him, he is not a member of Bristol, but he is a member of *Parliament*. If the local constituents should have an interest or should form an hasty opinion evidently opposite to the real good of the rest of the community, the member for that place ought to be as far as any other from any endeavor to give it effect." Edmund Burke, "Speech at Mr. Burke's Arrival in Bristol, 1774" in *The Portable Burke*, ed. Isaac Kramnik (London-New York: Penguin, 1999) 156.

[64] Jefferson to J. Taylor, 28 May 1816, *Writings*, 15:23.

[65] Ibid., 19.

[66] Jefferson to S. Dupont de Nemours, 24 April 1816, *Writings*, 14:488.

[67] Jefferson to J. Taylor, 28 May 1816, *Writings*, 15:19.

[68] Ibid.

[69] Ibid., 20.

[70] Jefferson to S. Dupont de Nemours, 24 April 1816, *Writings*, 14:491.

[71] Ibid.

[72] Jefferson to J. Taylor, 28 May 1816, *Writings*, 15:19.

[73] Ibid., 22.

[74] Jefferson to Samuel Kercheval, 2 July 1816, *Writings*, 15:33.

[75] Ibid.

[76] Cf. Ibid., 34–35.

[77] Ibid., 35.

[78] Ibid.

[79] Ibid., 36.

[80] Ibid., 37–38.

[81] Ibid., 38.

[82] Ibid., 39.

[83] Ibid., 40.

[84] Ibid., 42.

[85] Ibid.

[86] Ibid., 42–43.

[87] Ibid., 43.

[88] Jefferson, "Response to the Citizens of Albemarle County" (12 February 1790), *Papers*, 16:179.

[89] Ibid.

[90] Ibid.

[91] Jefferson to A. von Humboldt, 13 June 1817, *Writings*, 15:127.

[92] Jefferson to S. Dupont de Nemours, 24 April 1816, *Writings*, 14:490.

[93] Jefferson, "First Inaugural Address" (4 March 1801), *Writings*, 8:4.

[94] Gordon S. Wood, "The Trials and Tribulations of Thomas Jefferson" in *Jeffersonian Legacies*, ed. Peter S. Onuf (Charlottesville: University Press of Virginia, 1993) 408.

[95] Locke, *Two Treatises*, 2:304.

[96] Ibid.

[97] Ibid., 304–305.

[98] Jefferson to James Madison, 30 January 1787, *Papers*, 11:93.

[99] Locke, *Two Treatises*, 2:297 (italics added).

[100] Simmons, *On the Edge of Anarchy*, 175. For the "reassuring" passages of Locke, cf. *Two Treatises*, 328 and 344–45.

[101] Jefferson to Francis W. Gilmer, 27 June 1816, *Writings*, 10:32 (italics added).

[102] Jefferson to J. Cartwright, 5 June 1824, *Writings*, 16:48 (italics added).

[103] Jefferson to John C. Cabell, 2 February 1816, *Writings*, 14:422.

[104] Edmund Burke, *Reflections on the Revolution in France* and Burke, *Selected Works*, ed. E. J. Payne (Oxford: Clarendon Press, 1898) 2:36–37.

[105] Jefferson to John Adams, 17 July 1791, *Adams-Jefferson Letters*, 246. Although the letter is written in a conciliatory tone, it is clear that Jefferson was not displeased by the whole incident and was still convinced that the vision of the vice president was adverse to the spirit of the Revolution.

[106] This can be evinced by the confession made a few months before to Madison; cf. Jefferson to James Madison, 9 May 1791, *Papers*, 20:293.

[107] Cf. C. Bradley Thompson, *John Adams and the Spirit of Liberty* (Lawrence: University Press of Kansas, 1998) 269–74.

[108] Michael Lienesch, New Order of the Ages. Time, the Constitution, and the Making of Modern American Political Thought (Princeton NJ: Princeton University Press, 1988) 209.

[109] Jefferson to John Taylor, 28 May 1816, *Writings*, 15:19.

[110] John Adams, A Defence of the Constitutions of Government of the United States of America Against the Attack of M. Turgot in his Letter to Doctor Price dated the Twenty Second of March 1778, 3 vols. (London: J. Stockdale, 1787–1788).

[111] A. R. J. Turgot to R. Price, 22 March 1778, in Richard Price, *Observations on the Importance of the American Revolution, and the means of Making It a Benefit to the World*, 2nd ed. (London and Philadelphia: M. Carey, 1785) 74.

[112] Jefferson to Isaac H. Tiffany, 4 April 1819, *Political Writings*, ed. Joyce Appleby and Terence Ball (Cambridge, England: Cambridge University Press, 1999) 224.

[113] Ibid., 52.

[114] Ibid., 54.

[115] Adams, "Defence of the Constitutions…," in *The Works of John Adams*, ed. Charles F. Adams (Boston: Little Brown, 1856) 4:294.

[116] Jefferson, Notes on the State of Virginia, 65.

[117] Jefferson to J. F. Watson, 17 May 1814, *Writings*, 14:135.

[118] Ibid., 136.

[119] John Adams, "A Dissertation on the Canon and the Feudal Law" (1765) in *The Papers of John Adams*, ed. R. J. Taylor (Cambridge MA: Harvard University Press, 1977) 1:126.

[120] Jefferson to Elbridge Gerry, 26 January 1799, *Papers*, 30:646–47.

[121] Jefferson to J. Priestley, 27 January 1800, *Papers*, 31:341.

[122] Jefferson to J. Norvell, 14 June 1807, *Writings*, 11:223.

[123] Jefferson to W. Johnson, 12 June 1823, *Writings*, 15:443.

[124] Jefferson to James Madison, 6 September 1789, *Papers*, 15:397.

[125] Jefferson to J. Cartwright, 5 June 1824, *Writings*, 16:43–44.

[126] The historical myth of the Magna Carta has shown to be much more resilient than that of the "Saxon liberties" and the "Norman yoke," but it is nevertheless as "ideological" and baseless. For an analysis of the two historical myths in revolutionary America, cf. *The Roots of Liberty: Magna Carta, Ancient Constitution, and the Anglo-American Tradition of Rule of Law*, ed. E. Sandoz (Columbia: University of Missouri Press, 1993).

[127] Trevor Colbourn, The Lamp of Experience: Whig History and the Intellectual Origins of the American Revolution (Chapel Hill: University of North Carolina Press, 1965) 209.

Chapter 5

[1] Jefferson, "Autobiography" in *The Writings of Thomas Jefferson*, ed. Andrew A. Lipscomb and Albert E. Bergh (Washington DC: Thomas Jefferson Memorial Association, 1904–1907) 1:122 (henceforth cited as *Writings*).

[2] Franco Venturi, *Settecento Riformatore* (Torino, Italy: Einaudi, 1984) 4:133–34.

[3] Jefferson to J. Adams, 16 May 1777, *Adams-Jefferson Letters*, 4.

[4] Ibid.

[5] Jefferson to J. Adams, 23 February 1787, *Adams-Jefferson Letters*, 174.

[6] Although Jefferson was not aware of this fact, Raynal drew most fallacies about the American colonies from Abbot Cornelius de Pauw's *Recherches philosophiques sur les Américains* (1768). For a broad study on the European misconceptions and distortions about America, cf. James W. Ceaser, *Reconstructing America: The Symbol of America in Modern Thought* (New Haven CT: Yale University Press, 1997).

[7] Jefferson, "Answers and Observations for Démeunier's Article on the United States in the Encyclopédie Methodique" (24 January 1786) in *Papers, The Papers of Thomas Jefferson*, ed. Julian Boyd et al. (Princeton NJ: Princeton University Press, 1950) 10:17 (henceforth cited as *Papers*).

[8] Ibid., 19.

[9] Cf. Price, *Observations*.

[10] Jefferson to R. Price, 1 February 1785, *Papers*, 7:630.

[11] Jefferson to R. Price, 8 January 1789, *Papers*, 14:420.

[12] Ibid.

[13] Jefferson, "Notes on Professor Ebeling's Letter of July 30, 1795," 15 October 1795, *Papers*, 28:506.

[14] Ibid.

[15] Jefferson, "Answers to Démeunier's First Queries," 24 January 1786, *Papers*, 10:14.

[16] Jefferson to J. Adams, 13 November 1787, *Adams-Jefferson Letters*, 212 (italics added).

[17] Jefferson to E. Carrington, 4 August 1787, *Papers*, 11:678.

[18] Jefferson to J. Madison, 16 December 1786, *Papers*, 10:603.

[19] Jefferson to J. Blair, 13 August 1787, *Papers*, 12:28.

[20] Jefferson to G. Granger, 13 August 1800, *Papers*, 32:96.

[21] Jefferson to A. L. C. Destutt de Tracy, 26 January 1811, *Writings*, 13:13–21.

[22] Jefferson to R. J. Garnett, 24 February 1824, *Writings*, 16:15.

[23] Jefferson to J. Adams, 30 August 1787, *Adams-Jefferson Letters*, 196.

[24] Sydney A. Yates, Jr., "Address by Sydney" in *The Complete Anti-Federalist*, ed. Herbert J. Storing, (Chicago: University of Chicago Press, 1981) 6:108.

[25] Jefferson to T. Cooper, 26 November 1802, *Writings*, 10:341.

[26] Jefferson to J. Norvell, 14 June 1807, *Writings*, 11:224.

[27] Cf. Jefferson to J. Madison, 20 December 1787, *Papers*, 12:439–42.

[28] Ibid., 440.

[29] Ibid.

[30] Ibid., 441.

[31] Ibid., 442.

[32] Ibid.

[33] Jefferson to C. Rodney, 23 October 1805, Gratz collection, quoted in Joseph Charles, *The Origins of the American Party System* (New York: Harper, 1961) 86.

[34] Robert W. Hoffert, A Politics of Tensions. The Articles of Confederation and American Political Ideas (Niwot: University Press of Colorado, 1992) 142.

[35] On the Shays' Rebellion, cf. David Szatmary, *Shays' Rebellion: The Making of an Agrarian Insurrection* (Amherst: University of Massachusetts Press, 1980) and Mary Hull, *Shays' Rebellion and the Constitution in American History* (Berkeley Heights NJ: Enslow, 2000).

[36] Jefferson to W. S. Smith, 13 November 1787, *Papers*, 12:356. The letter to William Stephens Smith, son-in-law of John Adams, was written the same day on which Jefferson illustrated to Adams his doubts about the new Constitution.

[37] Lawrence Kaplan goes as far as to write that "the Revolution had a far greater effect upon his opinions of events in America than it had upon his opinions of contemporaneous developments in France." Lawrence K. Kaplan, *Jefferson and France: An Essay on Politics and Political Ideas* (New Haven CT: Yale University Press, 1967) 36.

[38] J. Jay to Jefferson, 27 October 1786, *Papers*, 10:489.

[39] Ibid.

[40] Cf. Jefferson to C. W. F. Dumas, 25 December 1786, *Papers*, 10:631 and Jefferson to W. Carmichael, 26 December 1786, *Papers*, 10:632–34.

[41] Jefferson to E. Carrington, 16 January 1787, *Papers*, 11:49.

[42] Jefferson to A. Adams, 22 February 1787, *Adams-Jefferson Letters*, 173.

[43] Jefferson to W. S. Smith, 13 November 1787, *Papers*, 12:356–57.

[44] "Come avete voi potuto convenire nella proposta costituzione di varj articoli, che preparano fulmini sterminatori alla povera libertà? Vi siete voi figurato Washington immortale?...Spero che non siate infettato della malattia, pur troppo endemica, della bilancia e dei contrappesi in materia di governo." F. Mazzei to J. Madison, 2 February 1788, *Filippo Mazzei: Scelta di scritti e lettere*, ed. M. Marchione (Prato, Italy: Cassa di Risparmio e Depositi di Prato, 1984) 2:9.

[45] J. Madison to F. Mazzei, 8 October 1788, *The Writings of James Madison*, ed. J. Hunt (New York: Putnam, 1900–1910) 11:278.

[46] Jefferson to D. Humphreys, 18 March 1789, *Papers*, 14:678.

[47] Jefferson to G. Washington, 4 December 1788, *Papers*, 14:328. In his writings, Jefferson shows time and again his dislike of Rhode Island.

[48] Ibid.

[49] Ibid.

[50] Patrick Henry, 9 June 1788, *Elliot's Debates*, 3:152–53.

[51] Jefferson to A. Donald, 7 February 1788, *Papers*, 12:571.

[52] Jefferson to Francis Hopkinson, 13 March 1789, *Papers*, 14:650.

[53] Ibid., 651.

[54] Cf. Forrest McDonald, Alexander Hamilton: A Biography (New York: Norton, 1979); Richard Brookhiser, Alexander Hamilton, American (New York: Free Press, 1999); Harvey Flaumenhaft, The Effective Republic: Administration and Constitution in the Thought of Alexander Hamilton (Durham NC: Duke University Press, 1992), Ron Chernow, Alexander Hamilton (New York: Penguin, 2004); Stephen F. Knott, Alexander Hamilton and the Persistence of Myth (Lawrence.: University Press of Kansas, 2002); Noble E. Cunningham, Jr., Jefferson v. Hamilton. Confrontations That Shaped as Nation (Boston: Bedford-St. Martin's Press, 2000); James H. Read, Power versus Liberty: Madison, Hamilton, Wilson, and Jefferson (Charlottesville: University Press of Virginia, 2000); and Karl-Friedrich Walling, Republican Empire. Alexander Hamilton on War and Free Government (Lawrence: University Press of Kansas, 1999). His fame as a "Machiavellian statesman" is persistent; cf. John L. Harper, American Machiavelli. Alexander Hamilton and the Origins of U.S. Foreign Policy (New York: Cambridge University Press, 2004).

[55] Lynton K. Caldwell, *The Administrative Theories of Hamilton and Jefferson* (Chicago: University of Chicago Press, 1944) 21.

[56] Cf. Alexander Hamilton, "Report on a National Bank," *Annals of the Congress of the United States*, 1st Cong., 14 December 1790 (Washington DC: Government Printing Office) 2081–2110; Hamilton, "Report on the Subject of a

Mint," *Annals of Congress*, 1st Cong., 14 December 1790, 2111–2140; Hamilton, "Report on Public Credit," *Annals of Congress*, 1st Cong., 28 January 1790, 2041–2080; Hamilton, "Report on Manufactures," *Annals of Congress*, 2nd Cong., 4 November 1791, 971–1032.

[57] Edward S. Corwin, *The Twilight of the Supreme Court* (New Haven CT: Yale University Press, 1934) 47.

[58] Cecelia M. Kenyon, "Alexander Hamilton: Rousseau of the Right," *Political Science Quarterly* 73/2 (June 1958): 168.

[59] Jefferson to the president of the United States (Washington), 23 May 1792, *Papers*, 23:538. It should be clear by now that when Jefferson spoke of "monarchy," he was not thinking of a King, but rather of the whole oligarchic system of mercantilism and corruption.

[60] Walling, *Republican Empire*, 162.

[61] The plan is sketched in Alexander Hamilton, "The Plan presented by Alexander Hamilton, June 18, 1787" in *The Origins of the American Constitution*, ed. Michael Kammen (New York: Penguin, 1986) 36–38. The larger version is to be found in *The Records of the Federal Convention*, ed. M. Farrand (New Haven CT: Yale University Press, 1911) 1:281–93.

[62] Russell Kirk, *The Roots of American Order*, 3rd ed. (Washington DC: Regnery 1991) 424.

[63] "There are some, who maintain, that trade will regulate itself, and is not to be benefitted by the encouragements, or restraints of government.... This is one of those wild speculative paradoxes, which have grown into credit among us, contrary to the uniform practice and sense of the most enlightened nations." Alexander Hamilton, *The Continentalist*, 5, quoted in Caldwell, *Administrative Theories*, 63.

[64] John C. Koritansky, "Alexander Hamilton's Philosophy of Government and Administration," *Publius* 9/2 (Spring 1979): 111.

[65] Daniel J. Elazar, "Republicanism, Representation, and Consent in the Founding Era," *Publius* 9/2 (Spring 1979): 7.

[66] Daniel J. Elazar, *Building Cities in America* (Lanham MD: Hamilton Press/Center for the Study of Federalism, 1987) 170.

[67] Cathrine D. Bowen, *Miracle at Philadelphia* (Boston: Little, Brown, 1966) 113.

[68] James Madison, "Madison Report" in *Elliot's Debates*, ed. James McClellan and M. E. Bradford (Richmond VA: James River Press, 1989) 3:148.

[69] Ibid., 131.

[70] For an investigation of banks and politics in the first ninety years of existence of the union, cf. the classical Bray Hammond, *Banks and Politics in America from the Revolution to the Civil War* (Princeton NJ: Princeton University Press, 1957).

[71] Fisher Ames to G. R. Minot, 17 February 1791, *The Works of Fisher Ames*, ed. William B. Allen (Indianapolis: Liberty Classics, 1983) 864.

[72] On the issue of constitutional interpretation and the congressional debates on the establishment of the First National Bank, cf. Benjamin B. Klubes, "The First Federal Congress and the First National Bank: A Case Study in Constitutional Interpretation," *Journal of the Early Republic* 10/1 (Spring 1990): 19–41.

[73] Jefferson to G. Washington, "Opinion on the Constitutionality of the Bank," 15 February 1791, *Writings*, 3:146.

[74] "Hamilton spent most of his career trying to reconcile the necessity of empire with the moral authority of consent, a problem that was perhaps most acute in his discussion of the federal courts and broad construction of the Constitution," Walling, *Republican Empire*, 154.

[75] It is likely that this feat required something more than the most part of the previous night, as stated in the letter to President Washington that accompanied the document; Alexander Hamilton, *The Papers of Alexander Hamilton*, ed. H. C. Syrett et al. (New York: Columbia University Press, 1961–1987) 8:62.

[76] Alexander Hamilton, "Final Version of an Opinion on the Constitutionality of An Act to Establish a Bank" (23 February 1791) in *The Papers of Alexander Hamilton* 8:98 and 100. Hamilton was also availing himself of a decisive advantage; he had already read Jefferson's report to the president.

[77] Ibid., 107.

[78] Alexander Hamilton, Federalist 23, in Alexander Hamilton, James Madison, John Jay, *The Federalist Papers*, with an introduction by Clinton Rossiter (New York: New American Library, 1961) 274.

[79] Ibid.

[80] Forrest McDonald, *The American Presidency. An Intellectual History* (Lawrence: University Press of Kansas, 1994) 208.

[81] Quoted in Felix Morley, *Freedom and Federalism* (Chicago: Regnery, 1959) 54.

[82] The rivalry between these two giants of the American founding had a very well known and unlikely ending, cf. Arnold A. Rogow, *A Fatal Friendship: Alexander Hamilton and Aaron Burr* (New York: Hill & Wang, 1999).

[83] Gouverneur Morris to R. Walsh, 5 February 1811, *The Diary and Letters of Gouverneur Morris* (1888), ed. A. C. Morris (New York: Da Capo Press, 1970) 2:523–24.

[84] Ibid., 524–25.

[85] Alexander Hamilton to G. Morris, 27 February 1802, *The Works of Alexander Hamilton* (1904), ed. H. C. Lodge (New York: Haskell House, 1971) 10:425.

[86] Ibid., 425–26.

[87] Jefferson, "Conversation with Alexander Hamilton, August 13th, 1791," "The Anas," *Writings*, 1:284.

[88] Jefferson, "The Anas," *Writings*, 1:279.

[89] G. Hammond to Lord Grenville, 19 December 1791, quoted in Malone, *Jefferson and the Rights of Man*, 396.

[90] George F. Will, Restoration: Congress, Term Limits, and the Recovery of Deliberative Democracy (New York: The Free Press, 1992) 167.

[91] Hamilton, "Report on Manufactures," 982.

[92] Ibid.

[93] Hamilton to Robert Morris, 30 April 1781, *The Papers of Alexander Hamilton*, 2:617–18.

[94] Hamilton, "Report on Manufactures," 971.

[95] Jefferson to N. Lewis, 12 April 1792, *Papers*, 23:408.

[96] Cf. Jefferson, "The Anas," *Writings*, 1:273–74. On that same occasion, the Congress approved the move of the federal capital city from New York to Philadelphia, pending the completion of the buildings in Washington.

[97] Jefferson to J. Monroe, 20 June 1790, *Papers*, 16:537.

[98] Cf. Ibid.

[99] Jefferson to the president of the United States (Washington), 23 May 1792, *Papers*, 23:536.

[100] Ibid.

[101] Ibid., 537.

[102] Ibid. Jefferson is clearly referring to the aforementioned speech by Hamilton to the Convention.

[103] For an investigation of the similarities between the theories advanced by Necker and the scheme devised by Hamilton to confront the issue of public debt, cf. D. F. Swanson and A. P. Trout, "Alexander Hamilton, 'the Celebrated Mr. Neckar,' and Public Credit," *William and Mary Quarterly* 3rd series, 47/3 (July 1990): 422–30.

[104] Jefferson, "Notes on the Constitutionality of Bounties to Encourage Manufacturing" (February 1792), *Papers*, 24:173.

[105] Eugene R. Sheridan, "Jefferson and the Giles Resolutions," *William and Mary Quarterly* 3rd series, 49/4 (October 1992) 591.

[106] Jefferson, "Memoranda of Conversations with the President" (1 March 1792), *Papers*, 23:187.

[107] Thomas Jefferson, *Notes on the State of Virginia*, ed. William Peden (Chapel Hill: University of North Carolina Press, 1955) 165.

[108] Jefferson to J. W. Eppes, 24 June 1813, *Writings*, 13:269.

[109] Ibid., 273.

[110] Ibid.

[111] Ibid., 274.

[112] Ibid., 277.

[113] Joyce Appleby, "Economics: The Agrarian Republic" in *Thomas Jefferson and the Politics of Nature*, ed. Thomas S. Engeman (Notre Dame IN: University of Notre Dame Press, 2000) 147. This essay was first published as Joyce O. Appleby, "Commercial Farming and the 'Agrarian Myth' in the Early Republic," *Journal of American History* 68/4 (1982).

[114] Jefferson to B. Austin, 9 February 1816, *Writings*, 14:390.

[115] Ibid.

[116] Ibid., 391.

[117] Ibid., 391–92.

[118] Ibid., 392.

[119] Ibid.

[120] Cf. Jefferson, "Note of Agenda to Reduce the Government to True Principles" (ca. 11 July 1792), *Papers*, 24:215. In a series of notes on which William Branch Giles fashioned a censure motion against Hamilton, cf. Sheridan, "Jefferson and the Giles Resolutions," 589–608.

[121] Alexander Hamilton, "The Public Debt" (23 January 1792), *Annals of Congress of the United States*, 2nd Cong., 1063–1070.

[122] John Taylor, *An Enquiry into the Principles and Tendency of Certain Public Measures* (Philadelphia: Thomas Dobson, 1794) 7. The pamphlet of Taylor, edited and published by Madison and Monroe, is a fundamental contribution to clarify the growing conflict between federalists and republicans. For a discussion of the historical context and the groundwork of Taylor's *Enquiry*, cf. Banning, *Jeffersonian Persuasion*, 195–200.

[123] William Findley (29 March 1792), *Annals of Congress*, 2nd Congress, 497–98.

[124] Ibid., 498.

[125] As further evidence of the parallel between the views of Anti-Federalists and Jeffersonians, it may be remarked that Mercer had been an Anti-Federalist. In all likelihood, he was the author—under the pseudonym 'A Farmer'—of a number of

articles published in Baltimore's *Maryland Gazette*, which raised much interest at the time; cf. *The Complete Anti-Federalist*, 5:29–36.

[126] John F. Mercer (29 March 1792), *Annals of Congress*, 2nd Congress, 500.

[127] Ibid.

[128] Ibid.

[129] Ibid., 504.

[130] Ibid., 506.

[131] Ibid., 511.

[132] Ibid., 507.

[133] Ibid., 512.

[134] Jefferson to the president of the United States (Washington), 23 May 1792, *Papers*, 23:537.

[135] Ibid.

[136] Ibid., 538.

[137] Ibid.

[138] For a discussion on the erratic Jeffersonian view of political parties, cf. Noble E. Cunningham, Jr., "Political Parties" in *Thomas Jefferson: A Reference Biography*, ed. M. D. Peterson (New York: Scribner's Sons, 1986) 295–310.

[139] Jefferson to H. Lee, 10 August 1824, *Writings*, 16:73–74.

[140] Jefferson to J. Adams, 27 June 1813, *Adams-Jefferson Letters*, 335.

[141] Jefferson to Lafayette, 4 November 1823, *Writings*, 15:493.

[142] Jefferson to W. Johnson, 12 June 1823, *Writings*, 15:444.

[143] Jefferson to Lafayette, 16 June 1792, *Papers*, 24:85.

[144] Ibid.

[145] Jefferson to J. Melish, 13 January 1813, *Writings*, 13:208.

[146] Ibid., 209.

[147] Ibid.

[148] Ibid., 210–11.

[149] Ibid., 211.

[150] Jefferson, "Notes on Professor Ebeling's Letter of July 30, 1795" (15 October 1795), *Papers*, 28:507.

[151] Ibid., 508.

[152] Cf. Ibid., 509–10.

[153] Jefferson to J. Sullivan, 9 February 1797, *Papers*, 29:289.

[154] Jefferson, "Notes on a Conversation with George Mason" (30 September 1792), *Papers*, 24:428.

[155] The infamous "Mazzei letter" raised an enormous outrage among Jefferson's opponents, mainly due to its manifest Francophilia. It was originally translated into

Italian by Mazzei himself, and some excerpts were successively published in the French translation in the Paris *Gazette Nationale* on 25 January 1797. Translated back into English, it was to appear in the pages of the Philadelphia *Minerva* on 14 May 1797; cf. "Editorial Note," *Writings* [Ford], 7:74. In his "Note," Paul L. Ford believes it to have appeared in an Italian paper; in actual fact, the French article was datelined Florence, 1 January 1797; cf. Mazzei, *Filippo Mazzei: Scelta di scritti e lettere*, 3:185–87. Howard R. Marraro, "The Four Versions of Jefferson's Letter to Mazzei," *William and Mary Quarterly* 2nd series, 22/1 (January 1942): 1–14, contains the four versions of the letter. The French version differs from the original in a few details and with the addition of a final sentence.

[156] Particularly during the presidential election of 1800, as John Ferling states, "For one Federalist scribbler after another, Exhibit A of Jeffersonian wrong-headedness was the so-called Mazzei letter," Ferling, *Adams v. Jefferson*, 153.

[157] Jefferson to F. Mazzei, 24 April 1796, *Papers*, 29:82.

[158] Jefferson to A. Stuart, 23 December 1791, *Papers*, 22:436.

[159] Ibid.

[160] Joyce O. Appleby, "Republicanism in Old and New Contexts," *William and Mary Quarterly* 3rd series, 43/1, (January 1986): 31–32.

[161] Cf. John F. Hoadley, *Origins of American Political Parties, 1789–1803* (Lexington: University Press of Kentucky, 1986).

[162] Cathy D. Matson and Peter S. Onuf, *A Union of Interest. Political and Economic Thought in Revolutionary America* (Lawrence: University Press of Kansas, 1990) 168.

[163] On this point, cf. the classic work by Alfred F. Young, *The Democratic Republicans of New York: the Origins, 1763–1797* (Chapel Hill: University of North Carolina Press, 1967).

[164] Cf. Appleby, *Capitalism and a New Social Order* and Saul Cornell, *The Other Founders: Anti-Federalism and the Dissenting Tradition in America, 1788–1828* (Chapel Hill: University of North Carolina Press, 1999). A work that correctly reads the triumph of Jeffersonism as a radically libertarian drive against any governmental interference in the lives of the individuals is Matthew Q. Dawson, *Partisanship and the Birth of America's Second Party, 1796–1800: "Stop the Wheels of Government"* (Westport CT: Greenwood Press, 2000).

[165] Cornell, The Other Founders, 8.

Chapter 6

¹ Jefferson to J. C. Cabell, 2 February 1816, *The Writings of Thomas Jefferson*, ed. Andrew A. Lipscomb and Albert E. Bergh, (Washington DC: Thomas Jefferson Memorial Association, 1904–1907) 14:423 (henceforth cited as *Writings*).

² Cf. Dumas Malone, *Jefferson and the Ordeal of Liberty* (Boston: Little, Brown, 1962) 402–406 and 419–20 and Merrill Peterson, *Thomas Jefferson and the New Nation. A Biography* (New York: Oxford University Press, 1970) 613–14 and 622–24.

³ Cf. Richard B. Bernstein, *Thomas Jefferson* (New York: Oxford University Press, 2003) 125–26.

⁴ Cf. Peter S. Onuf, *Jefferson's Empire. The Language of American Nationhood* (Charlottesville: University Press of Virginia, 2000) 72.

⁵ Bernard A. Weisberger, America Afire: Jefferson, Adams, and the Revolutionary Election of 1800 (New York: HarperCollins, 2000) 220.

⁶ Susan Dunn, Jefferson's Second Revolution: The Election Crisis of 1800 and the Triumph of Republicanism (New York: Houghton Mifflin, 2004) 111–12 and 237–39.

⁷ Quite properly, the best book on this subject, David N. Mayer's, *The Constitutional Thought of Thomas Jefferson* (Charlottesville: University Press of Virginia, 1994), gives much space to the Resolutions.

⁸ William J. Watkins, Jr., Reclaiming the American Revolution. The Kentucky and Virginia Resolutions and Their Legacy (New York: Palgrave, 2004) 116–17.

⁹ After lamenting the secrecy surrounding the meetings of the Convention in Philadelphia, Jefferson stated that "it is really an assembly of demi-gods" (Jefferson to J. Adams, 30 August 1787, *Adams-Jefferson Letters*, 196), and while it does not seem difficult to detect a note of little sarcasm in this remark, the common opinion among students is that he actually meant it.

¹⁰ Jefferson to A. L. C. Destutt de Tracy, 26 January 1811, *Writings*, 13:21.

¹¹ Watkins, Jr., Reclaiming the American Revolution, 55.

¹ Allan Nevins and Henry S. Commager, *A Short History of the United States*, 5th ed. (New York: Alfred A. Knopf, 1966) 151; cf. John C. Miller, *Crisis in Freedom: The Alien and Sedition Acts* (Boston: Little, Brown, 1951).

² Jefferson to E. Rutledge, 24 June 1797, *The Papers of Thomas Jefferson*, ed. Julian Boyd et al. (Princeton NJ: Princeton University Press, 1950) 29:456–57 (henceforth cited as *Papers*).

The Political Theory of Thomas Jefferson   261

[3] On the emergence of the party and the role played by Jefferson, cf. the classic Joseph Charles, *The Origins of the American Party System* (New York: Harper, 1961) particularly 74–90.

[4] Samuel E. Morison and Henry S. Commager, *The Growth of the American Republic*, 2nd ed. (New York: Oxford University Press, 1940) 1:273.

[5] Miller, Crisis in Freedom, 74.

[6] In fact, at the time, the states were empowered to naturalize aliens— Pennsylvania, for instance, required two years of residence in the country, while Maryland only requested one—and this measure had thus very little practical effect.

[7] James T. Callender, *A Short History of the Nature and Consequences of the Excise Laws...* (Philadelphia, 1795) 450, quoted in Michael Durey, "Thomas Paine's Apostles: Radical Emigres and the Triumph of Jeffersonian Republicanism," *William and Mary Quarterly* 3rd series, 44/4 (October 1987): 666. On the political ideology of the Jeffersonian party and the many contributions from across the Atlantic, cf. particularly Richard J. Twomey, *Jacobins and Jeffersonians: Anglo-American Radicalism in the United States, 1790–1820* (New York: Garland, 1989). This investigation of the radicalism of the Jeffersonians shows to advantage the variegated social and ethnic composition of the activists of this party.

[8] Cf. Durey, "Thomas Paine's Apostles," 666.

[9] The text of the two acts can be found in the *Virgina Report*, 17–21.

[10] Frederick S. Allis, Jr., *Government Through Opposition, Party Politics in the 1790s* (New York: Macmillan, 1963) 63.

[11] The First Amendment, only approved seven years before, reads: "Congress shall make no law abridging the freedom of speech or of the press; or the right of the people peaceably to assemble and to petition the Government for a redress of grievances."

[12] Thomas Paine, *The National Intelligencer* (22 November 1802) *The Complete Writings of Thomas Paine*, ed. Philip S. Foner (New York: The Citadel Press, 1945) 2:917.

[13] Thomas Paine, "*Philadelphia Aurora* (14 May 1803)" in *Complete Writings of Thomas Paine*, 2:936 and 938.

[14] For a brilliant and accurate historical investigation of the fact that the First Amendment was really intended to abolish the ancient common law action against "seditious libel," cf. Leonard W. Levy, *Freedom of Speech and Press in Early American History. Legacy of Suppression* (New York: Harper & Row, 1963) 1–18.

[15] Thomas Cooper, "Preface, Th. Cooper from the Prison of Philadelphia" (1 May 1800), An account of the trial of Thomas Cooper, of Northumberland; on a

charge of libel against the President of the United States; taken in short hand. With a preface, notes, and appendix, by Thomas Cooper (Philadelphia: J. Bioren, 1800) 2.

[16] On this figure and the intellectual legacy of his famous grandfather, cf. Jeffery A. Smith, *Franklin and Bache: Envisioning the Enlightenend Republic* (New York: Oxford University Press, 1990).

[17] This is the constitutional view of Hamilton and, in particular, of Joseph Story, and it was definitively accepted by the Supreme Court only in 1923, in *Massachusetts v. Mellon*. In the decision the Court stated that providing for the general welfare is a broad and autonomous federal power, cf. Morton Grodzins, *The American System*, ed. D. J. Elazar (Chicago: Rand McNally, 1966) 47.

[18] Quoted in Gilbert Chinard, *Honest John Adams* (Boston: Little, Brown, 1933) 278.

[19] John Ferling, *Adams v. Jefferson. The Tumultuous Election of 1800* (New York: Oxford University Press, 2004) 110. On the election of 1800, cf. the important contributions in Appleby's *The Revolution of 1800*, as well as Weisberger, *America Afire.*

[20] Harry J. Carman, Harold C. Syrett, and Bernard W. Wishy, *A History of the American People* (New York: Knopf, 1967) 1:301.

[21] Saul K. Padover, *Jefferson* (New York: New American Library, 1943) 256.

[22] Quoted in Allis, Government Through Opposition, 60.

[23] James M. Smith, Freedom's Fetters. The Alien and Sedition Laws and American Civil Liberties (Ithaca NY: Cornell University Press, 1956) 14.

[24] Jefferson to T. Lomax, 12 March 1799, *Papers*, 31:77–78 (italics added).

[25] Jefferson, "The Anas," *Writings*, 1:281–82.

[26] "The Federalists…left no stone unturned in their attempts to link the Republicans with the bloody excesses of the French Revolution. Jefferson and his adherents, they charged, embraced the same 'cant of jacobinical illiberality' as their radical friends in France," Ferling, *Adams v. Jefferson*, 151.

[27] Smith, *Freedom's Fetters*, 20–21.

[28] Jefferson to S. T. Mason, 11 October 1798, *Papers*, 30:560.

[29] Jefferson to J. Taylor, 4 June 1798, *Papers*, 30:389.

[30] Jefferson to A. Adams, 22 July 1804, *Adams-Jefferson Letters*, 275.

[31] Bruce Ackerman, The Failure of the Founding Fathers. Jefferson, Marshall, and the Rise of Presidential Democracy (Cambridge MA: Harvard University Press, 2005) 5.

[32] Appleby, "Thomas Jefferson and the Psychology of Democracy," 155–56.

[33] "The Virginia and Kentucky Resolutions, Madison's 1799 Report, and the oratory that accompanied them became known as the Principles of Ninety-eight and

would for decades be regarded as almost sacred to the adherents of the states' rights faith." Forrest McDonald, *States' Rights and the Union. Imperium in Imperio, 1776–1876* (Lawrence: University of Kansas Press, 2000) 43.

[34] Cf. John C. Calhoun, *The Works of John C. Calhoun*, ed. R. K. Crallé, 6 vols. (New York: Appleton, 1851–1855).

[35] Cf. Charles H. Ambler, *Sectionalism in Virginia from 1776 to 1861* (1910) (New York: Russell & Russell, 1965) 25–48.

[36] "Ratification of the Constitution by the State of Virginia" (26 June 1788), *Elliot's Debates*, 1:327.

[37] Noble E. Cunningham, Jr., *The Jeffersonian Republicans. The Formation of Party Organization 1789–1801* (Chapel Hill: University of North Carolina Press, 1957) 129.

[38] Cf. *State Documents on Federal Relations*, ed. H. V. Ames (Philadelphia: University of Pennsylvania Press, 1900) 95–96.

[39] For a contemporaneous defense of the Alien and Sedition acts, cf. Charles Lee, Defence of the Alien and Sedition Laws. Shewing their entire consistency with the Constitution of the United States... (Philadelphia: John Ward Fenno, 1798) and The Address of the Minority in the Virginia Legislature to the People of that State; Containing a Vindication of the Constitutionality of the Alien and Sedition Laws (1799) (Albany NY: L. Andrews, n.d.).

[40] Cf. The Virginia and Kentucky Resolutions of 1798 and '99;...with other documents in support of the Jeffersonian doctrine of '98, ed. J. Elliot (Washington, 1832) 15.

[41] Cf. Cunningham, *Jeffersonian Republicans*, 127.

[42] Cf. Adrienne Koch and Harry Ammon, "The Virginia and Kentucky Resolutions: An Episode in Jefferson's and Madison's Defense of Civil Liberties," *William and Mary Quarterly* 3rd series, 5/2 (April 1948): 145–76. This otherwise valuable essay is slightly affected by contemporary concerns. In 1948, the loyalties of American citizens were already subject to governmental scrutiny (a harbinger of the witch-hunt to come), and, understandably, the authors preferred to emphasize the defense of civil liberties over constitutional construction.

[43] Charles M. Wiltse, "From Compact to National State in American Political Thought" in *Essays in Political Theory. Presented to George H. Sabine*, ed. M. R. Konvitz and A. E. Murphy (Ithaca NY: Cornell University Press, 1948) 156.

[44] Alexander Hamilton to T. Sedgewick, 2 February 1799, *The Papers of Alexander Hamilton*, 12:452.

[45] Ibid., 453.

[46] John Ferling, *Adams v. Jefferson: The Tumultuous Election of 1800* (New York: Oxford University Press, 2004) 115.

[47] Cf. Madison, Hamilton, Jay, *The Federalist Papers*, 23, 26, 152–57, and 168–74.

[48] Jefferson, "Draft of the Kentucky Resolutions of 1798," *Papers*, 30:536.

[49] Ibid., 539.

[50] The statement by Dumas Malone that "To the best of my knowledge, his [Jefferson's] use of the word 'nullification' in 1798 was not known at the time of the Nullification Controversy in South Carolina" is thus totally unfounded. Cf. Malone, *Jefferson and the Ordeal of Liberty* and Ethelbert D. Warfield, *The Kentucky Resolutions: An Historical Study* (New York: Putnam, 1894) 406.

[51] Jefferson, "Drafts of the Kentucky Resolutions of 1798," *Papers*, 30:539. The one significant addition to the second Kentucky Resolution of 1799 was the sentence: "That the several states, who formed that instrument, being sovereign and independent, have the unquestionable right to judge of its infraction; and that a nullification by those sovereignities of all unauthorized acts done under the color of that instrument, is the rightful remedy;" quoted in Warfield, *The Kentucky Resolutions*, 125–26.

[52] Interestingly, about thirty years before, Edmund Burke had sketched a similar notion, albeit, of course, in a different context: "Indeed, in the situation in which we stand, with an immense revenue, an enormous debt, mighty establishments, government itself a great banker and a great merchant, I see no other way for the preservation of a decent attention to public interest in the representatives, but *the interposition of the body of the people itself*, whenever it shall appear, by some flagrant and notorious act, by some capital innovation, that these representatives are going to overlap the fences of the law." Edmund Burke, "Thoughts on the Present Discontents, 1765," *The Portable Burke*, ed. Isaac Kramnik (London-New York: Penguin, 1999) 141–42.

[53] Warfield, The Kentucky Resolutions, 183–84.

[54] Cf. Frank M. Anderson, "Contemporary Opinion of the Virginia and Kentucky Resolutions. Part II," *The American Historical Review* 5/2 (December 1899): 236–37. It is the second of a two-part essay by the same title. The first part was published in the preceding issue of the same journal [5/1 (October 1899) 45–63].

[55] *The Communications of several states, on the resolutions of the legislature of Virginia, respecting the Alien and Sedition laws*, Richmond, printed by order of the General Assembly, n.d. (but 1799) 3. I am referring to this source, since it was certainly the one used by Jefferson when considering the answers of the several states, also published in *The Virginia Report of 1799–1800. Touching the Alien and*

Sedition Laws; Together with the Virginia Resolutions of December 21, 1798, The Debate And Proceedings Thereon in the House of Delegates of Virginia, and Several Other Documents Illustrative of the Report and Resolutions, ed. J. W. Randolph (Richmond VA: J. W. Randolph, 1850) 166–77.

[56] Communications of several states, 4.

[57] Ibid., 7.

[58] Ibid., 9.

[59] Ibid., 16.

[60] Miller, Crisis in Freedom, 170.

[61] Quoted in Anderson, "Contemporary Opinion of the Virginia and Kentucky Resolutions. Part II," 233.

[62] Estwick Evans, *Essay on State Rights* (Washington City [D.C.]: Greer, 1844) 15. On the cover of the book, the name of the author was followed by "of the North," just to emphasize how these positions were common throughout America. At the end of the book, there is a list of important figures who had purchased a number of copies of this work; John C. Calhoun had ordered a good nine copies.

[63] McDonald, States' Rights and the Union, 60.

[64] John Taylor to Jefferson, 25 June 1798, *The John Branch Historical Papers of Randolph-Macon College*, ed. William E. Dodd, 2/3–4, June 1908, 276.

[65] Jefferson to J. Taylor, 4 June 1798, *Papers*, 30:388–89.

[66] Jefferson to J. Madison, 23 August 1799, ed. Adrienne Koch and published in the *Library of Congress Information Bullettin*, 4–11 August 1947.

[67] Cf. Jefferson to W. C. Nicholas, 5 September 1799, *Papers*, 31:178–79.

[68] Koch and Ammon, "The Virginia and Kentucky Resolutions," 167.

[69] Malone, Jefferson and the Ordeal of Liberty, 421.

[70] Jefferson to J. Priestley, 29 January 1804, *Writings*, 10:447.

[71] Onuf, Jefferson's Empire, 119.

[72] Ibid.

[73] *The Debates in the Several State Conventions on the Adoption of the Federal Constitution*, ed. Jonathan Elliot, 5 vols. (Washington DC: Printed by and for the editor, 1836–1845) 1:487.

[74] Richard Henry Lee to J. Gordon, Jr., 26 February 1788, *The Letters of Richard Henry Lee*, ed. J. C. Ballagh (New York: Macmillan, 1911–1914) 2:463.

[75] Quoted in Paul C. Nagel, *One Nation Indivisible, The Union in American Thought 1776–1861* (New York: Oxford University Press, 1964) 20.

[76] William Pinkney, *Annals of the Congress of the United States*, 16th Cong., Senate, 15 February 1820, (Washington DC: Government Printing Office) 408.

[77] Jefferson to W. F. Gordon, 1 January 1826, *Writings* [Ford], 10:358–59.

[78] Jefferson to W. B. Giles, 26 December 1825, *Writings*, 16:146.

[79] Ibid., 147.

[80] Ibid., 148.

[81] Jefferson to J. C. Breckinridge, 12 August 1803, *Writings*, 10:409–10.

[82] Peter S. Onuf, *Jefferson's Empire. The Language of American Nationhood* (Charlottesville: University Press of Virginia, 2000).

[83] Ibid., 1.

[84] Ibid., 6–7.

[85] Ibid., 8–9.

[86] Ibid., 10.

[87] Ibid., 15.

[88] Stephen Howard Browne, *Jefferson's Call for Nationhood. The First Inaugural Address* (College Station: Texas A&M University Press, 2003).

[89] Ibid., 15–16. Colin Bonwik also speaks on Jefferson's "understanding of the need to maintain the existing union of states," albeit in a less inspired vein; cf. Colin Bonwik, "Jefferson as Nationalist" in *Reason and Republicanism: Thomas Jefferson's Legacy of Liberty*, ed. Gary L. McDowell and Sharon L. Noble (Lanham MD: Rowman & Littlefield, 1997) 152.

[90] Craig R. Smith, *Daniel Webster and the Oratory of Civic Religion* (Columbia: University of Missouri Press, 2005) 8.

[91] Daniel Webster, "The Constitution not a Compact between Sovereign States, Senate, February 16th, 1833," in *Writings and Speeches of Daniel Webster*, 17 vols. (Boston: Little, Brown, 1903) 6:211.

[92] James Bryce, *The American Commonwealth* (London and New York: Macmillan, 1888) 315.

[93] Cf. Harry Hansen, *The Civil War. A History* (1961) (New York: New American Library, 1991) 34–35.

[94] Abraham Lincoln, "Special Message to Congress (4 July 1861)," in Lincoln, *The Life and Writings of Abraham Lincoln*, ed. Van Doren (New York: The Modern Library, 1940) 671. Interestingly, in 1936 the Supreme Court (in *US v. Curtiss-Wright Export Corporation*) stated that the United States had declared independence as a single country and that the several states were immediately incorporated into that "one nation," but only as far as their external defense and foreign relations were concerned.

[95] Abraham Lincoln to A. G. Hodges, 4 April 1864, in *The Collected Works of Abraham Lincoln*, ed. R. P. Basler (New Brunswick NJ: Rutgers University Press, 1953) 7:281.

[96] Jefferson, "Drafts of the Kentucky Resolutions of 1798," *Papers*, 30:540.

[97] Mayer, The Constitutional Thought of Thomas Jefferson, 205.

[98] Koch and Ammon, "The Virginia and Kentucky Resolutions," 174.

[99] It is none other that Lance Banning who affirms that the concept of states' rights was for Jeffersonians no more than a subterfuge. "Both Adams and the Old Republicans identified the principles of '98 with the Virginia and Kentucky Resolutions of that year. To both, the party's creed in years of opposition centered on allegiance to states' rights. But...states' rights and strict construction of the Constitution were among the means to more essential ends.... They sought, instead, a federal government that would preserve the virtues necessary to a special way of life." Banning, *Jeffersonian Persuasion*, 284. Likewise, in a more recent work, Banning states that "the strategy of 1798 was not developed for the sake of the states as states, but for the sake of republican and liberal ideas that were the essence of the Revolution. The legislatures of Virginia and Kentucky were employed...as authoritative vehicles for the collection and expression of the public will." Lance Banning, *The Sacred Fire of Liberty. James Madison and the Founding of the Federal Republic* (Ithaca NY: Cornell University Press, 1995) 394.

[100] Quoted in Robert M. Johnstone, *Jefferson and the Presidency* (Ithaca NY: Cornell University Press, 1978) 167–68.

[101] Article 6 reads, "This Constitution, and the Laws of the United States which shall be made in Pursuance thereof; and all Treaties made, or which shall be made, under the Authority of the United States, shall be the supreme Law of the Land; and the Judges in every State shall be bound thereby, any Thing in the Constitution or Laws of any State to the Contrary notwithstanding."

[102] A broad discussion from a legal perspective can be found in Antonio La Pergola, *Los Nuevos Senderos del Federalismo* (Madrid, Spain: Centro de Estudios Constitucionales, 1994) 253–76.

[103] Laurence H. Tribe and Michael C. Dorf, *On Reading the Constitution* (Cambridge MA: Harvard University Press, 1991) 83.

[104] Calhoun, "A Discourse on the Constitution and Government of the United States" (1851), *Works*, 1:252–53.

[105] Koch and Ammon, "The Virginia and Kentucky Resolutions," 162.

[106] Cf. Virginia Report, 150.

[107] For an overview of recent scholarship, cf. Alan Gibson, "The Madisonian Madison and the Question of Consistency: The Significance and Challenge of Recent Research," *The Review of Politics* 64/2 (Spring 2002): 311–38.

[108] Kevin R. Gutzman, "A Troublesome Legacy: James Madison and the 'Principles of '98,'" *Journal of the Early Republic* 15/4 (Winter 1995): 570.

[109] Clyde N. Wilson, "Little Jimmy's Last Hurrah" in *From Union to Empire. Essays in the Jeffersonian Tradition* (Columbia SC: The Foundation for American Education, 2003) 67.

[110] For an ardent and brilliant defense of the consistency of the political views of the "Father of the Constitution," cf. Banning, *Sacred Fire of Liberty*; of the same author, cf. also "James Madison and the Nationalists, 1780–1783," *William and Mary Quarterly* 3rd series, 40/2 (April 1983): 227–55 and "The Hamiltonian Madison: A Reconsideration," *Virginia Magazine of History and Biography* 92/1 (January 1984): 3–28. Drew McCoy, in his *The Last of the Fathers: James Madison and the Republican Legacy* (New York: Cambridge University Press, 1989), makes the case that Madison, supporting the midway position between nullifiers and nationalists, was actually not only perfectly consistent, but also in harmony with the spirit and the letter of the Constitution.

[111] James Madison, "Notes on Nullification, 1835–36," *The Writings of James Madison*, 9:574–75.

[112] Cf. Virginia Report, 140.

[113] "The rightful authority to interpose...was meant, not the authority of the states *singly & separately*, but their authority as the parties to the Constitution," that is collectively. "It is manifest that the adequate interposition...must be not a single, but a concurrent interposition," Madison, "Notes on Nullification, 1835–36," 576 and 578 (cf. also 580).

[114] Ibid., 574.

[115] Ibid., 589.

[116] Henry Lee, Plain truth: addressed to the people of Virginia, by a citizen of Westmoreland County (Richmond VA: February 1799) 19.

[117] James Madison, "Report on the Resolutions, 1799–1800," *The Writings of James Madison*, 6:348.

[118] Cf. Alexander Addison, Analysis of the report of the committee of the Virginia assembly, on the proceedings of sundry of the other states in answer to their resolutions (Philadelphia: Z. Poulson, 1800) 6–8.

[119] The formation of a sort of "Jeffersonian consensus" is witnessed by a number of works, such as George Hay, *An Essay on the Liberty of the Press* (1799) (Richmond VA: Samuel Pleasant, 1803), Tunis D. Wortman, *A Treatise Concerning Political Enquiry, and the Liberty of the Press* (New York: George Forman, 1800), Madison's Report of 1799, *Virgina Report*, 189–235, and many lesser known works. On this subject, cf. Levy, *Freedom of Speech and Press*, 267–97, although the author focuses solely on freedom of the press, going as far as defining "libertarian" as "favorable to the utmost freedom of expression."

[120] Jefferson, "Draft of the Kentucky Resolutions," 537.

[121] Likewise, such a notion was shared by other Jeffersonians: "[During the debate of the Sedition Act, St. George] Tucker and other Republicans recognized that the several states possessed a broad police power and in the absence of a state constitutional provision they could restrict freedom of speech.... This Republican constitutionalism underscores that the Sedition Act controversy was essentially a question of federalism. Republicans prized liberty, but thought it best secured when power was exercised at the local level." Watkins, Jr., *Reclaiming the America Revolution*, 41–42.

[122] Jefferson to A. Adams, 11 September 1804, *Adams-Jefferson Letters*, 279. It may appear surprising that Jefferson was corresponding with the wife of his avowed political opponent. In fact, Abigail Adams had sent her heartfelt condolences to Jefferson on the death of his beloved daughter Mary ("Polly") in April 1804. The letter occasioned a friendly exchange between Jefferson and Mrs. Adams. The correspondence and the friendship with John Adams was only resumed in summer 1813.

[123] Jefferson to E. Randolph, 18 August 1799, *Papers*, 31:168.

[124] Ibid., 169.

[125] Ibid., 170.

[126] Ibid.

[127] Ibid., 170–71.

[128] Virginia Report, 211.

[129] Ibid.

[130] Ibid., 212.

[131] Ibid., 213.

[132] Cf. ibid., 215

[133] Ibid.

[134] Ibid., 216.

[135] Ibid., 217.

[136] James Madison to Peter S. Duponceau, August 1824, *The Writings of James Madison*, 9:199.

[137] Ibid., 200.

[138] 11 US (7 Cranch) 32 (1812).

[139] Ibid., 34.

[140] Peter S. Duponceau, A Dissertation on the Nature and Extent of the Jurisdiction of the Courts of the United States (Philadelphia: Abraham Small, 1824) 9.

¹⁴¹ Joseph Story's opinion in *United States v. Coolidge* [1816] quoted in Duponceau, *Dissertation*, 237.

¹⁴² Ibid., 238.

¹⁴³ However, as late as 1834 the Supreme Court rejected the idea of a federal common law asserting that "there is no principle which pervades the Union and has the authority of law, that is not embodied in the constitution or laws of the Union.... It is clear, there can be no common law of the United States." *Wheaton v. Peters* [1834] 33 US (8 Pet.) 591: 657–58.

¹⁴⁴ For the global salvation promised by a global welfare state and the social-rights democracy, cf. Jürgen Habermas, *The Postnational Constellation: Political Essays*, trans. and ed. Max Pensky (Cambridge MA: MIT Press, 2001) [*Die postnationale Konstellation: Politische Essays* (Frankfurt am Main: Suhrkamp, 1998)].

¹⁴⁵ John Rawls, *The Law of Peoples* (Cambridge MA: Harvard University Press, 1999) 36.

¹⁴⁶ The idea of the ward-republic was brought up again in the 1900s by two Jeffersonians: cf. Albert J. Nock, *Our Enemy, The State* (New York: Morrow, 1935) and Walter Karp, *Liberty under Siege: American Politics, 1976–1988* (New York: Holt, 1988).

¹⁴⁷ Jefferson to J. C. Cabell, 2 February 1816, *Writings*, 14:420–21.

¹⁴⁸ Ibid., 421.

¹⁴⁹ Jefferson to E. Carrington, 27 May 1788, *Papers*, 13:208.

¹⁵⁰ Jefferson to J. C. Cabell, 2 February 1816, *Writings*, 14:421.

¹⁵¹ Ibid.

¹⁵² Ibid.

¹⁵³ Ibid., 421–22.

¹⁵⁴ Cf. Immanuel Kant, *Perpetual Peace, A Philosophic Essay by Immanuel Kant, Published in 1795*, trans. Benjamin F. Trueblood (Boston: The American Peace Society, 1897).

¹⁵⁵ In a persuasive and rigorous analysis, Giuliano Marini (*Tre studi sul cosmopolitismo kantiano* [Pisa-Roma Italy: "Biblioteca di studi kantiani," 1998]) concludes that Kant was envisioning a world federation, departing in this from the scholarly consensus, which sees the German philosopher advocating a confederal framework for the world republic.

¹⁵⁶ Virginia Report, 195–96.

¹⁵⁷ Article 5 provides that two-thirds of state assemblies can submit an amendment to the Constitution, but it needs to be approved by the vote of the assemblies or conventions of three-quarters of the states. The true "supermajority" needed to amend the Constitution is thus three-quarters of the states.

[158] Jefferson to W. Johnson, 12 June 1823, *Writings*, 15:451.

[159] Cf. Jefferson to S. Roane, 6 September 1819, *Writings* [Ford], 10:140–43.

[160] William J. Watkins, Jr., Reclaiming the American Revolution, 118.

[161] Locke, *Two Treatises*, 230.

[162] For a critical appraisal of this dichotomy, based entirely on categories derived from the European juridical and political notion of sovereignty, cf. Luigi Marco Bassani, "Jefferson, Calhoun and States' Rights: The Uneasy Europeanization of American Politics," *Telos* 114 (Winter 1999): 132–54.

Conclusion

[1] Henry D. Thoreau, "Civil Disobedience" (1849) in *Walden and Civil Disobedience*, ed. Owen Thomas (New York: Norton, 1966) 239.

[2] Jefferson to J. Adams, 4 September 1823, *Adams-Jefferson Letters*, 595.

[3] Jefferson to W. Hunter, "Response to the Address of Welcome" (11 March 1790), *The Papers of Thomas Jefferson*, ed. Julian Boyd et al. (Princeton NJ: Princeton University Press, 1950) 16:225.

[4] Jefferson to J. Madison, 24 December 1825, *Writings* [Ford], 10:352.

[5] Jefferson to W. Johnson, 12 June 1823, *The Writings of Thomas Jefferson*, ed. Andrew A. Lipscomb and Albert E. Bergh, (Washington DC: Thomas Jefferson Memorial Association, 1904–1907) 15:449 (henceforth cited as *Writings*).

[6] Jefferson to S. Kercheval, 12 July 1816, *Writings*, 15:41.

[7] For a recent treatment of the issues related to the Louisiana Purchase, cf. Peter J. Kastor, *The Nation's Crucible. The Louisiana Purchase and the Creation of America* (New Haven CT: Yale University Press, 2004).

[8] Cf. James M. Banner, *To the Hartford Convention* (New York: Knopf, 1970).

[9] Michael Zuckert, "Response" in *Thomas Jefferson and the Politics of Nature*, ed. Thomas S. Engeman (Notre Dame IN: University of Notre Dame Press, 2000) 209; on the other hand, what he adds just a few lines later is also true: "Jefferson...'refreshes our recollection' of both our greatest hopes for and *our deepest disappointments in America*" (italics added).

[10] Timothy Ford was not in good company when he wrote that the notion of a state of nature was a "mere fairy tale" in [Americanus], *The Constitutionalist, or an Inquiry of How Far is Expedient and Proper to Alter the Constitution of South Carolina* (Charleston SC: Markland, M'Iver & Co, 1794) 13.

[11] Abraham Lincoln to H. L. Pierce et al., 6 April 1859, *The Collected Works of Abraham Lincoln*, ed. R. P. Basler (New Brunswick NJ: Rutgers University Press, 1953) 2:374–76.

[12] As an example, in the late nineteenth century, John W. Burgess offered a definition of sovereignty as an "original, absolute, unlimited, universal power over the individual subject and over all associations of subjects," and "the State...[as] the source of all titles to land and of all powers over it" (John W. Burgess, *Political Science and Comparative Constitutional Law* [Boston-London: Ginn, 1891] 1:47 and 52). Such a notion was completely foreign to the political thought of the American founding.

[13] To Charles Beard and a number of scholars who came after him, the Civil War was "the Second American Revolution, and in a strict sense, the First," since it produced the fundamental changes in social relations that the Revolution of 1776 had left untouched (Charles A. Beard and Mary R. Beard, *The Rise of American Civilization* [1927] [New York: Macmillan, 1969] 137–38). Cf. also James M. McPherson, *Abraham Lincoln and the Second American Revolution* (New York: Oxford University Press, 1992).

Liberty, State, & Union

Index

Habermas, Jürgen207
Halliday, E.M.14
Hamilton, Alexander6, 7, 15, 24, 35, 132,
133, 134, 135, 136, 137, 138, 139, 140,
141, 142,143, 144, 145, 146, 147, 150,
152, 154, 155, 157, 173, 175, 190, 194,
195,
Hammond, George143
Hamowy, Ronald49
Harrington, James26
Hartz, Louis24
Hayek, Friedrich von34
Hemings, James Madison8
Hemings, Sally8, 9, 167
Henry, Patrick 130
Hoar, George7
Hoffert, Robert W.127
Hooker, Richard24
Hopkinson, Francis131
Horowitz, Asher37
Hume, David115
Humphreys, David130
Hutcheson53
Huyler, Jerome39

Jackson, Andrew176,
Jay, John128
Jinnah, Muhammad Ali5
Johnson, Lyndon B.5
Johnson, William213
Jordan, Winthrop9

Kant, Immanuel207, 210, 211
Kaplan, Lawrence12
Katz, Claudio57
Kenan Jr., William R.10
Kendall, Wilmoore98
Kenyon, Cecelia62, 134
Kercheval, Samuel83, 104
Keynes, John M.34, 144
Kirk, Russell21, 136
Kirzner, Israel78
Koch, Adrienne62, 190, 193
Koritansky, John136

Lafayette, Marquis de64, 65, 73, 154, 155
Lansing Jr., John135, 157
Laski, Harold96
Leclerc, Georges Louis79
Lee, Richard Henry 51, 184, 197, 198
Leggett, William13
Leveller215
Levy, Leonard8

Lienesch, Michael38, 113
Lincoln, Abraham5,10, 54, 55, 161, 186,
188, 189,
222
Locke, John15,16, 19, 24, 25, 26, 27, 28,
29, 31, 33, 34, 37, 38, 39, 43, 45, 47, 49,
51, 52, 53, 54, 57, 58, 60, 61, 63, 67, 72,
75, 76, 78, 84, 86, 87, 88, 89, 90, 91, 92,
93, 94, 95, 96, 97, 98, 99, 107, 109, 110,
111, 213, 215
Lutz, Donald92
Lynd, Staughton74
Lyon, Matthew167

MacArthur, Douglas5
Machiavelli, Niccolò26, 35, 36
MacIntyre, Alasdair33, 35
Macpherson, Crawford B.75
Madison, James2, 10, 15, 18, 19, 47, 50,
55, 61, 72, 73, 80, 81, 107. 119, 124,
125, 129, 130, 137, 138, 147, 159, 160,
162, 173, 177, 178, 179, 182, 191, 193,
194, 195, 196, 197, 198, 202, 203, 204,
212, 220
Madison, Rev. James75
Malone, Dumas8, 161, 183
Mansfield, Harvey C.10
Marshall, John141, 168, 213
Marx, Karl11, 34
Mason, George157
Matthews, Richard24, 37, 52
Mayer, David190
Mazzei, Filippo129, 158
McDonald, Forrest43, 54
Melish, John155
Menger, Carl78
Mercer, John Francis 150, 151
Merriam, Charles E.55
Miller, John Chester8, 179
Mises, Lugwig von34, 78
Molinari, Gustave de71
Monroe, James145
Montagu, Charles147
Morgan, Edmund56
Morris, Robert142, 143, 144

Necker, Jacques147
Nedelsky, Jennifer55
Newton, Isaac24, 52
Nicholas, Wilson Cary173, 182
Nozick, Robert78

O'Brien, Conor Cruise12